OPENED

COURTNEY BOYER

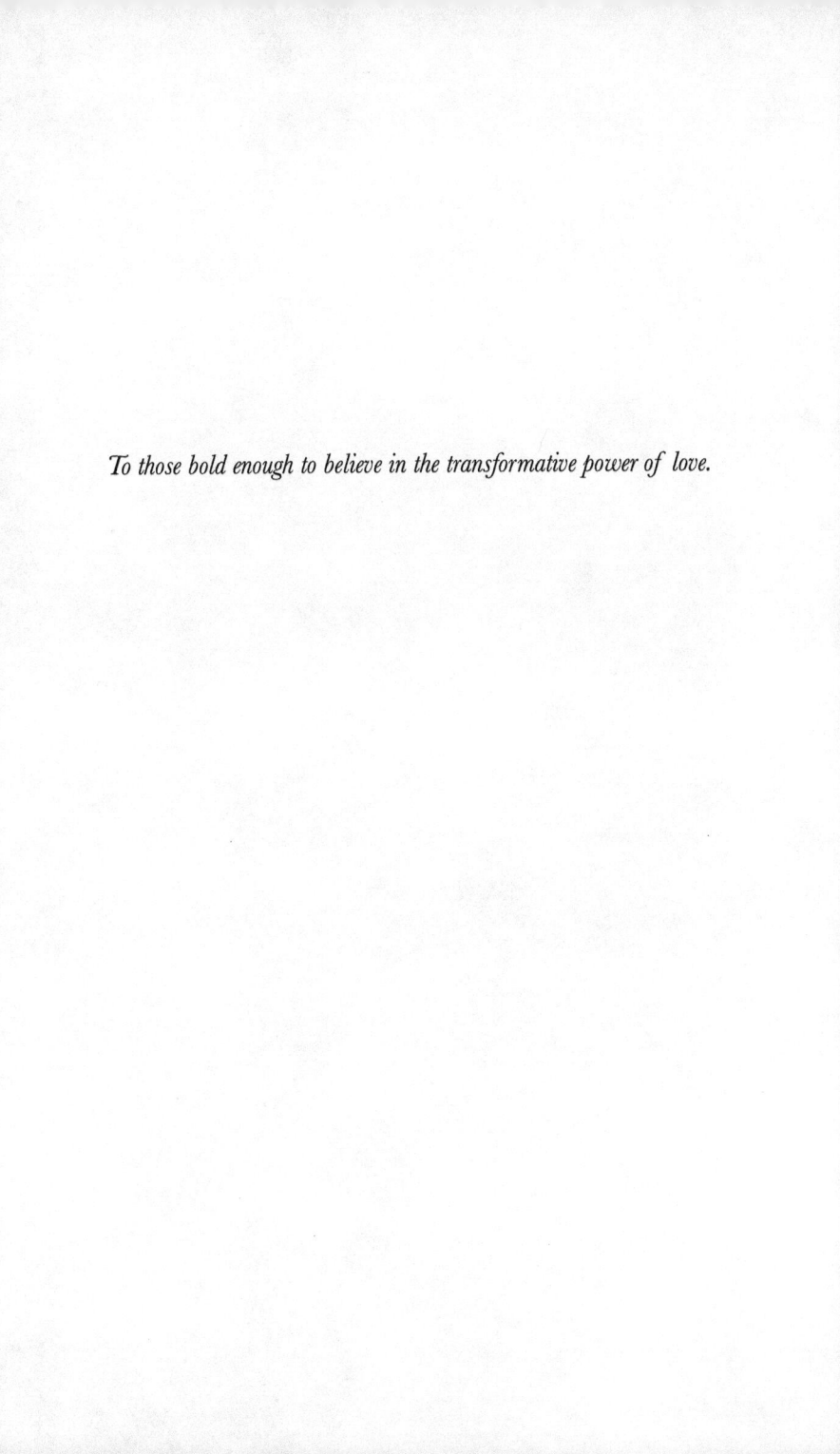

To those bold enough to believe in the transformative power of love.

To those bold enough to believe in the transformative power of love.

"Maybe the journey isn't about becoming anything.

Maybe it's about unbecoming everything that isn't really you, so that you can be who you were meant to be in the first place."

-Paulo Coelho

INTRODUCTION

If you picked up this book and thought it was going to be a how-to guide on opening your marriage, I've got bad news for you. This isn't it.

Which may be surprising since I'm a trained therapist-turned-relationship coach. In fact, you may often ask yourself throughout this book, how can she be trained in this field and still have such unhealthy relationships?

That is a great question. One that acknowledges the murky space between knowing and doing. Between complication and clarity. And boy, are some of these relationships in this book complicated. Not because they had to be.

See, when we have no idea who we are or what we believe we're allowed to have, that's when complications arise. Throw in some deep-seated patriarchal and purity culture conditioning, then top that sucker with performative perfectionism, and you've got yourself a recipe for, well. You'll see.

During the writing process, I would often cringe at some of my behaviors, decision-making, and ethos as I recalled the events that have reshaped my life. For better or worse, these are my lived experiences, presented to you in the most honest and vulnerable way.

It is incredibly easy to look back now and criticize, chastise, and contemplate what in the actual fuck I was doing. This memoir is a reflection of what I was believing about the world. About a woman's way in it. And, of course, about myself, during a select period of time.

My beliefs and ethics continue to evolve. That's the beauty of our time on earth. We never arrive at a final destination. There is always more deconstructing and dismantling to be done. For evolution doesn't stop. It slows. Rests. But time moves forward and as it does, it reveals to us the opportunity to shed another layer. To truly open ourselves up to growth and change.

I offer these pages to you—mired in tears, pain, pleasure, and triumph—with grace and humility.

CHAPTER ONE

January 2022
Germany

"WHAT IF WE HAD A THREESOME?" I blurted out.

It was our seventeenth wedding anniversary, and we were twenty-one stories up, overlooking the darkened city of Kaiserslautern, Germany, where we had moved for my husband's job.

His denim blue eyes flashed, narrowing in on me. "What?"

I looked down at my white linen napkin, folding it between my fingers as I fumbled for the words. "I just... like we don't have sex that often and you're always tired and..." I trailed off, hoping he'd interject at some point, saving me from the feelings that had been bubbling up in me for months, maybe years.

"You want a threesome?" Nate asked me as he wiped his mouth with his crisp white napkin.

I tried to clear the nerves from my throat. "Sure," I casually said, ignoring the tension building in my chest.

He took a fry from his plate. "Okay, how about with another woman?"

He was calling my bluff. Honestly, I didn't even really want a threesome. Just something more than what we currently had—sex every two to three weeks, date nights a couple times a year, annual weekend getaways where we argued most of the time because I wanted to go out and have sex while he wanted to rest and go to bed early.

I furrowed my eyebrows and shook my head. "What? No, not with another woman."

He grabbed another fry, popping it into his mouth. "Not with another guy, that's for sure."

I sighed so hard, my shoulders slumped. I bit my inner lower lip, considering my next words carefully. But before I knew it, I uttered, "What if we opened the marriage?"

Nate set down his beer and looked at me with disgust, his lips curling upward. "Is there something wrong with you?"

The man I had been with for nearly two decades looked around uncomfortably, leaning toward me. He narrowed his eyes once more and sternly said, "Seriously, what is wrong with you?"

Heat flashed through my face. The knot in my stomach tightened and expanded simultaneously. Shame flooded my thoughts for even considering this.

I'm a disgrace.

Was it so difficult for me to just be content with a husband that worked hard and provided for his family? Who was a good dad and a decent partner. Why did my heart, my soul, crave more? I fought back the tears as the waiter walked next to our table.

"What is wrong with you?"

I considered Nate's question. I mean there had to be something wrong with a woman who was asking to rewrite her marital rules at her anniversary dinner.

I'm desperate. I don't know what else to do anymore. I'm so tired of begging for attention. For affection. Of carrying the mental load of our family. Of having my sexual advances consistently rejected. I'm exhausted from feeling like I don't matter. That I'm too much and not enough all the

time. I just want to be seen. To be valued. Why am I not allowed to ask for more?

I opened my mouth to speak, but nothing came out.

"I'm not talking about this anymore," Nate said firmly as he took a drink of his beer. "This is not how I want to be spending our anniversary dinner, Courtney."

But I can't let this go. Not now. He's already mad anyway. If he could just see that an open marriage would allow me to have my needs met without him having to change a thing, then we could keep our family together. Then we can live the life we've been building. I'm so tired of feeling alone in this marriage—of feeling bad for wanting sex more than he does.

I swallowed the shame that threatened to silence me. "Would you be open to learning more about non-monogamy? I could send you some information."

He crossed his arms, leaning back in his chair. His candlelit shadow loomed against the cream-colored wall. "I can't see myself supporting that or doing that, so I don't see the point in you sending them to me."

I sighed again. Tears crept to the front of my eyes, but I pushed them back, something I had been doing for years. I was trapped in a cage cast by the patriarchy, where my roles as wife and mother were solidified by the cold steel bars of subjugation, submission, and the silencing of women. The gold-plating of that cage had convinced me that privilege came at a cost. When I had said "I do" at the age of twenty-two, I had no idea the price I'd be paying. That being married to a successful doctor meant navigating most of this life alone.

For the past year, I had been fervently staring at the cage I'd been in for nearly twenty years. Admiring its stability. Its shine. Contemplating its curve that always led me back to the same end.

I could no longer shake the belief that no matter how much that cage glittered, I didn't belong in it. This cage, this life, felt like a prison, and I was appealing to the warden to reconsider my sentence.

I ignored the pit in my stomach and went in for one last try. "Would you at least think about it? Please?"

Give me a reason to hope, Nate, please. I can't do this for another forty years of marriage. I don't have a clue what an open marriage looks like for us, but I will wither if we keep going the way we are.

With a sigh, he agreed. "Sure."

I took his reluctant agreement as a sign of hope. I had to believe that things could get better, and I truly believed that Nate and I were meant to be married. To be partners. But he had failed for years to even come close to meeting half of my needs, let alone all of them. He had rejected my requests for couples therapy. He hadn't opened the books I had bought for him on strengthening relationships. Their presence on our dusty book-shelves was a constant reminder that my pleas to improve our marriage, our connection, didn't matter.

Several months later, during a psychedelic mushroom trip, this became even more clear.

"Are you still in love with him?" Rachel, the guide, asked.

For the first time in our marriage, I couldn't quickly give an answer to that question.

My upper lip curled slightly as I contemplated her inquiry. "I don't know. I know I love him. And I'll do anything to keep our family together. But I also know I can't stay in a marriage where I'm not seen. Where I'm not desired sexually."

Rachel tilted her head the other way, bringing the pen to her lips again. "Does Nate not desire you sexually?"

"I think he does," I explained. "Sometimes. My weight has been an issue before. He's never called me fat or anything that's disrespectful. But he has shared that he's struggled with being sexually attracted to me when I'm not as active and I've gained weight. I mean, I get it. You want to be physically attracted to your partner."

Rachel leaned back in her chair. "So you struggle with body image issues?"

I nodded. "I have, on and off throughout the years. I just struggle to see myself as attractive and desirable, which I know affects my confidence, which impacts my attractiveness to Nate."

"You mentioned before that you had grown up in purity culture. Do you think that contributes to your body image issues?"

"I don't see how it couldn't. I always felt like I was too big. Taking up too much space, both literally and figuratively. I was told that, basically, my existence caused my brothers in Christ to stumble. I've spent the past several years deconstructing my faith. Really trying to understand my relationship with the Divine/God/whatever you want to call it. The more I do, the more I realize how oppressive and toxic this messaging was. But just knowing that doesn't seem to disconnect me from the trauma of purity culture. And I think I'm finally ready to break free from this cage I've been in my entire life."

"You said that you opened the marriage recently. How has that been going?"

I laughed. Rachel did not.

"Depends on who you ask. For me, it's going great. I've connected with this one guy, and I feel alive for the first time in years. But if you ask Nate, it's not great. I mean, I can't imagine having your partner after seventeen years of marriage ask you to do something so counter to who you are."

Rachel nodded. "Yes, I can imagine that's hard."

"I guess that's what I'd like to focus on. My feelings about my marriage and my body image issues."

Rachel smiled. "We can do that." She set her clipboard down and stood up. "You ready?"

I smiled slightly and nodded.

Ready as I'll ever be.

I slipped off my shoes, tucked one foot under my leg, and wrapped the cozy, soft gray blanket around my shoulders. Rachel handed me the first two grams of mushrooms to ingest. And one of the most transformative experiences of my life began.

Those next ten hours revealed some things to me I'm still processing, two years later. It's hard to describe what I experienced, but I do remember having felt some of the most intense love during my trip. When I thought about each of my kids, I cried with pure joy. An immense feeling of pride for just how incredible I thought they were.

But when I thought about Nate... I felt absolutely nothing. Just complete neutrality. Not anger. Not happiness. There was no physical reaction when I thought about him like I had with my children. It felt like staring at a blank wall.

How could I feel nothing for the man I had spent almost two decades with?

Exhaustion and rejection had led to desperation. I was drowning in my current life, and an open marriage was the life preserver floating by. Things felt bleak, but I could not shake the feeling that this might be our saving grace.

Could non-monogamy be my marriage's salvation?

CHAPTER TWO

I FIRST LEARNED about ethical non-monogamy (ENM) when I was twenty-four and in graduate school. I was getting my master's in education in human sexuality, and it was the first time in my life I had been exposed not only to non-traditional lifestyles, but also to people who were actually living them.

I could see how something like polyamory, a subset of non-monogamy where the focus tends to be more on romantic relationships and not just sex, was playing out with one couple and another classmate that was part of a throuple—three people in a relationship where they all date each other. I learned that ENM means different things to different people. Some people just enjoy the sexual freedom and variety (often referred to as swinging). Some people have no sexual desire but still crave emotional connection (this is common with those who identify as asexual). And some desire more than one romantic relationship (polyamory).

Polyamory and polygamy are not the same, I learned, but are often confused or used incorrectly by people outside the community. Polygamy refers to a man having more than one wife and is often quite oppressive to women because while the man can have multiple wives, the wives must be monogamous. Women in these arrangements are considered subordinate to the man and are treated as acquisitions/status symbols for him rather than being equal partners in a relationship.

I don't believe (and those in this community would agree) that any of these relationship styles are forms of cheating. Cheating is defined as intentionally deceiving or lying to someone. Of course, cheating can occur if a relationship agreement is violated, but the relationship models are not inherently based on cheating. They're based on non-monogamy.

I found some of my classmates' way of living fascinating. I marveled at how they could live boldly according to their own rules. How they had bucked the system and told anyone who didn't agree that they could shove off. Their confidence and commitment to intentional living was inspiring.

But this way of life went against my conservative religious upbringing steeped in purity culture that said marriage was between a man and a woman. And while I no longer believed that homosexuality was a sin or that gay marriage shouldn't be legal, I couldn't quite get on board with the whole multiple partners thing. I didn't see how one person couldn't be enough for someone.

I mean, why would Disney lie to us?

Throughout my teens and early twenties, it was ingrained in me by the church that my purpose was to find that one man who was going to adore me. Once I had that, I had reached the highest achievement level, one that is only surpassed by then becoming a mother. My focus was on finding that because that's what good, obedient girls did. I believed that once I obtained a husband, everything else about my life would fall into place.

This was one of the main reasons I married young. That and sex outside of marriage was one of the worst things you could do. And I couldn't follow Nate to medical school across the country if we weren't married. Don't get me wrong. I was totally in love with him and don't regret marrying Nate, but my religious background heavily influenced my decision to marry before my prefrontal cortex was fully formed.

Even though it was common for couples to get married young in my community, it was still kind of odd to the rest of the world. On our honeymoon, people were shocked when they learned that Nate, at the age of twenty-one, had made such a commitment before going off to medical school.

I tried to block out the naysayers. I truly believed that if a person just worked hard enough, they could make their marriage last. That when someone took those vows before God, it meant something. It meant that neither partner would ever quit—ever give up on each other, or the love they shared.

That wasn't the only thing fueling my commitment to matrimony. I used my "I've been married for X years" as a banner for being a great sex therapist. My self-righteousness for being in a "successful" marriage grew after each anniversary we celebrated.

Look at me! See. You can *have a happy marriage with great sex and an incredible emotional connection. God rewards those who are faithful to Him!*

But that wasn't even the truth. Nate and I didn't have great sex in our early years. I was still struggling with the guilt and shame purity culture had ingrained in me for this type of intimacy. I covered my naked body quickly in front of my husband. I craved his touch but wondered why I didn't react the way women did in the movies. I thought that I must be broken or that there was something wrong with me.

I believed God must be punishing me for having had sex with Nate before marriage. I hadn't remained "pure" and had brought sin into my marriage. Now I was paying the price for my lack of self-control.

I couldn't share how I was feeling with anyone. What if my friends didn't think I had all the answers? What kind of mental health and sex therapist would I be then?

So I examined the messaging I had received about sex. About marriage. About being a woman. Both in the church and outside of it. And what I found wasn't encouraging—it was enraging—

and it led me on a slow descent into deconstructing my faith, which included examining the impact purity culture had, not just on the women I worked with, but also on me personally.

After almost fifteen years of critically examining my beliefs while giving everything I could to my marriage, I found myself coming back to the concepts of ENM, a relationship style rooted in radical honesty, communication, and transparency.

Maybe a single person can't meet all your needs. Maybe some of us are hardwired to love more than one. Maybe compulsory monogamy is meant to keep women contained.

I had always assumed that my husband would meet my efforts. He would welcome my personal development and "aha" moments. But that didn't happen. In fact, the more I worked on myself, the farther I felt from Nate. The more I saw the holes and hiccups in our marriage. But divorce—failure, as I saw it at the time—was not an option.

When I asked Nate for an open marriage, I had no idea what I wanted exactly. I just knew I felt-suffocated. And I knew I wanted to feel free.

Nate had made little effort in our marriage. What made him a great doctor—emotional distancing, logic, and facts—didn't make for a great partner. I found it easier to do things myself than to involve him in the daily operations of the house. Asking for help and consistently being met with resistance took a toll on me. Unfortunately, I underestimated how draining three kids, two dogs, a home, and my own business would be on me. Nate and I didn't split those responsibilities evenly. The heavy lifting fell on my shoulders. And so did resentment.

With non-monogamy, I believed I had found a solution that wouldn't require more from him. He wouldn't have to finally go to therapy or journal or talk about his feelings like I had been asking him to do for years. He could continue to be consumed by his work and keep giving me his breadcrumbs. I could meet a guy, go on some dates, have great sex, and then come home to my family.

I never considered the idea that I could love another man or that another man would even want to love me—a married, middle-aged woman with three kids. That felt complicated and messy. A friend with benefits felt like a happy middle. Not something casual, but not something that was all that serious or threatening to my marriage—threatening to my family.

I saw this as a win-win. I saw it as our marriage's salvation. I never, ever expected non-monogamy to completely transform us both.

CHAPTER THREE

December 1988
Maple Valley, Washington

I TUGGED at the hem of my dress as I sat on the brown velour couch next to my grandparents.

"So…" my grandpa began seriously. "How's school going?"

I shrugged. "Fine. We're reading *The Boxcar Children,* but I've already read most of the series."

"That's because you're a smart one. Make sure you don't get distracted by any of those boys."

My grandma laughed. "Of course she won't be distracted by boys, but she doesn't want to outshine them too much…"

I reached for a handful of red and green peanut M&Ms on the coffee table in front of me and put two in my mouth when my grandma's familiar scolding began.

"Courtney, now, you don't want to eat too many of those. It's important that you watch your weight from a young age. You don't want the same struggle your mother had, do you? Or that one friend of hers? Goodness, she is so heavyset."

At the mention of my mom, my seven-year-old blue eyes searched the party for the woman I admired most. I found her across our living room talking to my aunt, her hazel eyes sparkling as she laughed. She floated on to the next member of our family, helping them out of their winter coat and welcoming them to our annual Christmas celebration.

Weight was something I was constantly aware of. My mom would pinch the fat on her slender sides anytime she tried on an outfit. She would complain that something had too many calories so she couldn't eat it. I'd hear my dad comment that she should go to an aerobics class and work on getting back into shape, despite her body size being only slightly above average.

Anytime we had a family gathering, my body was evaluated. Had I gained weight? Were my cheeks still chubby? Did the recent perm make my fine hair look any thicker? My appearance —along with my sister's, cousins', and aunts'—was always up for conjecture and comment.

"When I was your age, I played outside all day long. Didn't come home till it was dark out," my grandma said.

"Now these kids just sit around," my grandpa added. "No wonder so many of them are getting fat."

The M&Ms slowly melted in my clammy hands. I knew if I got chocolate on my Christmas dress that my mom would be furious. I quickly popped the remaining candy into my mouth.

My grandma looked at me with disgust. "Courtney! Did you not hear what I just said? You have to watch what you eat. I mean, do you think anyone is going to want to date you if you look like this?" She puffed her cheeks out and then shook her head.

I slowly chewed the M&Ms, unsure if I should spit them out or swallow them. Nervously, I itched the lacy tights that my mom had ordered for me to wear that night. As soon as my hand returned to my lap, I could see the evidence of my gluttony smeared across my left outer thigh. Quickly, I pulled the hem of my dress back down, praying no one saw the green and brown candy marks.

Guilt flooded my little body. Shame threatened to spring from my stomach. My silence was drowned out by my thumping heartbeat. I wanted to disappear. But all I could do was sit there and listen to the judgment.

CHAPTER FOUR

July 1997
Maple Valley, Washington

I QUIETLY KNOCKED on my mom's office door.

"Come in," she said in the tone she used when she was in work mode.

I cautiously opened the door and took a step in. "Are you and Dad okay?"

She didn't look up from her piles of papers. "You know your dad…"

I did know my dad. Hearing him threaten to leave was now a monthly occurrence. And even though I believed it was just his way of throwing a temper tantrum, my anxiety about losing my home and family permeated all facets of my behavior.

So I did everything I could to keep my family together. I obeyed. I overachieved. I dismissed my needs so they wouldn't disrupt the delicate ecosystem I was living in.

And when I would release the breath it felt like I had been holding in for weeks, start to relax, and relish the reality that I had kept the peace once again, he would say two words that would pull me back into the cycle I had no idea how to break.

Pebble Cove.

"You see those apartments right there." He would point at them, his finger tapping against the driver side window. "That's where I'm going to move if your mom doesn't start acting different." The stoplight would turn green, and we'd drive past the beige apartment buildings peacefully named Pebble Cove.

My mom feared public judgment more than anything, and my dad was a master at knowing how to motivate her. What was the behavior he abhorred so much that he regularly threatened to break our family apart?

According to him, she didn't prioritize him enough. She would forget her phone or not answer his calls when she was out running errands. A girl's night out to the local Mexican restaurant once every three months would run "long" (she was never home later than 11:00 p.m.).

Any time my mom chose herself over my dad, there was hell to pay. Yelling. Swearing. Threatening to leave. My mom would push back, but every time it would approach the possible point of no return, she gave in. She'd apologize. She'd promise to be "better." She'd shrink herself for the sake of my dad's fragile ego.

Relief would flood my adolescent body. And I would feel like I could breathe again. But the cycle always continued. And I believed that my mom's behavior, her giving in, was how you make a marriage work—by abandoning yourself for the peace of others.

CHAPTER FIVE

June 1998
Auburn, Washington

I WANTED BOTH OF THEM. But even at sixteen, I knew I couldn't. I had to choose. When you grow up in 90s Christian culture, steeped in purity principles, you don't date for fun. Dating had one purpose—to find a suitable spouse. And in order to prevent compromising your virtue, you never put yourself in suggestive situations that would tempt you to "give away" your virginity.

Chris had eyes like the Mediterranean Sea. His sandy blonde hair would fall across his sun-tanned face anytime the hot summer wind picked up. And don't even get me started on his washboard abs. He was wild and free. A drummer who went through life at his own beat.

Tom was... sensible. He was wicked smart and funny. Kind and patient. His luscious lashes framed his gorgeous sky-blue eyes.

I wanted them both.

I knew I couldn't.

Chris wasn't a Christian. I had been raised to believe that he would likely want me to compromise my decision to save myself for marriage. Tom would honor it. So I buried my desire for the Disney-manufactured dream of passionate love and pleasure, and made the responsible choice. The choice I knew would please my parents, pastors, and friends.

After a week of debating what to do, I decided I had to end things with Chris so I could pursue things with Tom.

I drove to Chris' house and knocked on his faded red front door. His thirteen-year-old sister told me I could find Chris in the garage. I walked slowly to the detached unit, noticing the paint-chipped siding and the garden gnome tipped on its side. There was nothing polished about Chris or where he came from. And yet I was drawn to his expansive way of looking at the world.

The door to the garage creaked as I slowly stepped inside. The shade was a welcome break from the blistering summer heat, and I found Chris working on his navy-blue VW Cabriolet.

He stood there shirtless—his golden skin glistening with sweat. I tried to ignore the beauty standing before me.

I interlaced my hands in front of my body, tightening up any parts of me that threatened to betray the reason I was there.

"Hey." I didn't go to Chris for my usual greeting of a hug. I stood stiffly several feet away from him.

"Hey," he said turning to me as he wiped his hands on the stained green towel hanging from his jean shorts.

"We need to talk," I said flatly.

Chris put his tools down and took a step toward me. "Okay."

The air around us hung thick, and it wasn't just the summer heat. I hated that it seemed tense even though we'd barely said any words. I hated having to do this. But it felt like the right thing. I had to believe it was the right thing to do. Chris wasn't marriage material.

I stared at the ground, twiddling my thumbs against my inter-laced palms, trying to muster the courage to end it.

My gaze slowly panned up to Chris. "I can't see you anymore. I'm sorry."

I was sorry. Truly sorry, but I wasn't exactly sure who I was apologizing to—him or myself.

He took a short breath, his gaze darting away from me. "I heard you've been spending time with Tom."

I shrugged and looked at the Cabriolet. A small smile creeped across my face when I thought about seeing him drive up with the top down, country music blaring.

Chris shifted his weight, and I returned to my present reality. "Yeah. I have. We share the same beliefs, and I'm interested in getting to know him better."

He pursed his lips slightly and raised his left eyebrow. "Okay."

My hands fell to my sides. "I didn't want to hurt you. That's why I came here today. To tell you…"

Chris waved his hand dismissively. "It's fine."

I could tell he was irritated by my decision and wasn't interested in my explanation.

Why does this feel so hard?

I shrugged. "I don't know what else to say. Spending time with you, Chris, was…"

Magical. I shared moments with him where I felt free and alive. Moments I felt desired even though I knew how dangerous that was. Dating Chris was like playing with a match that could set a whole forest ablaze with one careless flicker.

His jaw tightened, his cheekbones becoming even more prominent, as I considered the word that would complete my sentence.

Before I could finish, he nodded at the door. "You should go."

My head dropped slightly, and I turned to walk out. Stopping at the metal door, I turned to Chris who had already returned to working on his car. "I'll miss you."

He didn't look up.

As I got into my car, I fought back the tears. Ending things with him didn't bring me closure. Sure, I had some excitement now that I was going to be with Tom. But I wanted to grieve what I could never have with Chris. I felt like I had lost. And I couldn't fully explain why.

CHAPTER SIX

May 2000
Auburn, Washington

MY CLASSMATES and I filed into the chapel we spent every Wednesday morning at. But today was a Monday. I noticed a large whiteboard with writing already on it set up at the very front. Standing next to the whiteboard was a petite woman with short, curly brown hair. Her small hands were clasped in front of her floor-length skirt, and she slowly rocked back and forth. Without smiling, she watched our class as we made our way toward her.

None of us looked forward to this "special assembly." We had been told by our administrators that it was a type of family life education and was mandatory. When you attended a small, Christian school, you never knew what kind of guest speaker you were gonna get.

I looked at the woman whose lips slowly pursed into a tight smile and then to the whiteboard as I took my seat next to my friends. My eyes zeroed in on the words "Safe Zone" written in green and then to the words below it, "Danger Zone" written in bright red. I rolled my eyes, sat back in my chair, and crossed my arms.

Please, no.

The woman spoke somewhat softly, attempting to get a bunch of seventeen-year-olds to settle in and quiet down.

"My name is Mrs. McIntosh and today we're going to be talking about a very important topic. Purity."

Again?

I had heard this talk before. So many times, I had lost count. At youth group. At summer basketball camp. The most awkward being when teachers were forced to give these lectures by our administrators. The elements were all the same for these pep talks: fear of disappointing God and our families, guilt in desiring something that was so dangerous, and shame for our innately sinful nature (i.e., for merely existing).

Mrs. McIntosh pulled out a white piece of paper.

"Do you see this?"

We obediently nodded our heads.

"Every time you have sex with someone other than your spouse, you give a piece of yourself away."

Rip.

Mrs. McIntosh ripped the paper in two and continued.

"Every time you give in to the lustful temptations and don't save yourself for your future spouse, you disappoint God."

Rip.

"Every time you engage in some behavior in the danger zone, you are disrespecting your future husband or wife."

Rip.

Rip.

Rip.

She continued until all that was left was a small shred of white in her hand. Her gaze fell to the torn pieces at her feet, then slowly panned to the adolescent eyes staring back at her.

Mrs. McIntosh nodded once, put what was left in her pocket, and began her lesson.

I will never forget when a female classmate asked the following question.

"But like, shouldn't you test drive a car before buying it? It doesn't make sense to not have sex with someone you're going to spend the rest of your life with, does it? Shouldn't you know if you're sexually compatible?"

My heart raced at the boldness of her question. I wondered why she was even considering such a blasphemous thought.

Doesn't she know that sex outside of marriage is sinful?

Mrs. McIntosh, who I later discovered had no formal training in sexuality education or teaching, and was a stay-at-home tradwife and mother, shot down my classmate's question with so much venom, everyone could feel the sting.

She cocked her head slightly. "My dear, don't you trust God?"

She waited for my classmate to answer. Everyone turned to look at the young woman who had bravely raised her hand a moment ago.

"I guess."

Mrs. McIntosh blinked repeatedly and smoothed the top of her floor-length skirt. "You guess? Well, I am not sure what there is to guess about. You either trust the Creator of the Universe or you don't. And frankly, I would much rather put my trust in Him who knows the exact number of hairs on my head than anything else."

She shook her head. "I want you to imagine chewing a piece of gum. Every time you have sex with someone just so you can take a test drive, it's like having them chew your gum and then they give it back to you. Then you give it to the next person. And the next. And then what happens when you meet your spouse? You give them a wadded up used piece of gum."

Gross.

"Don't you think your future husband deserves a fresh piece of gum?"

My classmate hung her head and shrugged her shoulders.

I thought about what Mrs. McIntosh had said. What other leaders had preached on purity. It made sense. Who wants a used piece of gum? Aren't I worth saving myself for? Isn't my future husband worth the wait?

I obediently complied with expectations. I could hold out for a few more years. It wasn't going to be easy, but I believed my faith and future were worth it. Because then, once I met the man of my dreams, everything would be wonderful. And we'd live happily ever after. Just like everyone said we would.

CHAPTER SEVEN

February 2003
Spokane, Washington

IN MY SOPHOMORE year at Whitworth College, I found myself observing a certain guy, noticing how he interacted with everyone. He completely caught me off guard when he kept saying things that made me laugh. I just wasn't sure if he was boyfriend material.

"Who's that guy who's always in Jessica's room?" I asked one of my closest friends, Landis.

She thought for a moment. "You mean Nate?"

"I don't know. I know everyone else who hangs out on our floor, but not him."

"Oh, while you were gone for Jan-term, he went out with SaraBeth."

"The girl across the hall from us?"

"Yeah. Anyway, it didn't work out between them but he still comes around. I have a couple of classes with him since he's pre-med."

Pre-med. Now that's potential.

"Interesting…"

Landis looked at me with a twinkle in her eye. "Or do you mean *interested?*"

I laughed. "What?! No. Nooooo."

"Why not?"

"I don't know. SaraBeth and I have completely opposite personalities. If he liked her, I doubt he'd be interested in someone like me."

"Yeah, but it didn't work out between them. Do you think he's cute?"

I crinkled my nose slightly. "I mean, I guess. He's pretty nerdy, which you know I have a soft spot for. I swear he's always got a large textbook with him. But there is something about him I find…"

I didn't know exactly how to describe it. Nate and I had never talked directly. I had just stopped by my hallmates' room a few times and the last two times he had been there.

And even if he wasn't boyfriend material, it might not be a problem. My mom had instilled the "makeover mentality" into my sister and me. Basically, any man with potential could be molded or made over into whoever we thought was the successful version of him. It was a bit like the 1990s film, *She's All That*, where the female main character became the project of the male main character to become popular. There was no accepting people for who they were, at least when it came to a love interest.

Landis could see me contemplating. "I'll talk to him. Feel it out for you. See if he's interested."

"Interested in what?!"

Landis shrugged, and a mischievous grin spread across her face. "I guess we'll see."

Landis told Nate he should get to know me, and a couple weeks later, we went on our first date. Everything about Nate felt great. Except one major thing.

My mouth gaped in shock. "Wait, you're not a virgin?!"

Nate shook his head. Not an ounce of embarrassment was visible in his expression. "No."

"What do you mean *no*?"

Anger surged through my veins. My entire body tensed.

"I had sex with my high school girlfriend. We were together a couple of years."

His calm response was the opposite of my inner world, which was crumbling.

I can't marry someone who's not a virgin! I mean we just started dating but what's the point in dating him if I can't marry him?

"I thought you were a Christian. Didn't you grow up in the church?"

"I am and I did, but not like you did. Like my high school youth pastor was a lesbian."

"A lesbian!" My hands quickly covered my mouth. I didn't mean for my response to come out so appalled. So judgmental.

My parents are gonna freak when they find out he goes to a liberal church.

"I didn't become a Christian till later in high school."

"But then you became like a born-again virgin?" My words sounded like more of a plea.

He shrugged. "I guess."

You guess?! How do you not know? How can he be the spiritual leader of our house if he doesn't care about things like purity?

My head began to spin as the anger dissipated into frustration. I couldn't understand why God would bring someone like Nate into my life, who hadn't saved himself for marriage like I had. Was God punishing me? Wasn't I worth waiting for? That's what all the pastors and youth conferences and books had told me—I was worth waiting for. My future husband was worth waiting for. And now I was dating someone who was so flippant about his previous sexual history. He didn't even feel bad!

I tried to calculate how this might impact our potential marriage. Our potential future. Was it really a good idea to partner with someone who valued sex so differently than me?

June 2003

"We should stop," I told Nate as I pulled away from his kiss.

I was so tired of being the sexual gatekeeper of our relationship. Nate didn't see the problem with having sex before marriage, but I was committed in my decision to remain faithful to God's commandment not to sully the marriage bed. Holding the line of no sex was getting harder and harder the more I fell for this man.

For the past three months, I had been resisting. Fighting temptation. And being angry at God. It had felt so unfair. I had followed the rules. I had done everything that was asked of me. And I was promised a God-fearing man who had saved himself for me. So then why had I fallen in love with a man who wasn't a strong Christian and wasn't a virgin?

I was angry that another woman had shared something with Nate that I wasn't able to. I was envious that she had experienced something so special with my future husband. I had spent so much of my life feeling controlled and playing by other people's rules. It wasn't fair.

In an act of defiance and desire, I gave myself to my boyfriend in the most cliché way possible—one night in a college dorm room. Nate was doing summer research at a university where I happened to be attending a leadership conference. We had hung out the past two nights, pushing my sexual boundaries, and on my last night there, I told him, "I'm ready."

It wasn't something I had thought through, but I was tired of saying, "we should stop" or "no, we can't." Nate never pressured me, but he also didn't hide his desire to go all the way. And that —his desire for me—was something I was no longer interested in resisting.

"Do you really want to?" Nate asked me.

I stared at his tanned, defined abs and sparkling blue eyes. "Sure."

"But we don't have a condom."

I smirked slightly, raising my eyebrows. "Just pull out before you come."

I hadn't thought through the logistics of this. Afraid of losing my nerve, I pulled him on top of me. We locked eyes, and he prepared me as best he could.

"This may hurt a little. I'm sorry if it does. If you want to stop at any point, just tell me."

He was right. It did hurt a little, and it wasn't the passionate and climactic experience I had watched on TV countless times. To be honest, sex was pretty underwhelming and a little stressful. Nate was focused on making sure he pulled out, which then made me nervous that he'd come faster than he expected.

All the horror stories of women getting pregnant from their first time flooded my mind. But I wasn't backing down. We were doing this.

After it was over, we cuddled in bed for a little while. I laid my head on Nate's chest and fought back the feelings of disappointment and shame. This wasn't at all how I had imagined my first time would be. It wasn't magical. It wasn't romantic. I had dreamt about giving all of myself to my future husband for years, and now... my virginity card had officially been turned in.

It was getting late, and I needed to get some sleep before my presentation the next day. Nate didn't ask if I wanted to spend the night, and I didn't ask if I could. Shame was sprouting, and I held it at bay for as long as I could.

He kissed me goodbye, and I walked to my car alone. The night was filled with the chorus of cicadas. The darkness clung to me as I approached my car. I got in and my legs stuck to my leather seat. The second my car door closed my anxiety erupted.

I gripped the steering wheel, willing myself to drive the five minutes back to my hotel room. My breathing shallowed and my heart pounded in my chest.

What did I just do?

I closed my eyes, my hands glued to the wheel.

I'm not a virgin anymore. This is what it feels like to have had sex.

My mind quickly spiraled.

I'm going to hell. Like I'm actually going to hell. Why did I think that was a good idea? Is Nate still going to want to be with me after we had sex? Who is going to want to be with me after I've been deemed "used goods?"

I couldn't control my breathing. I couldn't control my thoughts. It was ironic that in my attempt to take control of my sexuality and body, I found myself paralyzed and panicked.

What is wrong with me?

CHAPTER EIGHT

September 2003
Spokane, Washington

PARENTS' Weekend at Whitworth College was just a few weeks away. I needed to call my mom to do our usual weekly check-in and discuss the upcoming festivities. I had recently started my junior year of college and was working in my office in the Student Life building as an intramural sports coordinator.

I picked up my office phone, staring out the large glass window that overlooked the campus quad, and dialed my mom. As the phone rang, I noticed that some trees were still brimming with brightness while others were showing signs of the impending season change. I loved this time of year. It felt like possibility.

We chatted, and she asked how Nate and I were doing. My parents had been disappointed when I ended things with my high school boyfriend, Tom, a year prior. They knew Tom and his family well and expected we'd get married in a couple of years. But as much as I appreciated and respected Tom, I wasn't in love with him. I didn't desire him. And I couldn't continue to date someone I didn't look forward to having sex with someday.

I twisted the phone cord around my finger. "Nate and I are doing great! He actually asked me to go away with him next weekend."

Sharing that information made me feel so grown up. Real couples traveled together. Adults did things like go away for the weekend and have crazy, passionate sex. Right?

My mom didn't share my enthusiasm. Her silence was deafening.

Finally, she asked, "Are you guys having sex?"

The cord unraveled from my finger. I sat up in my chair. I could hear my heart beat in my temples.

I'm not going to lie to her. I'm twenty years old!

Confidently, I responded, "Yes."

I could imagine my mom shaking her head. "I thought you were waiting until you got married to have sex."

Don't back down.

"I was, but I plan on marrying Nate so what's the difference?" I asked.

"The difference…" my mom began sternly, "is that you're sinning. Wait until your dad finds out about this."

My stomach sank. I closed my eyes picturing his reaction.

I should've lied.

"You're going to tell him?" I asked in disbelief.

"Courtney, I'm not going to hide this from him."

Disappointing my mom was one thing. But disappointing my dad… that was a whole other level.

I knew it was merely a matter of hours before he'd call me. Any time my phone rang for the rest of the day, I feared it would be my dad. As time ticked on, the knot in my stomach grew. Finally, he called me on my way home from work that night.

Rain pounded against the windshield, and I found it difficult to differentiate between the rain and my tears. Both blurred my vision so hard I pulled my car over to the side of the road.

My dad told me how disappointed he was in me and how sinful I was. He threw Bible verses at me and told me he couldn't approve of a relationship that was so contrary to what God had intended.

"Why do you care?!" I screamed into the phone, tears streaming down my face.

"Because I'm your father," he said flatly. "It's my job to protect you until you're married."

Looking back, I know now that what he meant was that it was his job to control me until that responsibility was handed over to my husband. I truly believe my dad thought he needed to protect the people he loved most—through control. But in that moment, I wanted nothing more than to break free from it.

I sobbed. "I don't need your protection! I need your support!"

I heard him take in a deep breath. "I can't support you in your sin, Courtney. I love you too much."

I had heard those same sentiments, even saying them myself many times—hate the sin; love the sinner.

He hung up. I stared at the wipers going back and forth across my windshield, trying to clear my vision. Rain now pounded even harder. The wipers tried to keep up, but it was still difficult to see. I decided to wait until the storm passed. I wondered just how long that would be.

The next day, my mom sent me a text telling me they would not be coming to Parents' Weekend. And until I had repented from my sinful ways, they wouldn't be speaking to me either.

Did I really expect them to roll out the "you're a responsible adult capable of making your own decisions" carpet? Why can't they just be happy that I'm doing great in school, involved in my community, have supportive friends, and a great boyfriend? It's never enough.

I felt gutted. And angry. How was this fair? I was a great kid and they were cutting me off until I did what they wanted. And really, they had all the power. They paid for school, my car, my rent, my cell phone bill. I felt confined to the golden cage I had been born into. Wasn't that what college was all about? Learning to spread my wings?

How am I going to survive on my own? Why couldn't I just go along and do what they wanted? What do I do?

I loved Nate. I loved having sex with him. And I also loved my parents. It felt like I would lose no matter what I chose. I would hurt someone either way.

I never even considered how I was hurting myself. Instead, I shoved down my anger, desiring to be loved and supported by my parents, and contemplated my own shortcomings.

Why was this wrong? What was wrong with me for wanting something I shouldn't?

I had been raised to believe that desire would only lead me astray. Proverbs 3:5-6 was my life verse: "Lean not on your own understanding but in all your ways acknowledge Him and He will make your paths straight."

If I believed the Bible was true, which I did, then I couldn't rely on myself to make the best possible choices. My sinful nature would only betray me.

I didn't speak to my parents for two weeks. The longest I had ever gone in my entire life without any contact with them. My anxiety grew every day we didn't speak.

Am I prepared to navigate this world without them?

Parents' Weekend came and went, and I felt like a fool without my mom and dad by my side those two days. I pushed down the shame that threatened to show itself when friends asked why my parents didn't end up coming. Nate's parents, however, did come for the weekend. They trusted their son to make his own decisions for his life, something my parents clearly didn't.

Nate made up some excuse about why my parents didn't come that weekend; his parents never questioned what he told them. They took us out to dinner the last night they were there, and I fought back the sadness creeping in. This was the weekend our parents were supposed to meet each other, but it didn't happen because of me. At least that's what I believed at the time —my disappointing choices had real consequences, and I was the bearer of those consequences.

My parents' no contact plan worked because after two weeks of anxiety at sky-high levels, I shamefully tucked my tail and entered my golden cage once again. My independence would continue to be an illusion as I agreed to stop having sex with Nate until we were married.

Thankfully, Nate was supportive. He knew how much my religious convictions mattered to me, and he didn't want to drive a wedge between me and them (or between himself and my parents). Looking back, I think he was a bit relieved with my decision because an unplanned pregnancy would have derailed his dreams of becoming a doctor. Plus, I was the one who was initiating sex and wanting it more than him. We continued to push the boundaries, engaging in other sexual activities, but vaginal sex was off the table.

I considered lying to my parents, but I just could not shake the guilt that I was disappointing God in my decision to defy His desire for me to remain chaste until marriage. I truly believed that if I was obedient, God would reward me with a strong sex life once we got married. This was my main motivator (that and avoiding an unwanted pregnancy) for me to keep my promise.

Nate secretly plotted his proposal. Three months later, he asked me to be his wife. A year after that, we were married.

CHAPTER NINE

July 2013
San Antonio, Texas

TEN YEARS and two thousand miles later, brown cardboard boxes filled every room of our 1950s ranch-style home. There was no escaping the move. I had left my thriving private mental health and sex therapy practice, my university teaching job, my friends, and my parents for Nate's medical fellowship in southern Texas.

Nate and I had spent the past three years in my home state, about forty minutes from my mom and dad, where Nate did his medical residency. Being around my parents as a wife and mom continued to shape and heal our previously rocky relationship. They respected me greatly in these roles. I mean, what Christian parent doesn't want their child to grow up, marry a doctor, and have healthy grandchildren that are being raised in the church?

I was thankful to have been near my parents because those three years were incredibly lonely. Nate worked eighty to one hundred hours a week at the hospital and was constantly stressed.

I stayed at home with our daughter, Addison, working on my second master's degree, and by the end of the three years in Washington, I had had two more kids, Avery and Asher, and started my own therapy practice.

This was when I started to carry the mental load of our growing family. Nate's drive to become a specialized doctor consumed him, and even though I had ambitions of my own, they took a backseat to my husband's. Because that's what I believed a good and dutiful wife did. She elevated her spouse so he could be the provider. The breadwinner.

I kept telling myself it would all be worth it someday. All those Sundays I took the kids to church alone. All the doctor appointments I had to drag the kids to by myself. All the missed dinners and holidays and birthdays that went unnoticed and uncelebrated. I thought if I just wasn't so needy—if I lost the baby weight faster, if I anticipated his needs more—then he'd be more present and patient.

But I couldn't see that it was never about me. Nate had his own issues; he just wasn't ready to face them. So he took his stress and insecurities out on me, and I was happy to serve in that role because I was taught that that's what a supportive wife does. You absorb it all, make it all better, and keep smiling so no one knows that anything is wrong.

It had been six days since I had flown with our five-week-old, two-year-old, and four-year-old from Washington to Texas. Despite spending significant chunks of time unpacking those boxes and caring for three small kids and two dogs, it wasn't enough.

Nate had come home from a fourteen-hour day at the hospital and could no longer handle the pace at which I was unpacking. His lips curled up and his chin dropped. "This place is disgusting! Have you made any progress? I mean, what do you do all day?"

Shame filled my face, and anger flooded my body. It hadn't even been two months since having my third C-section, and I spent most days trying to survive and keep tiny humans alive. This was our second move in three years. Both times had been for Nate's career.

But somehow, I wasn't meeting his standards.

"What do I do all day?! Are you serious?"

He pointed to the boxes still piled high in the living room. "It looks like there's even more boxes in here than before. How is that possible?!"

What do you do all day?

The words resounded like a gong in my ears.

"What do you think I do all day, Nate? Hmm?"

He shook his head. "I don't know. It sure isn't vacuuming. There's dog hair everywhere."

I took in a deep breath. I had just put the kids to bed, and I would do anything to keep them from waking up. Because I was the only one who got up with them every night. For the past four plus years, I was the one who took care of a sick kid or changed a dirty diaper or bathed a kiddo because of a blowout. Nate slept soundly thanks to the earplugs he wore.

My resentment was building. I wanted to scream at him. I wanted to tell him that I busted my ass to keep our family afloat. That I took on everything so that the only thing he had to do was go to work and go to the gym. I managed it all so that he could be happy.

Back then, I managed Nate's feelings so I could keep the peace. Growing up in a chaotic household where we communicated by yelling and being passive aggressive was something I didn't want my kids to experience. I thought if I shrunk myself and minimized my needs… if I played by the rules and overdelivered on what was expected of me, then I'd get the happy life the patriarchy promised I would. I'd get the God-fearing husband my teachers and pastors told me I'd be rewarded with.

The price of admission for that? My mind, body, and soul.

CHAPTER TEN

March 2015
San Antonio, Texas

TWO YEARS LATER, while visiting my friend, Serena, on a rare child-free evening, I ran my hand across her smooth, white-marbled countertop. "You know what would make life *so* much easier?"

She poured me a glass of wine. "What?"

I took my attention off the new countertops she and her husband had just installed in their kitchen and looked at her. "Group marriage."

Serena laughed, but I could see her wheels turning. She was an incredibly smart attorney with two young daughters and a husband who also worked all the time.

She nodded her head. "Yeah, I could use a sister wife or two."

We both laughed.

"No, no, no. I mean like couples with similar values and goals living together. Like in the same house or property. More commune and less *Sister Wives*."

I tucked my hair behind my ears and set down my wine glass. "I'm serious though. It's hard enough raising a family without grandparents nearby. My kids don't have any cousins. And honestly, I've always wondered what it'd be like to have sex with someone other than Nate."

Serena took a small step back, looking a little surprised. "You've never been with anyone but Nate?"

I laughed. "No! I grew up really conservatively. Christian school. Christian church. No sex before marriage. Lots of body shame on women for being temptresses, and edicts to submit to your husband. I was a *good girl*."

"I'm so glad my parents didn't expose me to that whole purity culture thing. Not that I don't have my own issues, but damn, that's a beast to overcome."

"Yeah, it's incredibly harmful. I work with so many women who grew up like I did and their marriages are struggling. They're depressed. Anxious. Ugh. I hate it. I hate that women are taught that we have to abandon who we are, disconnect from our bodies, just so men aren't tempted. It's ridiculous, really, that men can't take responsibility for their actions."

She took a sip of her wine. "Back then, why didn't you just do what you wanted?"

I smiled, laughing slightly. "Why don't you just tell your mom to butt out of your business?"

She raised her wine glass to me, the liquid swirling. "Point taken."

I crossed my arms, leaning against the counter. "I was afraid, you know. Afraid of disappointing my parents, afraid of going to hell for sinning, afraid of people thinking I was a slut or a compromised woman." I swallowed hard. "I think I'm still afraid of what I truly desire."

But Serena didn't hear the last part. Her youngest daughter

had come into the kitchen crying. My eyes fell to the crimson-colored wine, and I contemplated what I had just shared.

Words I had finally acknowledged—feelings that had been simmering beneath the surface. I had no idea what it meant, but I knew I was afraid. Afraid of where that desire would lead me. Afraid of who I might become. Afraid of what I could lose.

It would take another five years before I was finally ready to face those fears. And after that anniversary dinner, I could no longer ignore what was bubbling just below the surface. I also knew one of the fastest ways to accelerate that acceptance would be through psychedelics.

It's funny how that moment of fear with my friend felt so different from what I experienced during my mushroom trip years later.

It's incredibly hard to put into words what was revealed to me. It was as if a gorgeous gardenia was slowly unfolding before me while simultaneously wrapping its silky petals around me. During my trip, I felt the power of the feminine collective, and my gosh, was it incredible.

I cried. I marveled. And for a brief moment I understood.

I get it now.

And just as quickly I realized, I understood absolutely nothing except this one thing—love. The force that binds us and alchemizes us and brings us to our knees. Love propels us while it permeates our every cell. It is constant, yet asks us to change.

I had been so afraid of embracing women. Truly loving and accepting them. Why? Because they always felt like my competition. That if they won, that meant I automatically lost. I saw the world as a zero-sum game and every (wo)man for themselves. But now, good goddess, I felt received by my sisters and mothers, and it was glorious.

After the mushroom trip, I spent the next several days in a

state of reflection. I considered what I felt, what I saw, what I released. And no matter how much I tried to dismiss what I uncovered, I could no longer ignore two takeaways that would completely rock my life.

I knew I wasn't in love with Nate.

And despite fighting the label for the past several months since our anniversary dinner conversation, I knew a new identity reflected who I truly was: polyamorous.

CHAPTER ELEVEN

June 2022
Germany

ONCE I DISCOVERED what I truly wanted, I was more motivated than ever to share information and stories of successful non-monogamy with Nate. Now that he was willing to consider the possibility, I did a lot of research so I could share it with him and appeal to his scientific and logical side. Every few weeks, I'd send him an article. A podcast. A YouTube interview. Anything to convince him that monogamy wasn't for everyone. That, in fact, non-monogamy might be an excellent alternative to the narrative we had been blindly led to believe was the way, the truth, and the path to a happy life.

I truly believed that an open marriage would solve all our problems. Divorce was something I was not ready for, but I knew I couldn't continue in a marriage where I wasn't seen or valued. Where my desires didn't matter.

I'll get what I need occasionally from another man or two—it'll fuel me up. Then I'll have more energy and joy to serve my family. And Nate won't have to change at all.

Our marriage wasn't improving. If anything, it was even more strained from my desire to open it. Thankfully, I had a girl's weekend planned. I needed some space.

To celebrate winning our league, my women's soccer team took a trip to Amsterdam. The easiest and most economical way to get a team of women to Amsterdam from Germany is via train. We made the connection in Köln and boarded our final train.

I surveyed the car we had gotten into and spotted some empty seats. I noticed a group of five men, four occupying a table, and one across the aisle surrounded by three empty seats.

"Are these seats taken?" I asked the lone German guy, a bit embarrassed I hadn't asked in German.

"No," he simply replied, without a smile.

I turned to my teammates behind me. "These seats are game."

I slid into the seat closest to the window, and Mindy sat beside me as the train began to move. As I settled into my seat, I sensed that I was being watched.

My eyes met the man's gaze across the aisle in seat 56B, as if he had read my mind.

Wow, he's cute. Fair-skinned, dark brown hair, sharp nose, and a little stubble along his jaw and chin.

Quickly, I dismissed any notion that he felt the same about me.

I'm pushing forty and am a married mom of three. Why would someone who's young and looks that good want me?

I pulled out my laptop and began typing.

"Are you working?" the lone German guy across from me asked. I wished it had been 56B who had wanted to strike up a conversation, but I could still feel his eyes on me, and I guessed he'd be listening.

I looked up from my laptop. "Yes."

He asked me what I was working on and peppered me with questions about my job.

He took a sip of his beer. "So, you're... uh... like a sex therapist?"

I closed my laptop, anticipating a longer conversation. "I'm a trained mental health and sex therapist. But I'm no longer licensed. I do more relationship coaching. But yeah, I help solve people's relationship and sex problems."

He pointed to my computer. "What are you working on, then?"

I rested my hands on top of my silver laptop. "I'm writing a book geared toward women who have a low interest in sex. It's called *Not Tonight, Honey: Why women actually don't want sex and what we can do about it.*"

A warm smile spread across his face. "Cute title."

While I was answering more of his questions, I could feel 56B staring at me from across the aisle, listening intently to my words. My smile grew as I pretended not to notice the attention, but secretly, I felt something ignite within me.

Heat coursed through my body, and my hands tingled. Curiosity and confidence emerged simultaneously as I considered the reality of what was happening—an attractive, younger man desired me. And damn, that felt incredible.

"You want a coffee?" Mindy asked me as she stood.

"Actually, yes," I said. "I'll go with you."

As I exited my seat and stood for the first time, I could feel the eyes of 56B roaming across my body.

Ignore it. You're reading way too much into this.

Carefully, I navigated toward the beverage car with Mindy leading the way.

After we ordered our coffee, Mindy turned to me. "I have to pee. Grab my coffee for me?"

I nodded, and she left.

While waiting against the wall of the cramped beverage car, a crisp white shirt came into the corner of my eye. Instantly, I smiled. I knew exactly who it belonged to—56B. I glanced into those green eyes once again. This time, I held his gaze. This time, I believed I wasn't the only one who felt something.

We stood, backs against opposing walls, eyes locked on one another. Neither of us moved. My breathing quickened, and I wondered if anyone noticed the electricity that seemed to run between us.

"*Entschuldigung*," was the word that snapped me out of my temporary trance.

Somewhat startled, I looked at the beverage attendant. "Right, yes, the coffees. *Danke*."

Grabbing the steaming cups, I walked back to my seat. Once I settled back in, I noticed how fast my heart was racing, the sweat on my palms, and damn, was it suddenly one hundred ten degrees?

A few minutes later, the man from 56B returned to his seat as well. After a while, the group of German guys he was sitting with —friends headed to Amsterdam for a bachelor party—began socializing with us. Mindy moved a couple seats back to talk to one of our teammates. Sensing an opening, 56B slid into Mindy's seat.

His leg pressed against mine. "I had to tell you that I think you are so beautiful."

His German accent is adorable.

Flattered and caught off guard, all I could say was, "Thank you."

I tried not to look at him for too long. Tried to ignore the sexy stubble along his jawline. But his woodsy cologne drew me toward him.

He pulled out his phone. "Can I have your number?"

He can't be serious.

I laughed. "No."

Nate was seriously considering opening up the marriage, but

I didn't yet have the full go ahead. I wasn't ready to cross that line.

Not deterred, he countered, "What about Instagram?"

I considered it.

What's the harm? It's my business account.

I conceded. "Sure. Here, give me your phone."

Our fingers touched briefly, sending minor shocks of excitement through my body as he handed me his phone.

I typed my account name into his phone, clicked the follow button, and handed it back to him. "There."

He smiled and leaned his lips toward my ear. "I want to touch you."

My heart raced even faster.

Careful, Courtney.

I smiled, trying to ignore the heat rising in my body. "I'm sure you do."

Mindy came back to her seat, and 56B returned to his. We arrived in Amsterdam and said goodbye to the group of men we had met only a few hours ago.

The man, whom I nicknamed Amsterdam, hugged me. "I'll message you."

He was German, but I thought the name was fitting since I had met him on a train to Amsterdam.

And he did. We messaged several times about what we were doing in Amsterdam. He told me he wanted to see me again, but I wasn't ready to take things further than intense flirting. Nate hadn't fully agreed to an open marriage yet, and I wanted to be careful not to cross a line.

The Sunday before I headed home, I found myself turned on from flirting with Amsterdam all weekend. I couldn't remember the last time I had desired sex this much. My roommate had already checked out so I had the room to myself for a couple of hours. I messaged Amsterdam to ask what he was doing.

ME

I'm just alone. In my hotel room.

AMSTERDAM

Oh I wish I was there.

ME

Me too.

I considered my next possible moves. I could stop messaging. Stop flirting. Or…

Just do it. Do it.

I had no idea how I mustered the courage, but Amsterdam had awakened something inside of me. I knew that I should wait until Nate was completely in agreement about how exactly we would go about opening our marriage, but this moment felt like a great opportunity to tiptoe into it, without actually getting into a situation that might go too far too fast. Amsterdam wasn't even in the room, after all.

ME

What if you knew I was touching myself right now…

Oh my gosh. Oh my gosh. Did I really just send that? What am I doing? What if I do this wrong? What if he doesn't like what I say?

AMSTERDAM

Are you?

ME

Yes.

Right then, something inside of me broke open. A bolder version of me had finally been born. Even though part of me felt guilty for crossing this line without Nate's support, I could no longer resist whatever was pulling me deeper into myself. It wasn't about connecting with Amsterdam. It was about unlocking the desire for more. More joy. More passion. More excitement. More sex. More love.

How can I show Nate how much opening our marriage would benefit him? He could continue his focus on work, while I have these experiences that make me come alive, so I can be a happy, fulfilled person, and better able to take on the challenges of our family life.

CHAPTER TWELVE

June 2022
Germany

THE OVERTURNING OF *ROE V. Wade* was on every news page and all over social media. For nearly fifty years, women in the U.S. had had a constitutional right to obtain an abortion (prior to fetal viability). That right had just been revoked by the U.S. Supreme Court. Women, mainly those of lower socio-economic status living in conservative states, would lose access to this reproductive choice.

Is this really happening? This can't be right.

I went through page after page, trying to find proof they were wrong. They had to be wrong. The more I scrolled, the more anger built in my body. I felt like I was about to erupt as I dove deeper into the coverage on the ruling.

We don't matter. What we want, what we desire to do with our bodies... none of it matters to men in power.

I felt disgusted. Disappointed. Powerless. Anger continued to build until it erupted into a sea of sobs.

I was tired of men deciding what millions of women and I were allowed to do with our bodies. I was tired of not being trusted with the ability to make my own decisions. Tired of feeling caged and believing that the only ones who held the keys to my freedom were the men in my life. The men of this world.

I was exhausted from society telling me I had to play by their rules. I had done that my entire life. I had disconnected from who I was, suppressed my desires, followed the path that was supposed to lead to a life of success. And yes, if you glimpsed my life, you could label it "successful."

But at what cost? When did what I want matter? When do I get to matter?

The weight of the Supreme Court ruling fell heavily on me. I no longer saw my desire for an open marriage as a mere personal quest. The restriction of women's rights spurred a resistance in me. I just wasn't sure how it would take shape or when it would fully emerge. Or if anyone would rally with me.

———

A couple weeks after I first met Amsterdam, Nate encouraged me to take a weekend to myself to focus on writing my first book, *Not Tonight Honey*.

I drove to a hotel in southern Germany to work. The deeper I dove into this project, on understanding women's sexual desire and pleasure, the more my soul stirred. My sexuality felt stifled. It was as if I couldn't get enough air into my lungs most days. I was trying to put on my breathing mask first, like the flight attendants advise us to, all the while feeling shame for wanting to have my needs met. I could not stay in a marriage where my need to be seen and desired was ignored. I felt trapped and craved freedom. But I didn't want to break up my family.

Once again, I brought up non-monogamy to Nate on a phone call after I arrived at the hotel.

"I might be coming around to the idea, but I'm still not sure," he said.

FINALLY.

The cage door was finally cracking open.

I sighed. "Nate, I think you'll be surprised at how well this is going to work for us."

"Once you've made up your mind about something, you achieve it. And that's what you've done here. So, sure, you have my permission, or whatever, to do what you need to do. But to be honest, I don't want to know about it. Don't tell me any of the details, okay?"

Recently, I asked Nate why he finally agreed to my non-monogamy at that time—this turning point in our relationship. Why he tolerated six months of conversations about a topic he thought he would never have to consider.

His answer was simple: "Because every time you talked about opening our marriage, about non-monogamy, you started to come alive, and I could not ignore that."

I don't know if either of us knew at the time how powerful the advocating for my needs would be and where it would lead us.

I frowned. "Okay. I understand."

"I have to go," Nate said.

He hung up, and I sat there staring at my phone wondering what to do next. It felt like the shackles of my marriage had fallen off.

Amsterdam had messaged me the day before and had asked what I had planned this weekend. I told him I was getting away to work on my book but didn't tell him where I was going.

A smile crept across my face.

You know what would be fun…

Without hesitating, I opened up Instagram, pulled up my chat with Amsterdam, and messaged him.

ME

Come take me out to dinner.

After I hit send, I contemplated deleting the message. My heart was racing. It felt like I was going to escape from my body at any moment.

What did I just do?

I had to reassure myself—I wasn't doing anything wrong. I finally had Nate's permission, and I knew that once we got into the lifestyle, he would feel more positive about it.

AMSTERDAM

Okay. Send me your address.

He and I had stayed in touch off and on since we'd last said goodbye at the train station. His English wasn't great, but I didn't care. He wanted me, and that was all that mattered.

Holy shit! He's going to drive ninety minutes just to take me out to dinner.

Wait? Is he expecting sex? I do want to have sex with him, don't I? Is this a date?

WHAT AM I DOING?

I sent him the address.

AMSTERDAM

Okay, I need to shower and change. I'll be there in about two hours.

What. Is. Happening?

I threw the phone on the bed. Then myself. I rolled over and stared up at the ceiling. I put a hand on my heart. Still racing. I rolled over onto my stomach and watched out the window as a sailboat slowly drifted by.

I can't believe I'm doing this. Maybe he won't show up.

My emotions see-sawed as I stared at the clock. Two hours later, I received a message:

AMSTERDAM

I'll be there in thirty.

Not exactly punctual. It's not like I'm on the verge of a panic attack or anything.

Twenty minutes later, I headed to the lobby and waited. I stared out the large glass revolving doors and saw a white sedan pull into a parking spot. I walked outside and waited for Amsterdam to emerge from his car.

Gosh, he looks great.

That smile. Sly. Mischievous. His six-foot, slim frame walked toward me and pulled me into a hug. I breathed him in. My nose twitched. I could smell a hint of cigarettes on him, layered with his cologne.

He pulled back from me and smiled. "It's wonderful to see you. You look great."

I hadn't stopped smiling since he emerged from the car. "Ah, thank you. It's nice to see you. Long drive?"

He ran his hand through his brown hair before putting it in his pocket. "Yeah. I ran into traffic. *Stau.*"

I nodded and looked around the parking lot.

Now what?

I hadn't been on a date with someone other than my husband in almost two decades.

He looked around the parking lot, then back at me. "So you want to go get something to eat?"

I nodded. "Sure, that sounds great."

He turned his body, inviting me to walk beside him. "There's a restaurant I've been to a long time ago. It was excellent. Let's walk to it."

"Yeah, okay," I said.

The heat was sweltering, and my jeans were sticking to my

legs as we walked for forty-five minutes in ninety-degree heat to a restaurant he apparently only vaguely remembered. I should have learned by then never to trust a German when they suggest a walk—it's either a hike or a trek.

Finally, he stopped in front of a bustling Italian restaurant. "This is it. If I remember… Do you want to sit outside?"

"Sure," I said, relieved to finally be there.

It's not like there's air conditioning inside.

Amsterdam spoke to the hostess in German, and I was melting—not just from the heat. She took us to our table outside, and immediately, he ordered something for us in German.

I had to say it. "I think it's sexy that you speak German. I mean, yes, I know, that's your native language, but it's hot watching you order in German."

He laughed, and I wondered if I sounded like a moron. As someone who didn't speak German well, I appreciated those who could speak more than one language.

You think his talking normally in his native language is sexy? Get. It. Together, Courtney.

We spent the next two hours laughing and talking. Occasionally throughout dinner, he put his hand on my leg. I didn't flinch. It didn't feel weird. I liked the light pressure against my thigh. In fact, at times, it helped keep me from floating away from this magical moment.

I had my second glass of wine and finally relaxed. For the first time all night, I took in my surroundings and marveled at where I was, soaking in the moment. I was sitting in a beautiful courtyard—the streets lined with cobblestone. The sun gleamed off the sparkling lake and the mountains. The majestic Alps took my breath away.

Amsterdam caught my eye. "You are gorgeous."

I couldn't tell if my face was flushing from the heat or the wine or this moment, but I didn't even care. My lips curled into a smile, and I nodded. "Thank you."

I finished my wine, and he paid the bill.

Confidently, Amsterdam stood up. "Let's go for a walk."

We sauntered along the boardwalk toward the lake lookout. I boldly looped my arm with his and we walked in silence, letting the tension between us build. As we came closer to the dock, we noticed a wall of locks.

We stood in front of a stand-alone chain-link fence with hundreds of locks fastened to it. I ran my fingers along one of the blue-painted locks and marveled. "Look at this one. It's got like birds or something on it."

I could feel Amsterdam staring at me the way he had on that train weeks before. My body remembered how it felt, and in response, my heart raced. A feeling that had been reserved for Nate finally emerged—intense desire. I wanted the handsome German who stood before me.

What if he doesn't want me the way I want him?

CHAPTER THIRTEEN

AMSTERDAM MOVED CLOSER to me to see the lock I was holding. I knew his interest in the locks was feigned, and I sensed his eyes were fixated on me. He grabbed my hand holding the lock, and turned me to face him.

Before I realized what was happening, he pulled me in and put his lips to mine. His scruffy beard lightly scratched my face, contrasting with his soft kiss. Our mouths moved together as his tongue slipped against mine.

This. Is. Amazing.

My body pulsed as if I had just run a forty-meter dash. Behind my closed eyes, I conjured the image of the locks beside me, praying they would secure me to the dock I was on.

I don't want to leave this moment.

Seconds later, my stomach dropped.

Wait. What if someone saw me? Oh my gosh. Maybe this wasn't a good idea.

As I contemplated my exposure, Amsterdam peeled his body away from mine, grabbed my hand, and pulled me next to him. We continued to walk and talk, stopping occasionally to rekindle the ever-growing passion.

We spent the next several hours bar-hopping. Drinking. Talking. Touching. Laughing. Kissing. I didn't want the night to end. Amsterdam paid for everything. I ordered whatever I wanted at each stop. I felt incredibly liberated not having to worry about money.

The enchantment I was under lessened when I saw a text from Nate telling me he was going to sleep.

I wasn't sure how to respond. He had made it clear that he didn't want to know details, and I wanted to respect that.

I sent him a message asking if he wanted to call to say good-night, like we usually did when one of us was away. I was grateful when he responded with a simple, "No."

Even though I was having fun with Amsterdam, I felt guilty. I wondered if there would ever be a night where I went out on a date, and Nate not only knew about it, but was also able to tell me, "I hope you have a good time."

It was nearly 1:00 a.m. when we began walking back to my hotel.

Oh, shit. Is he staying over tonight? Should I have sex with him? I'm a little drunk, but not out of control. I know exactly what I'm consenting to if this goes where I want it to. I do want it to, don't I?

As I contemplated consummating things, Amsterdam pulled me into a dark alley. Our lips furiously met one another's as he pushed me up against a brick wall. His lips moved to my neck as his hand slid down my pants. I let out a small groan as he skill-fully fingered me.

Dear God, this is incredible. Please, do not stop what you're doing.

I could hear people passing by on the street, but neither of us cared enough to change venues. Shadows shielded us from being seen, but it didn't matter since we were completely lost in our own world. After what felt like hours, we took things back to my room.

We held hands as we walked into the hotel lobby and continued kissing in the elevator up to my floor. I swiped my key card and opened the door, disappointed to not find relief from the heat that still hung in the air this late at night. Amsterdam led me to the bed and slowly took off my clothes, kissing me as each item was discarded.

I stared up into his eyes as I unbuttoned his crisp, white shirt, revealing his tanned chest. I pressed my lips against his skin, inhaling his scent, but more so solidifying this moment in my memory.

This is really happening. Holy shit!

My fingers moved from his chest, down his stomach, and landed at the buttons on his jeans. I fumbled with unbuttoning them, and no matter how hard I tried, they would not budge.

Why are these buttons and not a zipper?!

Thankfully, Amsterdam took over. We laughed as he slid off his jeans and boxers. I sat on the bed, naked, while he went to grab a condom from his wallet. The sex educator in me wondered how long that condom had been in there.

Heat degrades the efficacy of condoms.

As if he could see my wheels turning, he said, "I only have one. I got this from the bathroom in the bar tonight."

One. Magical. Condom. Gotta make it count, I guess.

He stood in front of me, his hardness mere inches from my face. I reached for him, taking his cock in my hand, slowly rubbing his thickness.

"Fuck," he moaned.

I bit my lower lip as he looked down at me. His patience had expired, and he moved my hand so he could slip on the condom. I scooted to the top of the bed and laid my head against a pillow. Without breaking eye contact, he slowly climbed onto the bed, then on top of me.

I felt him enter and it was, well, a bit underwhelming. After a few minutes and one position change, his fun was over, and he pulled out of me.

"Did you come?" he asked me breathlessly.

Is he serious?

Without hesitating, I answered, "No."

I had no intention of lying. Didn't he know that most women need ten to seventeen minutes to orgasm, and that's after they're already aroused? And most women, myself included, need more than just vaginal penetration to climax.

"Damn, you are so hot," he said. "I didn't think I'd come that fast with how much I drank."

And yet, here we are.

So romantic. I didn't know what to say. I was hot and aroused, but pretty unsatisfied. And being drunk meant I likely wouldn't get off. Especially not in the heat. Despite having an air conditioner, it was still like eighty degrees in my room.

I turned to face him, my naked body exposed. I thought about telling him what I needed to finish off the evening satisfied, but then my fear of taking "too long" changed my mind.

"Let's call it a night. Do you want to sleep here?"

I mean it's 3:00 a.m., what's he supposed to say, Courtney?

He sat up, his legs hanging over the bed. "Yeah, I need to shower first though. Can I borrow your toothbrush?"

Nate would never have shared his toothbrush. What an interesting thought…

Considering his tongue had been in my mouth most of the night, I agreed. We headed to the bathroom. I watched him shower and longed to be in there with him. Even though he was just inside me, the act hadn't felt intimate—I craved more closeness. Showering with someone is intimate, right? But I didn't feel like we were close enough for me to join him. So I didn't.

We finished getting ready, hopped into bed, and Amsterdam rolled onto his side.

So much for cuddling.

Even though it was still incredibly warm, and the last thing I wanted to do was touch someone for a prolonged period, I deeply desired to be held. To be loved. Valued. Seen.

I slept like shit, spending most of the night tossing and turning. Not just because of the heat, but also because Nate had no idea I was with another man. I hated that I had to hide this from him. It felt wrong, but I also knew the truth would hurt him, and he had asked to be kept in the dark.

When I awoke the next morning, I realized I hadn't spent the night with another man in twenty years. I had no idea how I felt about that, but was soon distracted by Amsterdam's wandering hands. He pulled me into his body and started kissing me. I knew there'd be no sex since we had already used our only condom. But that didn't stop us from utilizing our hands and lips and tongues to explore each other's bodies.

Our time that morning was playful. Easy. And damn, I loved how he looked at me with that mischievous grin and hungry desire.

I checked out of the hotel, and we walked to our cars together. He carried my suitcase, and I wondered if I would ever see him again.

Do I want to see him again? Does he want to see me?

He put my suitcase in my car and closed the door.

I smiled at him and coyly said, "Well, thanks for dinner. This was fun."

He stepped closer to me, his green eyes shimmering. "It was. I hope to see you again."

I moved my hands to his chest, smoothing out his white shirt. "I'd like that."

He leaned in and kissed me hard before we parted and went our separate ways.

When I got home, I didn't tell Nate what happened, because I wanted to honor his request. But that's not the whole truth. I also didn't want to tell him because I didn't want him to make me feel bad for what I had done. I wanted to savor the romantic rendezvous I'd just had. And I didn't want to apologize for a single minute of it.

I was tired of apologizing. It felt like I had spent most of my life apologizing. For taking up too much space. For not being thin enough. For being too emotional. For having desires of my own outside of motherhood and marriage. For wanting something more than what I already had and should be grateful for—a beautiful life as a doctor's wife.

It was exhausting—I was exhausted. And the only thing that seemed to spark joy was the allure of an expanded life.

Amsterdam and I texted for a few days after. I kept waiting for him to ask to see me again. I knew that what we had wasn't special, but somehow, I felt special with him, and I couldn't quite figure out why. Our conversations were not riveting or even that engaging. But I loved how he looked at me. How he desired me. It continued to stoke the fire that had been ignited a few weeks before.

Later that month, Nate encouraged me to go to Heidelberg and take another night to write. He was incredibly supportive of my writing and knew that I worked best without distractions. Even though I should have been going to write, my body craved being with Amsterdam again. I texted him.

ME

I'll be in Heidelberg tomorrow. Meet me there.

He read it. But never responded.

I drove to Heidelberg wondering if I'd have another night with Amsterdam. I hoped he would surprise me. That I'd have a message that said, "I'm here. I had to see you again." I checked my phone constantly that afternoon and evening.

The message never came.

My disappointment led to reflection. It wasn't that Amsterdam was an amazing guy. He wasn't. What made that one night magical was that it was the first time in my life where I boldly chose myself. Where I willingly waded into the unknown and opened myself up to the possibilities and pleasures of something that felt crazy.

It was magical because of who I became on the banks of that German lake. That version of me was bold. Confident. Carefree. That version of me laughed with ease and kissed with passion. I wanted to fully become that version of me, but I didn't know how.

How does this version of me exist in a world where a woman like me, married and a mother, isn't supposed to also be those things?

I wanted to be both versions. I wanted both.

CHAPTER FOURTEEN

July 2022
Germany

IT HAD BEEN a couple weeks since my encounter with Amsterdam, and I had pretty much given up any hope that I'd see him again, but the memory of our encounter still thrilled me.

"Well, I just embarrassed myself with a local German guy," I told my best friend, Abby, as I walked into her kitchen.

"Oh, no, what happened?" She motioned for me to follow her outside to her backyard.

I'd known the Johnsons for a couple of years. They had been married almost as long as Nate and I, and were also newer to Germany. Abby had hired me as a relationship coach, then Carlos did, and then about six months after we finished working together, Abby invited me to a Bible study. We'd been besties since. The fact that the Johnsons were also in the transition of opening their marriage was serendipitous.

"I thought he was into me," I explained on the way to their patio table. "We've known each other for a year. He plays on the men's soccer team in our village. We've texted over the past month and he seemed interested. I got tired of playing these games of not knowing so I just said, 'hey, I want to come over and spend the night with you.' He said he didn't see me 'in that way' and just wanted to be friends. What was I thinking?!" I rubbed my forehead in frustration.

"I'm sorry you're feeling that way," she said, grabbing my hand. Her curly auburn hair framed her kind face beautifully.

I plopped down on the patio barstool across from her, next to her husband, Carlos.

"Men troubles?" He asked me sincerely, putting his phone down.

"Yeah. I just don't know where I'm going to meet anyone. Like where do I even start?"

"So have you heard of this app?" Abby began with a smile. "It's called Feeld. It's for non-monogamous folks, and I think you'd enjoy it. There are some people who are looking for three-somes or more kinky stuff, but since you're super sex-positive, I'm sure you'll be fine."

I groaned. "An app? I thought I avoided this whole scene by getting married pre-smart phones."

"It's not that bad," Carlos added. "We both are on it. Haven't really talked to anyone yet, but figuring things out."

"Who is going to want to date me? I mean seriously. I'm almost forty, married, and have three kids."

Carlos' head fell back, and he let out a huge laugh. "I can guarantee you that you won't have a problem on these apps. Come on, Courtney. You're beautiful. Who wouldn't want to date you?"

Abby smiled and nodded in agreement. "Just do whatever you feel comfortable with. Here," she said, putting out her hand. "Give me your phone. I'll download it for you. We can set up your account together."

I protested, shaking my head. "I have to create a profile?! Like with pictures. You guys, no. I can't do this."

Abby raised her eyebrows at me, her pale blue eyes twinkling. "It'll be fun. Come on…" She still had her hand outstretched, waiting for my phone.

Rolling my eyes, I handed it to her.

"Yeah!" she exclaimed, and downloaded the app.

"How's Nate doing with all of this?" Carlos asked.

I shrugged. "He doesn't want to know about any of it. He doesn't want to talk about it. It's like the elephant in the room. I don't know what to do."

My lips curled downward, and I felt a pang of sadness in my chest. "I guess I'm on my own."

Abby reached for my hand again and looked at me. "You always have us. You're not alone in this."

She was right. And what a gift they had been to me through it all.

"Okay, some basic demographics. Birthday, check. Heterosexual still?" she asked.

"Yes. Though maybe this would be easier if I were into women…" I said flatly.

"What do you want to put in your bio?" Abby asked.

I pushed against the table. "Bio?! I don't know…"

Abby continued, eyes fixed on the screen. "What are you looking for?"

I put my head on the table, banging it slightly. "I have no idea."

Carlos sweetly put his arm around my shoulder. "You don't have to have a bio or know what you're looking for. Just leave it blank and see what happens. But I can guarantee you'll have like fifty guys like you by tomorrow."

I quickly raised my head. "Fifty?! There's no way. You're delusional."

"No, Courtney," Carlos countered. "You are if you don't think you're a catch."

Abby handed me back my phone. "You swipe like this, and if you like someone, you click this here"—she pointed to the heart icon—"And if someone likes you, then you can decide if you want to like them back. Also, you may get a 'ping.' That's where someone really likes you. I think that costs extra. Oh, you have to pay to see who likes you."

"I have to pay for this?!" I exclaimed.

I had no idea why I thought this would be painless and free.

Carlos laughed. "There's a free version, but then you don't get to see who matched you. You have to match blindly back, which I don't recommend for you. It's like thirty dollars a month. Just try it for a month and see."

I stared at my phone, convinced this was a terrible idea.

What have I gotten myself into? I wish I could talk to Nate about this…

I looked at Abby and Carlos and smiled. "Thank you. I should probably get home. I'll let you know if I get any likes."

With a laugh, Carlos said, "Not *if*, Courtney. You'll see."

Later that night, I scrolled through what felt like a catalog of men. I had absolutely no idea what I was looking for. Sure, I had been attracted to men I'd seen over the years, but I'd never seriously considered dating them.

Oh, this guy is cute. Thirty-two?! That's seven years younger than me. Probably too young. Right? Well, I'll just keep scrolling.

A notification popped up on my phone: *A liked you.*

OMG! Someone liked me! Okay, let me see.

I clicked on A's profile and saw a blond, German-looking man, drinking a coffee outside some café.

Let's see… he's forty-one. About my age. That's good.

I scrolled through his pictures.

He's attractive. In shape. Also, good. No bio, though. Hmm. I guess I should match him back.

My finger hovered over the heart icon on his profile.

Am I really doing this?

My heart raced. I couldn't tell if I was excited or about to have a panic attack. My finger touched the heart icon.

You've matched with A popped up on my screen. *Chat now or later?*

Wait, do I have to message him now? Good night nurse, why are there so many steps? What do I even say?

Suddenly, I forgot how to flirt. Or talk. Words would not form. I closed the app. That was enough for the night. I put my phone on my nightstand and rolled onto my back. I stared up at the ceiling, wondering what in the actual fuck I was doing with my life.

I woke up the next morning to thirty-two likes. Not the fifty Carlos had told me to expect but still, thirty-two?! I opened the app and went through my likes, looking at the first match.

Oh, geez, no. Next.

Damn, he's got a great body, but you can't see his face in any pictures. Next.

I whittled my way down to five guys I liked back. I noticed I had a conversation alert. When I opened it up, I saw a message from *A*.

A

Guten Morgen.

Oh, shit. He thinks I speak German. Or that I am German. Clearly, Germans speak German, Courtney. Focus. Um… okay, I know how to talk to people. Get it together, girl.

ME

Hey! Good morning. Es tut mir leid aber ich spreche kein Deutsch. Sprechen Sie Englisch?

I think I said that I don't speak German. I guess we'll see if he can speak English.

Within a few minutes, he responded.

A

Yes, I speak English. How are you today? Getting ready for work?

Do I tell him what I do for work? How much information do I give about myself? Is there a guidebook on this? Is it too early to start drinking?

> ME
>
> I'm good. Just got my kids off to the bus, and I'll finish getting ready soon. Drink my coffee.

Another message alert popped up.
Someone else messaged me?
I clicked to the conversation.

> SWISSDOC
>
> You are gorgeous.

I smiled and clicked on his profile, which read a bit more explicit than I was expecting.
Thirty-six. Younger, but not too young.
He didn't show his face in any of the pics, though.

> ME
>
> Thank you.

> SWISSDOC
>
> Ever had a moresome?

That escalated quickly.

> ME
>
> Nope. Can't say that I have. I'm assuming you have though.

> SWISSDOC
>
> Oh yeah. I love them. Do you ever come to Switzerland?

I am already not enjoying this.

> ME
>
> I've been a couple of times but we're three hours from the border.

SWISSDOC

> You could make a special trip. I'd make it
> worth it.

This guy barely knows me. And it's taken him all of thirty seconds to invite me to a moresome. Gross.

I see a message from A come in.

A

> Oh you have kids. How many? I have two.

When do I tell him I'm married? Aren't most of the people on this app in open relationships? How am I this clueless?!

ME

> Yes, I have three.

A

> Three? Wow. You look great for having three kids.

I continued my conversation with him, ignoring Swissdoc. More likes continued to come in. By the time I was done chatting with A, ten more guys had liked me.

Maybe I'm not too bad, after all.

A told me he would message me later, and I found myself excited about the thought of hearing from him again.

Throughout the day, I checked the app regularly. Anytime I saw a notification of someone liking me, a surge of excitement, a ping of joy, pulsed through my body. I still had no clue what I was doing, but so far, this online dating thing wasn't so bad. It was actually kind of fun.

Whoever said online dating is hard probably was doing it wrong.

After a few days, my confidence in interacting with men online began to grow. I liked flirting. And, I loved the attention; it was a huge ego boost. Growing up in a small, religious community didn't make for the kind of environment where I would get attention from men. But now… it felt incredible to be seen. Desired. Even if it was only because they thought I was pretty.

I found that I kind of had a type at this point. Intelligent, charming, funny, athletic, and tall. I hadn't matched with anyone older than A (who was forty-one) and didn't think I should look at anyone under thirty. That just felt weird. Plus, I doubted they would be into someone my age anyway.

I decided to put in my profile the type of man I was looking for and a little about myself. I found the app to be pretty diverse and didn't want to attract guys who were just looking for a dominatrix or a third (someone to join a couple). The app was marketed as "dating for the open-minded" and that it seemed to be.

Bio: Hi! New to all this. I'm married. American. I enjoy sports, travel, reading, and drinking wine.

I read what I had written.

This is the lamest profile.

I still had no idea what I was looking for. I kept the changes I had made to my profile and figured I could update it when I did figure out what I wanted.

Better than nothing, I guess.

My conversations with A, whose actual name was Andreas, were nice. Easy. I learned he was a divorced dad who used to live in Munich. His marriage ended when his wife left him for his best friend. He shared that he enjoyed dating married women because they were less complicated than single women.

I didn't push him on what that meant. I just enjoyed talking with him. The details didn't seem to matter.

ANDREAS

I'd really like to meet you.

ME

Are you asking me out?

ANDREAS

Yes.

ME

I leave for the U.S. tomorrow. I'll be back in two
and a half weeks. I can message you when I'm
back.

ANDREAS

I'd like to stay in touch if that's okay with you.

My heart began to race. It surprised me that he wanted to keep messaging me when I'd be on another continent with a nine-hour time difference.

And we did. We texted and video called. I woke up to "good morning" each day and texted him "good night" before I went to sleep. I could feel myself falling for this charming, funny, handsome German.

I felt giddy. I couldn't eat or sleep, and it wasn't just jet lag. Andreas consumed my thoughts. I didn't even open the app or text with other guys. I had found what I didn't even know I was looking for.

Maybe this open marriage thing isn't so hard, after all.

I was wrong.

CHAPTER FIFTEEN

I WANTED to tell my mom and sister about opening my marriage and my new identity in person. Maybe that was just my way of kicking the can down the road. But since my mushroom trip revelation, I knew that now was the time to share this truth with them.

After my sister left the church when she was eighteen, my parents realized that maybe there was more to the whole "hate the sin, love the sinner" concept. Gone were the days of them cutting off contact with someone because they vehemently disagreed with their lifestyle (i.e., sexual behavior) choices. Thankfully, we had worked through my "sinful ways" and I agreed to their and our pastor's terms—delaying sex until marriage.

Once again, I chose what I thought was the right thing to do in order to keep the peace for everyone else. I buried my desires and ignored the longings deep within me. But they didn't go away. No, they tugged at my heart, and every time they did, I was filled with shame for wanting something I shouldn't.

Since my dad had passed away in 2017, my mom, sister and I had become close, even to the point where my sister felt comfortable sharing with us that she was bisexual.

I wasn't worried about telling Katie that I was polyamorous. She knew it was a much bigger deal for me to realize this truth about myself than to have to share it with her.

"I love you no matter who or what you are, Courtney. You know that," she said as she hugged me.

Comforted, I told her, "I know," and squeezed her tightly.

"Have you told Mom?"

I laughed. "Not yet. Obviously, I'd tell you first."

She laughed, too. "Obviously."

Growing up, sex was not something that was discussed in our house. I attended a Christian school and went to church three times a week. There was an expectation that sex was saved for marriage, which was why my parents had blown up about me having sex with Nate before we got married. I had never heard of individuals who were polyamorous or non-monogamous until I went to graduate school. If I had, I'm sure they would have fallen into the shameful "sexual deviant" category.

After I got married, my parents' beliefs about the world started to change. They no longer blindly accepted the dogma of the church and even became accepting of "alternative" lifestyles. Despite my parents being previously judgmental, they loved my sister and me fiercely. So when I considered telling my mom I was polyamorous, I never feared she would love me less. She had truly evolved in her own views of the world despite still fervently identifying as a Christian.

I decided to take my mom to lunch at Panera and tell her my truth.

How could telling your mom that you're polyamorous over a delish bowl of broccoli cheddar soup be a bad idea?

As we waited to order our food, my heart began to beat faster. I knew I couldn't put this off. I had to do this now.

I picked a table tucked in the corner, away from others, and we both sat down in the hard brown chairs. I couldn't eat yet, but my mom picked up her sandwich to begin.

The tension felt like tumbling in my stomach.

"Mom, I have something to tell you."

She put down her turkey sandwich and gave me her full attention. "This sounds serious."

I did what I always did when I was nervous—massaged my cuticles with the back of my fingers.

"It is," I told her. I didn't want to scare her, so I gave the standard preamble. "My health is fine. The kids are fine, but I need to share something with you."

I paused, swallowing hard. "I'm non-monogamous. Well, actually, I'm polyamorous."

I saw the wheels in her head turning. She narrowed her eyes a bit considering my words and then asked inquisitively, "What does that mean?"

I laughed a little and explained what it meant to me. I wanted her to understand that I loved Nate, but currently wasn't in love with him.

"Non-monogamy is an umbrella term," I explained, motioning a half-circle with my hand. "And polyamory is one of the spokes that falls under it. Swinging is another. Anyway, polyamory means different things to different people. I'm still figuring out what it means for me, but I do know that I desire a romantic relationship with another man, but still want to stay married to Nate."

"That makes sense. I know he hasn't been the most attentive husband."

Suddenly, a memory flooded my mind. A few years ago, Nate had yelled at me in front of the kids and his mother. About what? Who knows. But I remembered my face reddened with embarrassment, and I tried to minimize my feelings so the argument (and my shame) would end, a habit I had become accustomed to. Later that night, his mother said to me, "Why do you put up with that? I would have left him a long time ago."

I knew our families were aware that Nate was a great provider, but not a great husband. This truth felt like it might cushion the blow of me sharing my new identity of being polyamorous.

"How does Nate feel about it?" she asked, leaning toward me.

That seems to be the million-dollar question.

"Well…" I began. "He's still adjusting and processing. I haven't actually used that word with him yet, 'polyamorous,' so I'm not sure. I don't know if this is who I've always been or it's just a by-product of our marriage."

My mom reached her hand across the table and squeezed my arm. "Okay, well, you know that you're my kiddo and I love you no matter what. We can talk more about it if you want, but we don't have to."

A sense of relief washed over me. My shoulders relaxed, and my breathing became more expansive. I had no idea how this conversation was going to go, but this smoothly wasn't what I was expecting. Yes, it had been nearly twenty years since we had had the epic conversation that threatened to sever ties with my parents. But that version of my mother was just as different as who I was all those years ago.

After my dad died five years ago, my mom stopped holding on to the life she thought she was supposed to have and started to embrace change. When your world falls apart, you get to decide what pieces you pick back up. Thankfully, she left the judgement and purity culture behind.

"Thanks, Mom," I said, as I squeezed her hand back.

Later that night, I reflected on how lucky I was that two of the people I loved most in this world now knew my truth. And that didn't make them love me any less. I knew that no matter what happened in my marriage, I always had a safe landing place to come back to. A place where I didn't have to pretend to be monogamous or happy or fulfilled or fine. A place I could let out a big exhale, pull the blanket over my head and know that when I was ready, loving arms would wrap around me and tell me it was going to be alright.

While having the love and support from my mom and sister felt incredible, the gnawing shame of hiding this from Nate, the kids, and everyone else in my life continued to grow. The echoes of Nate's words, "What's wrong with you?" continued to chime in my mind.

The steady drumbeat of shame was accompanied by the resounding gong of dread. Of others discovering my deviation from what was expected of me—a woman who dutifully supported her husband and didn't take up too much space or have too many desires of her own.

And the cymbal of disgust. That I couldn't just be a "normal" monogamous wife and mom who happily put the needs of her husband and children before herself.

In a few days, he and the kids would meet me in Oregon. I knew I had to talk to my husband about what I had realized. I also knew that this could mean the end of our marriage—the end of our family as we had known it.

CHAPTER SIXTEEN

AFTER NATE and the kids arrived in Oregon, I asked him if we could go for a walk privately.

Later, as we walked through my mom's cookie-cutter neighborhood, I poured my heart out to him. I told him that I had felt neglected for years. That I was tired of getting nothing but his breadcrumbs. I told him that I needed a partner who was emotionally available. And then I told him I was polyamorous.

"I'm not asking for your permission anymore, Nate," I said with unwavering confidence. "This is who I am and this is what I need, and if you can't get on board with it, I totally understand."

He tried to shame me into staying small. "Then I'll tell my parents. I'll tell your mom and sister. I'll tell the kids."

I hated hearing him threaten me. But I would be damned if I let him try to shut the cage door on me. I had tasted freedom. I had soared on the winds of non-monogamy, and whatever had been awakened in me refused to return to life as it had been for all those years.

Despite his threats, I felt steadfast in who I was—a woman who *knew* she deserved more. I wasn't hurt by his words. I knew why he was resorting to threats. He was trying to maintain control of his life and ours, grasping at whatever he could to stop this new ship from sailing. We both knew that he was scared and desperate.

Confidently, I told him my mom and sister already knew, and that I didn't care who knew. But the kids…

"If you tell the kids without my permission, and before I'm ready, it will hurt them, and I will never forgive you," I said.

Nate continued to hurl anything at me that could deter me from my newfound truth. "There's no way you could stay in Germany if we're separated or divorced. You'd have to get a work visa and that could take months. You'd have to go back to the U.S., be away from the kids…"

He was right, but I was tired of living in fear. I would not settle for a marriage where my needs weren't met, where I couldn't be my authentic self, just to keep the peace for everyone else.

Calmly, I said, "I will work as a janitor and clean toilets if it means keeping me and the kids in Germany."

Our conversation felt like a game of badminton. Every time Nate smashed the birdie to my side, I lobbed it right back. I wasn't backing down.

After talking and walking for nearly thirty minutes, his heart broke. Call it grace or divine intervention. But something inside of him softened for me, and he finally understood what I needed.

"I don't want to get a divorce," he said, fighting back the tears.

"I don't, either."

I would do anything to keep our family together, but I wouldn't—I couldn't—go back to being monogamous. I had experienced life as a non-monogamous woman, and that freedom was liberating. I would not shrink who I was before because it made him or anyone else uncomfortable.

"It just feels like…" Nate began. "We've been playing a game for the past twenty years and I show up one day to play and you're like, 'oh, we're playing a whole new game now. And if you don't like it, well then don't play.'"

I nodded in agreement. "Yeah, I can see how you'd feel that way. That was never my intention. To change the rules or change the game, but yeah, I guess that's what's happening."

"It just doesn't feel fair," he said, his head dropping in defeat.

Neither was having to walk on eggshells and carry the mental load of the household for nearly two decades.

"You're right," I said in agreement. "It's not fair. And I am sorry about that. I don't know what to do. I just know that I can't go back to monogamy. Gosh, I am so sorry for that."

Tears streamed down my face.

We weaved through an overgrown patch of bushes when Nate asked, "What about telling the kids?"

Anxiety surged through my stomach, acid threatening to rise into my throat. "Absolutely not. I'm not ready."

Nate cocked his head slightly. "I just don't like lying to them. We've always been honest with them."

Once again, he was right. We'd raised our kids in an open and honest home. We didn't keep secrets. We accepted people regardless of their sexual orientation or gender identity.

But what if they thought I was a monster? Disgusting? Depraved?

Those aren't actual exaggerations. I legitimately thought my kids might think of me as a horrible person and reject me as a mother if they knew I wasn't like most moms. Like most people.

I bit the inside of my lower lip. "I'm just… I'm not ready yet. But I want to tell them. When we get this a little more figured out, we'll tell them. I promise."

We continued to walk for a while in silence. The air between us hung heavy with sadness.

After a few minutes, Nate stopped dead in his tracks. I turned back to look at him and saw his lips curl into a half-smile.

"Let's figure this out, then. I've kept you small for a long time, Courtney, and I'm sorry. You deserve to be your most authentic self. I want to help you do that."

Surprisingly, I wasn't relieved to hear those words. I knew how much work this would be for both of us. But I was encouraged. The seeds of hope were being planted in soil that had been dry and barren for years. Now it was up to us to water them.

I looked at the man I had loved for half my life and offered a smile. "Thank you. This isn't going to be easy, but I want to figure it out. Together."

The truth was that I wasn't ready for my marriage to end. I wanted to keep my family together because that's what I thought a good mom did. I didn't want to give up on twenty years of love and adventures with my best friend. I believed in what Nate and I had built, and what was possible. I wasn't ready to throw in the towel.

But I didn't know exactly what I wanted our marriage to look like. I just knew I was miserable and something had to change. Because over the past couple months, I had changed. And whatever had been awakened in me was not interested in slumbering again.

That walk with Nate felt transformative. It was, in many ways. And for the first time in a long time, I was optimistic.

A few days after Nate and I agreed to a new start, we flew back to Germany. I had continued to message Andreas, and we agreed to meet for a date the day after I returned to Germany.

Nate was not ready for that.

CHAPTER SEVENTEEN

August 2022
Germany

AFTER OUR WALK IN OREGON, we agreed to be more transparent with my dating. Nate didn't want to know the details of what I did with other men sexually, but he would like to know when I was going on a date, and a little about who the men were. I never had to ask his permission, but I did need to coordinate it with his and our family's schedule. It was less about his approval and more about consideration.

I was pleased with this new change. I wanted Nate to be aware of this part of my life. I hated having to hide things from him. It hurt me that I hurt him. But I still didn't know how to navigate getting my needs met and honoring my husband. The two continued to feel diametrically opposed.

Before leaving for my date, I walked downstairs to our entryway and put on my shoes. Nate met me there. I could feel his anxious energy, his pain, even before he spoke a word.

"Please don't go," he said.

Tears welled in his eyes. I watched his chest—his breathing was quick and shallow. His body was tense.

My body countered his tension with its own. "I have to. It takes him two and a half hours to get here. He's already on his way!"

Once again, we began a game of badminton.

"No, please. I'm begging you, please don't go meet him."

Birdie coming at me.

The tears he had been fighting fell. I could sense his fear. I knew he was scared, but this felt manipulative.

I was pissed. Nate was trying to lure me back into the cage by making me feel guilty. I feared he was trying to close the door, or worse, clip my wings completely. The fear of never flying again emerged. The need to leave the house, to get out, get away, was so strong. My calm demeanor flipped, and I was ready for a fight.

Why can't he see I'm doing this for *us?! The attention and affection I get from Andreas takes the pressure of off Nate. Why is he being so selfish? When do I get to be happy? Because Nate sure as shit hasn't been interested in my feelings for the past twenty years.*

My anger erupted. "Why are you doing this? You said you'd be supportive!"

Birdie to Nate.

He crumbled. "We're not in a good place for you to go on dates with other men."

I shook my head. "How long am I supposed to wait, Nate? When will it be a good time for you?"

I slammed the birdie to his side.

Before he could answer, I told him I was leaving and I would be home in a couple hours. I walked out the front door, got into my car, and tightly gripped the steering wheel.

I hated that I had to leave like that. That I had to pretend when I met Andreas that my marriage wasn't on the verge of collapsing. So I pushed the anger deep down, put on a smile, and drove to meet the charming German I had been texting for the past three weeks.

I was incredibly nervous to meet Andreas. I was confident in our connection, but I did have one concern—how he would react to my body. Even though I had explored my body image issues with Rachel during my mushroom trip, to my dismay, they hadn't magically resolved themselves.

Andreas and I had never sent nude pictures or seen much below the waist of each other. I hadn't misled him that I was a different size than I was, but I'd also never sent a full-body picture of myself.

What if he didn't like what he saw?

We also never discussed sexual desires or preferences. I was too afraid to bring that up. I had grown up in purity culture where you didn't discuss those things. You took whatever God gave you. And even though I could help my clients successfully communicate in these areas, I was so insecure with being married and dating—I didn't feel like I deserved to ask for what I wanted. I believed I should just be grateful that I got to have sex with someone other than my spouse.

Don't be greedy, Courtney.

The longer Andreas and I texted and talked, the more my anxiety about how he would feel about my body grew. Amsterdam had met me in person, so he had all the information before pursuing things with me. Even though Amsterdam loved my body, that didn't seem to improve my insecurity.

When I arrived at our date, I gave myself a little pep talk.

You can do this, Courtney. He won't care what your body looks like. He cares about you.

But when I got out of my car and saw his reaction to me, it felt like he was disappointed. His mouth frowned slightly, and his energy seemed to close off. Maybe I was projecting. Maybe it was jet lag. But something shifted between us.

Andreas was wearing khaki shorts and a navy Ralph Lauren

polo shirt. His blond hair was slicked to one side, and his face was freshly shaven.

His slim, 6'1" frame hugged me. "You're wearing jeans?! In this weather!"

That German accent never fails to make me smile.

I waved my hand, dismissing his comment. "They're rolled up. It's not that hot."

I looked around the gravel parking lot and wondered what to do. The woods were nearby, so I suggested we go for a walk. I didn't find Andreas as attractive in person as I thought I would, but he was still incredibly charming. As we walked, I thought how much I wanted him to hold my hand. To stop and pull me in for a kiss. I wanted to feel the passion we had cultivated for the past three weeks.

It never happened.

We approached the end of our walk, putting us back at the gravel parking lot.

Think, think, think. What should we do? I know what I want to do…

Even though I wasn't hungry, I asked him if he wanted to get some lunch at the restaurant nearby. He agreed, and we walked to the outdoor eatery.

The waitress seated us at a small wooden table with four chairs.

Do I sit next to him? Is that weird?

I sat down, and he sat across from me. Jet lag and nerves had finally caught up with me. I was barely touching my salad, and I could feel Andreas watching me as I picked at it, moving the turkey around to different parts of my plate.

My frustration grew. Andreas and I had incredible chemistry texting and on calls. But now that we were in person, things felt different. Plus, we still hadn't really touched in the past hour.

I had left my husband at home, who begged me not to come, for this?

I knew German men weren't typically as forward as American or other European men, but this felt like I was pulling teeth to get him to be engaged with me.

Should I just finish my lunch and leave?

I put down my fork and looked at him. "It seems like you're disappointed or something in meeting me."

My boldness caught him off guard. He stumbled for his words. "Oh, um, no? Why do you say that?"

I wiped my sweaty hands on my napkin. "Well, you haven't really touched me. Haven't tried to kiss me. We're not even sitting next to each other. Are you not interested?"

Andreas raised his eyebrows and pouted his lips, his German accent punctuating the words. "No, I am. I don't know why…"

I wasn't going to wait around for him to figure out how he was feeling. "Can I sit next to you?"

"Yes, of course," he said, motioning to the open chair on his right.

I moved to the chair closer to him and put my hand on his leg. My bold approach worked because Andreas leaned in and kissed me.

I'd been dreaming about that for three weeks. His soft lips against mine felt incredible. Finally touching him in real life… It felt good to be here with him.

I leaned in close and whispered in his ear. "I'm not wearing any panties."

Andreas raised his eyebrows, a mischievous grin spreading across his face. "Oh?"

I smiled seductively, sitting back in my chair, my desire for him growing.

His hands gripped the table. "Let's go to my car."

He paid for our lunch, and we held hands as we walked back to his black Mercedes wagon. Anticipation tingled throughout my body.

We slid into the leather seats and closed the door.

"Where should we go?" he asked.

Is there a hotel nearby? What I wouldn't give to be in a bed with this man right now…

I laughed, put my hand on his leg, and raised my eyebrows. "Where do you want to go?"

He turned the car on. "I have an idea."

He drove for about five minutes to a secluded side road in a local forest. He pulled over next to a patch of bushes, turned off the ignition, and looked at me. We didn't speak, but I knew our next steps.

He opened his door, got out of the car, and turned his head back. "Get in the back."

I happily obliged, joining him in his backseat. Nothing in me hesitated. I couldn't think. He consumed all of my thoughts, and I wanted all of him in that moment. Our bodies moved closer and our mouths collided. Tongues flew, hands roamed, clothes quickly came off. In thirty seconds, we were naked in his backseat.

This is insane. Someone could walk by.

Reaching for his shorts on the car floor, he grabbed a condom from the pocket, tore it open with his teeth, and slid it on.

There wasn't much foreplay. Unless you count the three weeks of tension building via texts and calls. In seconds, Andreas was over me, in a modified missionary position. Sweat beaded down the side of his face as he looked into my eyes before sliding inside of me.

A small moan escaped my lips. Pleasure surged through my body.

Sex with Andreas felt like a delicious ice cream cone on a warm summer day. But damn, the heat in the car was about to melt it. Outside, it was ninety degrees. I can't imagine how hot it was in there with the windows rolled up. After twenty minutes of maneuvering and switching positions, Andreas began to lose his erection.

He wiped the sweat slowly dripping down his face. "It's so hot in here. I can't stay hard."

Even though I knew it had nothing to do with me, I took his loss of erection as a personal blow.

Maybe he's not attracted to my naked body.

We agreed to roll down the non-tinted windows a little, chancing someone hearing us. A little air movement made all the difference because after another ten minutes, Andreas climaxed.

We both sat back, breathless, exhausted, and covered in sweat. We awkwardly put our clothes back on—skinny jeans do not go on easily under these conditions—and headed to the large, weathered picnic table a few feet from his car. We each sat on our respective benches and talked across the table. As I stared at his attractive face, sweat gleaming on his forehead, I wondered what he was thinking.

Is he happy to be here? Enjoying this? Is he attracted to me?

My self-worth felt tied to his satisfaction. All the conditioning I had received growing up made me question myself. Women exist for a man's pleasure. A good woman keeps her man satisfied; if he's not satisfied, there must be something wrong with that woman. Men desire smaller women.

It was something I did with every man I had ever dated.

My insecurities made me hesitant to suggest another round, but I wasn't satisfied sexually. I wanted Andreas again. And again. And again. But these weren't exactly conditions conducive to a sexcapade.

Thankfully, I didn't have to ask. After fifteen minutes, he stood up, walked over to me, and grabbed my hand. Silently, he walked me into a patch of flowers, a little way off the beaten trail.

We stopped walking, and he turned to face me. He placed his hand behind my head and pulled me into his body; my face rested against his chest. He wrapped his other arm around me, pressing me tighter against him.

Thump. Thump. Thump.

I could hear his heart beating. His breath shallowing. And I could feel his desire rousing in his pants.

He leaned his face down towards me and pressed his lips passionately against mine. My hands gripped his back, still damp from our tryst in the car.

This feels so good. Please don't stop.

He pulled back and lifted my blue cotton shirt over my head; I did the same to his. He continued to kiss me, making his way down my neck, as I unhooked my bra, exposing my breasts to the outdoor elements. I took off my jeans while he slid out of his shorts.

Andreas laid his shirt on the ground and pulled me down to the forest floor. We looked around, hoping no one would walk by and interrupt us, but even if someone did, I didn't care. Andreas knelt down in the dry grass and laid me all the way back. It felt like we were moving in slow motion. I stared up into his piercing blue eyes, his golden hair shimmering under the summer sun as once again, he slid inside me.

I could feel the pressure in my pelvis building, pleasure just waiting to pulsate throughout my body. Andreas continued to move in and out of me, groaning faintly. After a few more minutes, he climaxed for the second time that day. He rested on top of me, his cock still inside me. My hands rested on his bare back, and I could feel the rise of his quickened breathing.

Wow, that was fun.

I couldn't shake the thought that this was our second sexual encounter, and neither time had he seemed to be concerned with my pleasure.

This is another area where purity culture leaves its mark. Despite having the academic and clinical sexual knowledge, I lacked experience in advocating for my sexual needs. I was sexually immature and inexperienced. I attributed my partner's performance to how he perceived me. Having had the same partner for two decades didn't lend me the skills needed to negotiate with a new sexual partner.

There was no safety to fall back on since this wasn't an established relationship. Even if I had had the skills, I lacked the confidence. Hell, I lacked the self-worth to believe that I was deserving of a partner who prioritized my pleasure.

After a brief recovery, we stood up and began brushing off the dirt and grass while quickly getting dressed. We laughed as we found random pieces of grass and smooshed flowers on different parts of each other's bodies.

Andreas smiled as he pulled something from my hair. "You've got some twigs in your hair. Will probably be finding these things for a few days."

There was nothing that could stop me from smiling. "Thanks," I said as I brushed my hands against my jeans.

Andreas drove me back to my car, and I wondered how to end this first date. As he pulled up to where I had parked, I felt an incredible surge of confidence.

I did this! I initiated this.

I felt like I had absorbed all the energy from the sun on the bed of that forest floor. Happiness beamed from every part of me. As I got out of his car, I turned back to him, leaned back over my seat, and put my lips on his. "I want to see you again."

He smiled. "Of course. Me, too."

I kissed him again. "Text me when you get home."

CHAPTER EIGHTEEN

OVER THE NEXT FEW DAYS, I didn't hear from Andreas much. His dad had some unexpected health stuff, and he started texting me less. I asked him if he wanted to meet up the following week, but he never responded to my request.

I could feel him slowly pulling away, and I didn't understand why. We had both agreed that we wanted something meaningful. Not necessarily a full relationship but something of substance. Now, it felt like he had only wanted to meet for sex.

I texted Abby.

ME

I don't want to get all clingy with Andreas and be like "oh we had sex and you feel distant now."

ABBY

Maybe he just wanted to meet for sex?

ME

He's the one who was like "I'm afraid I might fall in love with you." I don't want to play games but I also don't want to look needy. I'm overthinking this.

ABBY

Yeah, we get this way. It's so good that you're acknowledging your feelings. How are things with you and Nate?

ME

Better. But not. He's trying to be supportive of my non-monogamy journey. Sometimes he really is and other times he spirals and it's awful.

ABBY

Yeah, Carlos is having a hard time. I don't think this whole open marriage thing is working out the way he thought it would.

That's the thing—no one taught us how to navigate anything but monogamy. My entire relationship framework was based on finding one partner and staying with them for the rest of my life. I had absolutely no idea what I was doing or where I was headed.

I didn't want to leave Nate for Andreas—I wanted them both. But Andreas didn't seem to know what he wanted, and Nate's feelings were incredibly unpredictable.

I never knew what version of Nate I was going to get. It depended on his mood, or not. I didn't know. All I knew was that I was back to walking on eggshells, and I loathed that feeling.

NATE

Going to bed now. Not trying to upset you. I just see your cup being filled and for some reason it is hard for me tonight. I feel lonely. Not trying to change what you are doing. Just letting you know. Love you. Went for a walk.

My stomach dropped. I hated getting these kinds of messages

from Nate. I never knew what to do. Give him space or try to connect? I didn't know.

> **ME**
>
> Want me to go with you?

NATE

I don't want to bring you down. I will be okay.

Too late.

NATE

And of course I do. But you are doing what you need so I will just be back later. I won't interrupt you. Night.

> **ME**
>
> If you want me to come, then ask me.

NATE

I always want you to come on walks with me, but not this time. It feels different right now. You know it's hurting me and yet you continue on. I don't get it. You know I'm struggling right now.

> **ME**
>
> I don't know what to say.

NATE

Your actions said enough.

> **ME**
>
> You're hurting and I'm sorry.

NATE

Not enough to change anything and that hurts even more.

I understood where he was coming from. If you know that what you're doing is hurting your partner, you're supposed to stop, right? But what happens when it's not what you are doing that hurts your partner but *who* you are that is hurting them? Then what?

I was in a lose-lose situation. If I chose myself, I would hurt the man I loved. Who I had vowed to spend my life with. Who I was raising three children with. If I chose him… my heart would sink every time I even entertained that thought.

Because the truth was that I had chosen him. For almost two decades. I had given him everything. And I still felt empty and alone. I couldn't go back into the box I had meticulously built. The one adorned with accolades and achievements. The one people marveled at: "How does she do it all? She has such a beautiful family. Wow, a doctor's wife. What a great life she has."

And I did have a great life in many aspects. But the truth was that I burned that motherfucking box that had kept me small the day I told Nate I wasn't in love with him and I was polyamorous. I had set the life we had built up in a blaze. Now I was having to watch as it burned, wondering what would be salvageable after the fire went out.

Later that night, he wanted to talk.

"You're steering this ship, Courtney," he said coldly. "Not me."

I shook my head in anger. "What does that mean!?"

Resentment flashed in his eyes. "It means that you're in charge. I'm just along for the ride."

I threw my hands up. "Oh. So all this, our life now, is my responsibility?"

Nate shrugged. "This is the boat you're building."

You motherfuc—

This was the storm that had entered our harbor. Nate didn't want to give up control of the ship he had been steering for most of our relationship. He saw my stand not as an equal bid for power, but as mutiny.

For nearly two decades, I had managed Nate's feelings. Now, my husband was having to take responsibility for them. He suddenly had to deal with a wife who was no longer interested in polishing the bars of her pretty cage. Sure, I hadn't been a doormat for most of our marriage, but I was so focused on keeping the peace that I was willing to relinquish my power.

I was no longer interested in being a pushover and peacemaker. I was willing to lose it all, my family, our real estate investments, our retirement savings, all of it because something sang from deep within me. At my core, I knew I was meant to soar.

I put my hand against my chest. "This is just me?"

I tightened my jaw and squeezed my nails into my palms. "You know what? If you don't like it, find another boat."

I was tired of the guilt. Tired of shrinking myself for the convenience of others. I was no longer afraid of being alone. I wasn't scared of what others would think if they heard Nate and I had split up.

Yet, despite my sheer determination, I could feel myself splintering. As much as I wanted to shove Nate into the life raft and send him on his merry way, a large part of me felt tethered to him. Our lives were tangled together, and even though I knew I was capable of separating from him, he felt like the glue holding my fracturing pieces from floating away.

Yes, our marriage was crumbling. But I was breaking.

CHAPTER NINETEEN

August 2022
Germany

I KNEW that I needed help and quickly. Nate and I were sleeping in separate rooms. I told the kids that I was sleeping downstairs because of the jet lag and how hot it was upstairs, but the truth was that I couldn't be in the same bed as him. I needed space. I needed to process everything that had come up over the last few weeks and figure out how to function with this new crippling anxiety and depression.

For the first time in my life, I was depending on two of my closest female friends: Abby and Kaitlin. I could no longer shoulder my secret alone, and these two women showed up for me by listening, encouraging, and advising. After my high school best friend betrayed me, I had subconsciously vowed to never fully trust women again. Sure, I had girl-friends, but I always kept them at a distance, never sharing too much information for fear that it could be used against me. Used to hurt me.

Despite Jesus's message of love and unity, young women were

often pitted against each other because we were looking for the same valuable prize: a godly man. Since those weren't in abundance, Christian girls often covertly competed in the limited pool of potential husbands, using any means necessary to secure a solid spouse.

This planted distrust in my fertile soul for women and pedestaled men. A good man was the prize. The goal. Not a solid group of girl-friends. No, finding a spouse who would be your everything—that was the ultimate dream.

Yet, I had obtained that. I had checked the boxes and made it to the top of the mountain. But my husband didn't meet all my needs. Nate wasn't my everything. And I realized I wasn't the only one who struggled with this reality.

Abby, Kaitlin, and I met every week for "book club." We never actually ended up talking about the book we were reading. Instead, we shared about our lives. Our marriages. Our motherhood. These two women had front-row seats to my crumbling marriage and walked with me through all of it. But they also believed I needed professional help. So I went in search of it.

I tried to find a therapist, but that proved to be much harder than I thought. Many U.S.-based providers are unable to see clients outside of their state, even virtually. And finding providers in Germany who spoke English, and had availability, was almost impossible. I finally gave in and tried BetterHelp, a mental health platform that provides online therapy services.

I am a trained mental health and sex therapist, so I knew the type of therapy I was looking for. I was elated when I found a woman who had training in my preferred modality and signed up for a session. She was an older British woman. Her warm smile stood out to me, so I was not prepared for her reaction to my situation.

I laid it all out at the beginning of our first session. "I recently came out as polyamorous, and I'm having trouble navigating this new identity in my marriage. I'm dealing with a lot of anxiety and some depression."

I asked her if she was comfortable working with clients who were non-monogamous. Not all therapists are, so I wanted to make sure I was supported by someone who was.

She waved her hand, dismissing my concerns. "Yes, of course I'm fine with you being non-monogamous."

Apparently, we had different definitions of what "being fine" meant. During that first session, she kept referring to polyamory as "polygamy."

Yeah, sure, they sound alike. I'll give you that.

In the second session, she said that polyamory was "basically legalized cheating." I fired her after that.

Back to the drawing board.

I refused to give up. Therapy is like dating, which I realized was ironic in my situation—finding the "right one" takes some time. The next therapist through BetterHelp was great. I loved our first session and felt like I was gaining traction.

Until I showed up for our second session. And she didn't. Confused, I checked my email to verify the time. I was surprised to see that I had received a message stating that my therapist was "no longer practicing."

Are you kidding me?!

I was beyond frustrated at this point. My anxiety wasn't improving. My marriage was incredibly strained still.

I'm trying, Universe! Can't you see that?

At this point, I didn't make the connection that I had an anxious attachment. As a trained therapist, I was familiar with attachment theory, but it wasn't something I was able to apply to myself at the time. Everything felt overwhelming and most days I was drowning.

I shared my frustrations with a friend who recommended I try a local therapist. I called the woman who seemed lovely on the phone that same day. Thankfully, she was able to get me in for a session the next day.

Hallelujah!

At the beginning of our session, I was adamant that I was not there for marriage help. I knew she was a marriage and family therapist, so I made my disclaimer known. I just needed to talk about how I was feeling about myself—my identity—and not how to improve my marriage. That could come later.

Unfortunately, she must have missed the memo along with my reminder during the session that I didn't want to focus on my marriage.

I tried not to roll my eyes. "Yes, I am familiar with the four horsemen of the apocalypse…" I said. Several times. I didn't need a review of Gottman theory (a popular approach to couple's therapy founded by John Gottman.)

I left that session incredibly defeated. Zero for three in the span of three weeks. How could that be possible when I'm a trained therapist? How could getting mental health help be so hard?

I dreaded the idea of opening myself up to one more person. But I was hardly sleeping. Barely eating. Hiding my feelings from everyone. And Nate and I couldn't figure out how to navigate any of this. We were arguing all the time. The tension was so thick in our house, it felt suffocating.

If we had been in the U.S., I would have asked Nate to move out or asked if I could go stay with my sister for a few weeks. But living in a foreign country on official U.S. Government orders, on another continent from my family, made things complicated. It put pressure on me to make things work in my marriage that I may not have wanted had we been living in the U.S.

One day, I thought of tapping into my network from graduate school.

Someone HAS to be able to help me.

I reached out to a former classmate who had been practicing therapy for years. After emailing back and forth, we decided that Nate, he, and I should set up a session together.

It was one of the best decisions I've ever made. Dave, our therapist, provided valuable insight into our situation without judgment. We are forever grateful for him.

As great as Dave was for our marriage, that still didn't solve the problem of my identity crisis. After coming out to a friend as polyamorous, she told me about a woman she knew who did somatic coaching, a holistic type of coaching that incorporates the mind, body, and spirit through various techniques and exercises.

I was desperate enough to try anything at that point. Once again, I had to tell my story to a stranger. Fortunately, Stephanie was amazing, and I am incredibly grateful for her message of love and acceptance.

My sessions with Stephanie focused on reconnecting me to my body. I had never realized until working with her how disconnected I was from my physical form due to the messaging I received in purity culture. I was always taught that the body couldn't be trusted. It was weak and would lead us astray, away from God. My body was a temptation to men that would cause them to lust after me. I was taught that men who pursued women sexually usually did so because the women were "asking for it" with what they were wearing.

The more I worked with Stephanie, the more I realized how polluted my thought process was. The programming of purity culture had me believe I was only interesting, desirable or worthy if a man validated me as being those things. I was only able to know my own greatness if a man deemed me as great. And the ultimate way this was demonstrated was by a man choosing me.

Society had scared women into believing that if we were single, it was because a man hadn't chosen us. And since men want a wife, if you weren't chosen, there must be something wrong with you. Being single was declaring to the whole world that you were defective, unwanted, and undesirable. Because who would *choose* to be single? When partnership was the pinnacle of a well-lived life.

I slowly realized how powerful these beliefs had been for me, and for the first time in my life, I began to feel safe in my body. I learned how to regulate my nervous system so I wasn't always in a stress state. And I started to believe that maybe, just maybe, there wasn't anything wrong with me. Stephanie was exactly who I needed to begin the journey of coming home to myself.

Because that's what this was all about. Yes, my marriage was unraveling, and how I saw the world had completely shifted. But those deconstructions were a result of what had been awakened inside of me: the desire to connect with a part of myself that I had never considered—never explored—never even knew existed. For the first time in my life, I wondered who I actually was, and what I truly wanted my life to look like.

The circle of people who knew that I was polyamorous continued to widen, and that terrified me. I thought this part of me was something I could keep under wraps. I would NOT be one of those people who talked about her dating and relation-ships publicly—those people are annoying. We get it. You're so happy and have lots of love and sex. Yay for you.

Never thought I'd write a book about all of this. Oh, the irony.

I feared that the more people who knew, the less I'd be accepted, the less I'd be respected, the less I'd be loved. Being polyamorous was only a small part of who I was, right? So, I didn't need to share that with everyone.

Nate still thought we should tell the kids, but I was adamant we shouldn't. I just didn't feel ready. I was scared of the possi-bility that I could lose their love. I researched "how to come out to your kids as polyamorous" and all the advice was mixed. Most of it was focused on introducing a new partner to the mix, or the realities of dealing with both parents who date other people. None of it applied to my current situation. Of course, our kids not knowing added another layer of complication when they would ask, "What are you and dad fighting about?"

"Oh, you know, I decided to change the rules of our marriage after almost twenty years together. He's not adjusting well. It's fine. Everything is fine."

Having to say, "I'm polyamorous" felt foreign. Incredibly uncomfortable. It was easier saying it to distant friends or strangers rather than someone I cared about. I braced for the judgment and questions from others, often holding my breath, when I shared that information.

And you know what? It never came. Not once. Sure, I'd get questions. But no one in my life ever reacted negatively to me sharing my truth. I am beyond grateful for that because I know that's not the case for everyone.

But I couldn't keep ignoring that I was sitting on a ticking bomb. I was terrified that someone would confront me in front of my kids and launch accusations that I was a terrible person, a terrible mother. That they would reflect back to me what I already believed about myself—that there was something wrong with me.

Because there *had* to be something wrong with a woman who was willing to lose it all—a beautiful family, financial security, stability—just so she could be her authentic self. What in the hell did that even mean?

I had no idea. But I knew that the life I had before was gone, even if it didn't look like it to anyone on the outside. I kept wondering when I would feel that happiness. When I'd finally reach that moment where I could finally relax and all would be right with the world.

When does that happen? Is it even possible for someone like me? Someone who is willing to risk it all because the life she has no longer fits?

I just needed Nate to get on board fully. Then I'd be happy. Right?

CHAPTER TWENTY

August 2022

AS THE WEEKS PASSED BY, most things Nate did annoyed me: how he looked at me, his energy when he walked into a room, the love notes he started leaving on my computer, the emails he would send sharing about his feelings.

When we were first married and Nate was in the early years of medical school, he wasn't around much. And when he was, he was even less emotionally available than normal. All of his energy went into being a doctor, leaving me little to no attention or affection. Oftentimes, I would ask him if we could talk about how I was feeling.

"I don't have time to deal with this right now, Courtney," he would say.

One day, I needed him to know how alone and frustrated I felt.

"What if I sent you an email?" I asked.

"Sure," he responded in annoyance.

So I did. I crafted an email where I poured out how much I

missed connecting with him, how I desired him and how lonely I felt with the way things had been. I proudly hit the send button and eagerly awaited his response.

Days went by without a reply. Finally, I brought it up while we were getting ready for bed one night.

"Did you get my email?"

"Oh, yeah," he said nonchalantly.

"Did you read it?"

He put down his toothbrush and looked at me in the mirror. "It was like half a page long. I don't have time to read that. Can't you make it shorter next time?"

I suppressed the shame that bubbled up. I sequestered my needs and accepted that maybe I was asking for too much from the man I loved.

Fast forward fifteen years and those tables had turned. Anxiety would surge in my chest when I saw an email from Nate. I dreaded having to sift through his slew of feelings. It was exhausting and I had no idea how to give space to what we were facing.

This wasn't just an awakening for me. It was absolutely one for him as well. We were both struggling to adjust to all these changes. We were trying to chart a new course, and the map that had been handed to us (by the patriarchy) was no longer relevant. But our instruments were still calibrated to return us to our golden cages.

Nate was one of the most driven people I'd ever met. It was one of the reasons I fell for him. His dream had always been to be a doctor. Everything he did was designed to bring him one step closer to practicing medicine. That meant things like emotional awareness and communication took a back burner. Feelings got in the way of a profession that valued logic, focus, and hard facts.

For most of my life, my dad was this way, too. Logical, analytical, quick to judge. He didn't always consider someone's feelings, and his way of communicating was either passive aggressive or yelling. So when I married Nate, I didn't think twice about having an emotionally unavailable partner. This was what I had known. What my nervous system had associated with safety and love from growing up with an emotionally unavailable father, even though consciously I knew those behaviors were anything but loving and safe. Over time, as I grew in my own personal development, I deeply desired a partner who understood their emotions. Who understood mine.

It was one of the reasons I fell out of love with Nate. Our emotional connection was nearly non-existent. But now, after twenty years of having a partner disconnected from their feelings, I was suddenly faced with a man finally ready to feel. And when you're not used to it, experiencing emotion can feel overwhelming. Like finally being able to hear or see. Your body and mind go into sensory overload. And instead of meeting this new Nate with compassion, I met him with contempt.

No matter what he did, I felt like I was suffocating from his need to save our marriage. It felt desperate, and was a huge turnoff. Suddenly, he was complimenting me, wanting to touch me. He hadn't been the most attentive husband, so this sudden change irritated me.

I was repulsed by the idea of having sex with him. I had been begging him for years to open up to me emotionally. To desire me sexually. And it took a crisis like this to get his attention. I was angry. Resentful. I wanted to run away. But I couldn't. I couldn't abandon my family. I was ashamed of who I was and couldn't risk people finding out that my marriage ended because I wanted to be with other men.

I couldn't even imagine people's reactions. Actually, I could. Here's one scenario I often pictured. "Did you hear what happened to Courtney and Nate?" they'd ask each other in hushed tones. "She asked for an open marriage so she could shag a bunch of guys. What kind of mother does that? She probably needs mental help. Can you believe she thinks *she's* capable of coaching others on their relationships?! Madness!"

I assumed people would think the worst of me. Other women would shake their heads in disgust that I was so depraved and lacked the self-control to be a proper wife and mother. Men would shun me for the absence of moral character and see me as someone who abandoned my family for carnal desires.

Looking back on my resentment and shame, I realize that my disdain for Nate was simply a reflection of how I felt about myself. I didn't believe I deserved a husband who loved me for who I truly was.

To be fair, I didn't even know who I was. Purity culture and the patriarchy tell you what a good wife and woman looks like: you're slim, small, meek, pretty but unassuming, servant-like, with no needs and desires of your own. You exist to support and help the man in your life. Women who want things outside of their home and family are selfish.

These beliefs were simmering beneath the surface. I didn't think I was worthy of a life full of love and joy. At this point, I didn't even know if I could feel love and joy again.

Instead of deep-diving into my own underlying issues, which was emotionally labor intensive, I continued to spend time on the dating app. The attention and appreciation I received from men I had never met, who were handsome and funny and sexual, distracted me from my reality. It was just the escape I needed.

Greek liked you.

I saw the notification on my phone and opened the app.

Attractive. Athletic. Great smile.

My eyes came to his age. My mouth fell open.

He's twenty-eight?!

Anytime I matched with someone more than three years younger than me, it felt like I was doing something wrong. That I was violating the expectation that you could only date within a certain window. I was already challenging social norms by being married, a mother, and polyamorous. Why couldn't I just be attracted to men who were also around my age?

Greek didn't look like he was in his twenties. He was tall, had a nicely trimmed beard, and damn, that grin. Mischievous. Seductive. I wanted to know more. And since I hadn't heard from Andreas in a week, I figured I would see who this guy was.

We exchanged pleasantries and switched to the messaging app, Telegram. Greek was funny and witty and charming. It was easy to talk to him. Unlike Andreas, Greek asked a lot of questions about my marriage.

GREEK

What's the deal you have with him if I may?

ME

I just tell him when I'm talking to someone and then if I want to meet the guy for a date or do an overnight.

GREEK

Damn, okay so he is fine with it? Does he do the same?

ME

He does not. He's never had the desire to. I'd be fine with it if he did, but so far, he hasn't shown any interest.

GREEK

Has it been long since you opened the marriage? Just can't get how he is okay with it.

This sentiment is something I would experience often. A lot of people subconsciously (and some even consciously) believe that relationship equals ownership. I have been asked often how Nate "lets" me be with other men, as if he controls my body and sexuality (which he does not). The belief that a man could "let" his wife be with other men without deriving any pleasure from it has dumfounded many.

ME

He works a lot and just doesn't have time for another relationship, but really he doesn't have the desire. We opened the marriage two months ago.

GREEK

And for you it's just sex though, right? Or polyamorous as in getting in a relationship too? Sorry for the question bombing. This is an interview if you haven't realized.

ME

For me, that's something I'm still figuring out. I don't like one-night stands. I need to feel safe with the person to have sex with them. I like getting to know people and connecting with them. No, this is fun! You can ask me whatever you want.

GREEK

That is awesome of him. Poor guy on one hand, but super nice haha.

ME

I mean he got to do what he wanted to do for twenty years. I supported him through med school and residency and fellowship. Conferences and committees. Training for Tough Mudders and anything else he wanted to do. All the while, I took care of our three kids, paid the bills, did laundry, cooked, cleaned, etc. So he's had it made pretty well.

GREEK

For me it's mostly sex, I mean I love having time for myself you know... especially after breaking up after being with someone for six years. I have so much time to myself traveling and doing what I want. So I don't want anything serious.

The conversations with Greek were pretty sexual. He wasn't

interested in getting to know me as a person and never asked to meet up since he thought our ninety-minute distance was too far.

I enjoyed our conversations. They energized me and helped me escape the tension at home. Plus, I liked that Greek was younger than me. It made me feel empowered and sexy to be desired by an attractive younger man. My confidence about my body increased, and I started to feel good about how I looked.

Even though I was struggling in my feelings for Nate, I felt like I needed to help him transition into our new normal. I still didn't want my family to be torn apart. Working things out with Nate needed to happen. I wanted to know I'd given it my all.

After a few sessions with Dave, I truly believed we could figure this out. I knew we couldn't keep going the way we were. Everyone in our house was walking on eggshells, and that wasn't fair to the kids. It wasn't fair to any of us.

I started to open my heart back up to him.

NATE

Not trying to burden you but just want to keep you updated. I am doing very bad today. I slept horrible and have some stuff I would like to talk to you about in person, maybe before book club.

ME

Oh no! You're not bothering me. Now I'm scared.

NATE

I am too.

ME

Can we talk now? Very bad how?

NATE

Bad.

ME

Call me.

I called him. He shared that he felt like he wasn't enough.

That everything he had worked so hard for was for nothing. He vomited all of his emotions onto me. It was incredibly hard for me to hear. Once again, I was responsible for managing his emotions. I was overwhelmed with holding space for his fluctuating feelings and attending to my own identity crisis.

He texted me after our call.

NATE

Man, what is my deal? I am really an idiot here. I had a great day yesterday with you (minus a few minutes last night). I will get my shit together. I just feel raw right now and not handling it well. Love you. I hope you can still open up to me. I won't do this again.

ME

You're allowed to be upset. It's just hard right now for me to help you process.

NATE

Thanks, but questioning your commitment to the family, so dumb. I can't wait to see how amazing you will become after you heal from all this.

The more supportive Nate was, the more my heart opened to him. The more controlling and resentful he was, the more I wanted to escape. But I couldn't say that Nate wasn't trying; he really was. He would ask about the men I was talking to. Ask how he could support me. And my heart continued to soften toward him.

One day, when we were standing in the kitchen, all the annoyance and anger I had had for Nate seemed to vanish. I finally saw him as a man dedicated to his wife's growth. As someone who was as committed to keeping their family together as I was.

And damn, that aroused me. It was like seeing him in a whole new light. Suddenly, my body craved him. We hadn't had sex in weeks. We'd barely touched. But something inside me ached for him.

I tilted my head and leaned against the kitchen counter, fighting the awkwardness since it had been so long. "Do you want to go upstairs?"

Nate raised his eyebrows. "What?"

I took a step forward and repeated myself.

He put his work bag down and looked at me with wondering eyes. "Are you sure?"

I shifted my weight back to both legs. "Do you want to talk about it or do something else?"

He nodded to the door. "Let's go."

The next day, I texted him.

ME

How are you doing today?

NATE

Okay, I certainly slept better. Feel a little blah but still better. How are you feeling?

ME

We had sex three times yesterday and you're just blah?!

NATE

Not related, silly. Today I am worried about sliding back or not continuing to get better given how awesome yesterday was. And I mean awesome!

ME

Don't think that. I mean I understand how you feel. I feel great!

And that was the truth. Nate and I were finally on our way to a new normal. We both had no idea what we were doing but we were doing it together and that was what mattered.

It also didn't hurt that after that night we started having the most sex we'd ever had since the first few months of marriage. One week, we had sex fifteen times. Fifteen!

I felt free, yet still conflicted because I knew this was still so hard on him. But we were on the right track. Nothing could derail us. Right?

CHAPTER TWENTY-ONE

ONE OF THE things I've loved about living in Germany is that it allowed me to return to soccer, or Fußball as Germans call it. On August 28th, during a game, I went for a ball against a girl half my age, stepped wrong, and immediately collapsed to the ground.

Pain surged through my lower left leg. As hard as I tried, I couldn't get back up and couldn't feel much below my left knee. I was carried off the field and watched my team win from the sidelines. After the game, Nate told me to go to the ER and said he'd meet me there after he dropped off his brother and sister-in-law, who had just flown in from Seattle that day.

An X-ray later confirmed I had fractured my tibia and would need surgery. I had played soccer for most of my life. Played in thousands of games and never had more than a rolled ankle. Now, at thirty-nine, when things finally felt like they were looking up, I was told I couldn't bear any weight on my leg for three months after surgery because of an injury I sustained in a game. I was devastated.

I spent the next ten days before surgery trying to pivot my plans. We had booked travel, the kids had school starting, and I was essentially confined to the bed since I needed to keep my leg elevated. I had to rely on Nate and the kids for everything.

The cracks Nate and I had begun to repair quickly turned back into chasms. Everything I had done: cooked, cleaned, done laundry, drove kids, picked up around the house, he now had to pick up the slack for. At least for the next six to eight weeks.

All my coping skills were no longer available: exercise, soccer, getting a massage, getting out of the house and spending time with friends, traveling—no longer an option. Sure, I could've asked a friend to pick me up and drive me over, but I was depressed, and in a lot of pain, so being social was the last thing I wanted.

Nate was no longer reaping the benefits of having a wife fueled by her polyamorous adventures. Our sex life dropped off. We argued all the time because we both felt unsupported. Tensions were incredibly high, and I sank deeper into feeling alone.

To top it all off, I hadn't heard from Andreas in almost two weeks and that added to my depression. One night, Nate asked me if Andreas knew what had happened to my leg.

I shook my head. "No. Why would he? I told him I would give him the space he wanted."

Nate pursed his lips and looked at the floor. "I know this may sound weird, but what if I reached out to him and told him what happened? He should know."

Wait, what?

My eyebrows shot up immediately. "Are you serious?"

I was shocked. But more importantly, I felt an immense sense of pride for Nate. I couldn't imagine how hard that would be for him, yet he was willing to put my feelings first.

I considered his suggestion. "Do you think that'd be weird if you did?"

Without missing a beat, he looked at me and said, "This whole situation is weird."

Fair point.

I missed Andreas. I missed our connection. Our conversations.

Screw it. Why not? What's the worst that could happen?

I nodded. "Yeah. I mean, okay. If you want to. I'll send you his email."

On the day of my surgery, Nate emailed to a man he had never met. A man he had once begged me to not see because he was scared I would leave him for Andreas.

Andreas, this is Nate Boyer... Courtney's husband. I wanted to give you an update on Courtney. Just to be upfront, she is aware that I am emailing you and it was my idea. To start, I did not think that up until a few weeks ago I would ever be sending an email like this, but lots of things in my life have changed recently, and I wanted to email you for her.

About ten days ago Courtney was playing in a Fußball match (she plays for our town) and during the game, she had an injury where she fractured her tibial plateau. She has been on crutches for the past ten days and had surgery today to repair the fracture. She wanted you to know as she had not had a chance to tell you about this in the last week. The surgery went well, and she should be home tomorrow with a long recovery ahead.

That is not the real reason I wanted to email you though. What I wanted to tell you is how amazing Courtney is. I am admittedly biased, but she is one of the most amazing and beautiful people I know. She very much enjoyed the conversations and time you shared, maybe more than you know. Personally, I believe that she was/is in love with you. Not in an overly dramatic or obsessive way but as someone she wanted to continue to spend time with and to be a part of her life. I am not sure if you feel the same way or if there is something else/someone else that you are dealing with right now, but I am here to ask that you choose to be a part of her life or let her know that is not what you desire. It does not need to be all-consuming or encompassing but Courtney and I both feel that she has love to give and deserves to be loved.

If you want to know more or have any questions, I will do my best to update you.

Respectfully,

Nate Boyer

The next day, still at the hospital, I received a text from Andreas. My heart raced as I opened the message.

ANDREAS

Hey. How are you?

ME

I've been better.

ANDREAS

Yeah, I heard. Your uh, husband emailed me.

ME

I know.

ANDREAS

Don't you think that's a little weird?

Geez. Well, that wasn't what I was hoping he would think.

ME

Not really. I mean your presence in my life affects him too. Not sure how it makes it weird.

I wasn't going to back down. Andreas could go fuck himself if he thought what Nate did was weird. I thought it was one of the bravest things a husband in his position could do.

Andreas and I had semi-awkward small talk for a few more minutes. He was in Greece with his kids and didn't seem to be interested in reconnecting. I saw the conversation for what it was and told him to enjoy his time in Greece. It was the last time we ever spoke.

I set my phone down and wondered how I had gotten here. Even though my tibia had been repaired, and was now holding strong thanks to seven screws and a plate, I felt incredibly broken.

I looked at my bandaged leg, resting atop two hospital pillows, and reflected on my current reality.

Why this? Why now? Is the Universe punishing me, pushing me back down because I got "out of line?" Is this the price for wanting too much? Why can't I be content with what I have?

That night, I had a dream. Maybe it was the pain meds—maybe it was the Universe answering me back. No idea. But I will never forget how real it felt.

My tail flicked back and forth as I paced my prison. My home. I was a well-trained circus animal. When they let me out of my cage, it was only conditional. As long as I did what I was supposed to do, I could be free from captivity. But the moment I stepped out of line, the moment I bucked against my upbringing, I was led on a leash straight back to that iron cell. Where I would sit and stew until I realized who was in charge. Who I answered to. Acknowledged who held my freedom. Until I succumbed to society's expectations of me.

But suddenly, I realized I possessed power. I was no longer the circus animal. I was myself. Standing on two human legs. I walked to the front of my cell and wrapped my hands around the cold steel bars. Touching the bars transmitted a truth—this cage was never meant to protect me, as my captors often told me.

No, it was designed for their power to be preserved. A way to protect themselves from a woman who knew who she was and what she wanted. Because a powerful woman is a force to be reckoned with.

I stared at the keys that jangled at my captors' waists. I was always looking outside of myself for the answer to my freedom. Suddenly, I felt something cool against my chest. Instinctively, my hand moved to my neck. I felt a thin metal chain resting against my skin. I traced the chain with my fingers to where it apexed at my breastbone.

It was a key.

I stared at the lock as I held the key between my fingers.

And the most profound truth struck me: The key to my future, to my freedom, had been resting around my neck this entire time.

CHAPTER TWENTY-TWO

September 2022
Germany

A FEW DAYS after my surgery, Nate and I went over to a friend's house for brunch. I was mobile on crutches but still in pain. This was another new normal I was navigating.

After hobbling over to a chair and propping up my leg, I saw an alert on my phone.

Max liked you.

I opened the app and looked at his profile.

Cute pictures. Good description. Thirty-four.

I raised my left eyebrow as I pushed the heart button.

Not like I have much going on.

My days consisted of field trips to the bathroom and watching Netflix in bed.

He messaged me immediately.

MAX

I'm so glad we matched! Wow, you are hot. And you're American. I can't tell you why but for some reason, I just love American women.

ME

Oh really? Yeah, I'm from Seattle. You're German?

MAX

No, I'm actually French. I live in Munich though.

We continued to exchange basic details and switched over to Telegram.

MAX

Hi, Max here.

ME

Who?

ME

Just kidding.

MAX

Hahaha, good one.

ME

A sense of humor is important. I like to laugh.

MAX

For a second, I thought, wow, she knows so many Maxes. Same here. This is actually kind of my regret when speaking German or English. I can't be as funny as I am in French.

We continued chatting after Nate and I returned home, and until late that night. The next day, he asked me if I could meet for a coffee. As much as I would have loved to meet this charming and funny Frenchman, I was still only four days post-surgery.

ME

I'm sorry, I can't today. Funny story... I had surgery a few days ago.

MAX

Oh I'm sorry to hear that. Then we will do something another time. I wish you all the best for healing.

ME

Thanks. I mean I can still function. I meet with the surgeon Thursday and am hoping I get cleared to drive.

MAX

But in any case, I genuinely want to meet up with you. I rarely get such a positive feeling when chatting with a woman.

Later that night, I messaged him again.

ME

I told my husband about you. He was like oh you like this guy. I said how do you know? He said I can just tell.

MAX

You have no idea how it makes me happy to hear that. I feel so lucky that we are in contact. I can't explain exactly why but I can sense that you are a unique and very good person. I can't wait to get to know you better.

ME

Are you back in Munich?

MAX

Yes.

Disappointment made my stomach drop. I knew he lived in Munich, which was four hours away if there was no traffic, but I had kind of forgotten that—Max's charm allowed me to easily enjoy messaging with him.

MAX

I don't want you to be afraid by the fact that I am living far right now. If I want to meet with you, I will drive no matter how long. I could drive to your area, book a hotel for me to stay Saturday night. And we meet together for a drink on Saturday evening or afternoon as you like (I guess it is not always easy to schedule things with a family).

ME

I can schedule things. I like that idea. I would feel bad if you get here and meet me and you're like damn, she's lame. Do you want to do a video call first with me tomorrow to see how I am first? Maybe you'll be less attracted to me when you see me in real time. Geez, I'm really selling myself here.

It's important to note that my self-confidence and self-worth was very low still. Having been blown off by Amsterdam and Andreas certainly didn't make it better.

MAX

So Courtney, let me say a few things here. First of all it is extremely important to me that we have open and honest communication. So if you are disappointed when seeing me or talking with me on Saturday then of course you can quit after a drink. I won't be mad at all. It can totally happen that you don't have a good feeling. It is important that your enjoyment and pleasure is at the center of everything.

Who is this guy? Seriously. My pleasure and enjoyment at the center of everything? Um, yes please.

> ME
>
> I understand. I do want you to want me though.

MAX

And your positive energy just turned me on totally... I can't tell why it is really the first time that I feel such positive connection just by chatting with a woman.

> ME
>
> Women you talk to aren't like me? Really?

I wasn't using that question as a way to fish for a compliment. I genuinely had no idea what women on dating apps were like.

MAX

I chat with a few women from time to time but none as beautiful as you. And none has that positive energy that you seem to have. It seems that you are different. Am I wrong?

> ME
>
> I would say I have a different attitude than most monogamous individuals. I've worked hard to accept who I am and what I want.

MAX

I believe it is not easy to get into this lifestyle, especially with the pressure of society isn't it?

> ME
>
> Definitely not. I grew up pretty religious so that also didn't help. I feel more accepted now but still misunderstood. Some of my friends and family know. They've all been supportive.

MAX

That is nice! The one married woman that I dated, only one friend of hers knew. She had to keep everything secret.

I asked Max when his last relationship with a single woman

was. He shared that his last relationship ended a year and a half ago. He thought he was going to marry her but found out that she was still in love with her ex-husband.

The more I got to know Max, the more the Frenchman charmed me. He even kept his word and booked a hotel near me, about thirty minutes from my house. There was only one slight problem.

I texted Nate after my appointment with the surgeon.

ME

The doctor didn't clear me to drive and Max is coming here in two days. What am I going to do?!

CHAPTER TWENTY-THREE

I THOUGHT I would have been cleared to drive. I was beyond frustrated.

NATE

I'll drive you.

I'm sorry, did I just have a stroke?

ME

What?! No!

NATE

Is someone else going to drive you?

Um, gosh. There has to be someone else who could take me. I don't feel good about having a taxi just drop me off at some hotel thirty minutes away. This can't be happening.

NATE

It's fine. I'll drive you.

And he did. That afternoon, after Max confirmed he was almost at the hotel, Nate helped me load up into our car, me still on my crutches, and drove me the thirty minutes to the romantic hotel Max had booked for him and me.

As we drove through the small German villages, I looked out the window wondering if this was really happening. A tune by Luke Bryan played quietly in the background. I rested my arm against the door and cradled my chin in my palm, then closed my eyes.

I can't imagine how Nate feels right now. Ugh, I feel like the worst wife. But seeing Max also feels so right.

I opened my eyes and turned to Nate. He looked sexy in his black leather jacket. Nothing about him felt fake or tense. He was doing this out of pure love for me.

"How are you feeling about this?" I asked.

He shrugged, not taking his eyes off the road. "I'm okay. I know this is what you need."

I didn't know what to say to that. But he was right. This was what I needed.

Then why does this feel hard?

Surprisingly, our car ride wasn't uncomfortable. We talked and laughed and I felt incredibly close to the man I had married. We pulled into the hotel property, a mile of wooded areas that led to a complex of a restaurant, hotel, and beer garden. Little creeks ran along the road and wound into the forest. Being here felt like releasing a deep breath.

Nate pulled into an open spot, parked the car, and helped me with my bag. I stood there, staring at the graveled parking lot, feeling like a kid going away to camp for the first time. I didn't want to leave Nate, but I also knew I had to do this.

Nate sensed my uneasiness. He squeezed my arm but didn't say anything. He just kissed me goodbye and said he would see me tomorrow at 10:00 a.m. I awkwardly hobbled into the hotel lobby on my crutches, my bag over my left shoulder.

The automatic glass doors parted. I went into the lobby, turned my head to the right, and saw a 6'6" Frenchman with fair skin, short brown hair, and a huge smile waiting for me. This man, whom I had just connected with a week before, was now standing before me in a puffy dark vest, blue plaid shirt, and dark jeans.

Wow, he's a lot taller than I expected. Well dressed.

When I saw Max, my whole body lit up, like plugging in the lights of a Christmas tree for the first time that season. Sensations pulsed from my pelvis to my throat. Waves of joy. Anticipation. I was nervous, but calm and curious.

And unlike when I met Andreas, I didn't feel insecure about my body. Maybe it was the broken leg that was still swollen from surgery and the belief that I wasn't bringing my best physically due to something out of my control. But there was something about Max that went beyond him seeing me as an attractive woman. When Max looked at me, it felt like someone was seeing my heart, unveiling my deepest parts.

His long legs strode slowly toward me. He bent down and greeted me with a kiss on each cheek.

Next, he grabbed my bag from my shoulder. "Let me take that."

Hearing his French accent sent a smile across my face. He complimented me and asked if I wanted to join him for a drink at the end of the lobby. I nodded. Max led me over to a table with two oversized red chairs and a small glass coffee table in between. He took the chair on the inside so I could stretch my leg out.

As we sat down, my heart raced. I had no idea what to do. I found myself staring at his plump lips wondering when he would kiss me. I wanted him to make the first move. I wanted him to be overwhelmed with desire for me.

During the next hour of talking, my anticipation grew. Despite my nervousness settling, I was anxious to feel his lips against mine. There was something about Max that drew me in. Yes, he was attractive, but I was also incredibly captivated by his energy.

Finally, after another thirty minutes of chatting and flirting, he leaned toward me and put his mouth against mine.

You know the game Suck and Blow? Where you try to suck the card in and pass it to the person next to you by blowing it? That's what kissing Max felt like. Awkward. And without the laughing—like he was trying to suck the air from my lips.

His mouth remained on my parted lips for only a few seconds.

Not exactly the kind of kiss I was hoping for. Maybe it's just his nerves.

We continued to kiss a little as we talked and laughed. I kept waiting, hoping, for our kissing to feel magical. I wanted to experience the physical manifestation of my excitement for Max— that passion I felt for him emotionally.

I dismissed my disappointment—I told myself that I didn't care. I was so enamored at being in this beautiful hotel with him. Because of traffic, it had taken him nearly seven hours to get here. Just to meet me. He booked a hotel knowing that I may not want to spend the night with him. It was the most romantic thing anyone had done for me.

Max leaned in close, his yellow-flecked brown eyes looking deep into mine. "Do you want to go back to the room?"

My heart raced even more. "I'd like that."

He grabbed my bag and waited for me as I crutched along. We had to go down six stairs and into another building before we came to our room. I tried not to feel self-conscious, but the trek to our room was taking forever. Sweat dripped down my back from the amount of energy it was taking me to crutch through the hotel.

I wasn't sure what Max's expectations were when it came to sex. I hadn't thought that far ahead. I knew I wanted to have sex with him, but I wasn't sure how that was going to go with, you know, my leg wrapped and in a brace. There was also one other small issue…

Max opened the door to our room and set down the luggage. The bed was pretty standard German, two twin beds pushed together with individual white duvet covers. The open bathroom was on the left. I could see a glass shower with a rain shower head. A tinge of disappointment pinged in my stomach. My bandages couldn't get wet. I wouldn't be able to enjoy a shower with Max.

I crutched over to the bed and sat down, leaning my crutches against the wall.

Just tell him.

CHAPTER TWENTY-FOUR

I SMOOTHED the sheets on either side of me, wondering how not to ruin the mood with the information I was about to share with Max.

"I'm on my period."

Max was taking off his shoes and hanging up his vest. His face didn't even flinch.

"I don't care."

I frowned. "Okay. And I'm not sure how much movement I can really do because I can't bend my left leg. Like at all."

Max continued to undress, untucking his shirt from his jeans. "It's fine."

He was so focused on the impending intercourse that he didn't seem to care that I was bringing my less than stellar game to our first time together. He helped me undress, kissing me still awkwardly. He put a (white) towel down on the white sheets and slipped a condom on.

I had never been with someone over a foot taller than me so I'd never considered how that would work during sex. I was surprised to find that we didn't line up as easily as I thought we would. His head was way past mine so he had to arch his back like a cat to kiss me.

Not that it really mattered because Max came relatively quickly. I did not. The sex was good, but I felt off with my leg being in a brace. After we got off the bed to clean up in the bathroom, I looked back and saw bright red blood marks all over the white sheets. I had even bled through the towel. It seriously looked like someone had tried to clean up a murder scene, done a shitty job, and the only thing missing was the body.

What in the actual hell? Oh my gosh. It couldn't just be my leg. It had to be a murder scene and *a broken leg? This could not get any worse. Right?*

There was no hiding it. Unless I threw the comforter over it all. Fortunately, Max didn't seem fazed by it. A little while later, we began having sex again. After a few minutes, I could tell something was off.

I looked up at him. "What's wrong?"

Max pulled out of me and rolled over onto his back. I awkwardly propped myself on my elbows, turning to face him.

Is something wrong?

He stared at the ceiling. "Sometimes, this happens."

I furrowed my brow. "What happens?"

"I lose my erection."

Things weren't computing in my head. He's only thirty-four. We just had sex a little while ago, but he was quite aroused when we started again.

I cocked my head slightly. "I don't understand."

Max's tone was short. "I've been to doctors about it and they gave me some pills. Sometimes it helps, and sometimes it doesn't."

Is he talking about taking Viagra? What is happening right now?

I went into troubleshooting mode. "Is it the condom?"

He continued to stare at the ceiling. "Could be."

"I mean it's fine. We can try again later. There's no pressure."

This was not how I saw this overnight going.

I lay back and stared up at the ceiling. My leg was hurting, and I needed to take my medicine. Once again, I was faced with the embarrassment of the bloody sheets as I got up off the bed.

Max was quiet. I tried to curl up next to him, but he had shut down. I wasn't sure how to proceed. I asked if he wanted to watch a show but we ended up talking instead.

Later, after we'd had dinner at the hotel, we had sex again. Max lasted a little longer, but once again, lost his erection.

Maybe it was the pain medicine, or that I was on my period, but I fought back insecurity, doubt, and disappointment.

Max noticed my shift in energy. "It's not you, you know. It's me."

I gave him a half-smile. "I know that intellectually. I'm a trained sex therapist. I know how erectile dysfunction works. But I can't help but feel like it is me."

Nate drove me here for this?

Tears threatened to well up in my eyes. "Let's just go to sleep. Tomorrow is a new day."

I didn't know who I was trying to reassure with those words.

I slept horribly that night. I had to get up to pee, which required me to use my crutches. Shockingly, they are not quiet. That ordeal of moving from the bed to the toilet took me ten minutes.

We woke up around 8:30 a.m. I looked over at Max and considered initiating sex, but after the two failed attempts last night, I chickened out. I knew Nate would be there at ten which made me feel like my time with Max was slowly ending. The vibe in our room reminded me of party balloons that had slowly lost their air after a few days—limp and deflated. We didn't talk that much as we packed up and headed to breakfast. Max was kind and made me a plate of eggs, a croissant, and a bowl of yogurt at the buffet since I couldn't carry one with my crutches.

I continued to monitor the time. Even though this experience was not what I had expected, there was still something about Max that felt magical, and I didn't want to lose it. I didn't want this to be a one-time thing. I wanted it to matter. Because things that mattered lasted. Right?

Before I left, I told Max that I wanted a relationship with him. I wanted to continue whatever this was.

Maybe not the bad sex, but that could be improved.

When I shared my feelings with him, he didn't respond. He sat on the bed, his elbows on his thighs, hands clasped, staring at the ground.

"I'd prefer not to walk you out. I'm not ready to meet Nate," he said quietly.

Disappointment welled in my throat. I hadn't expected him to meet Nate, but I didn't like how this interaction felt.

I looked at the clock and saw that it was almost ten. "I need to go."

Max stood, his long legs stretching tall. He towered over me. Just like when we first met, he bent down, this time to tell me goodbye with a quick kiss. I grabbed my bag and crutched toward the door he was holding open for me.

The hall of the hotel felt eerily quiet as I went to meet my husband outside.

I stepped out just as Nate was pulling up. He smiled big and waved when he saw me.

I opened the car door and tossed my bag into the backseat.

While I slowly maneuvered my crutches, Nate asked me excitedly, "How was it?!"

CHAPTER TWENTY-FIVE

NATE'S SMILE showed he was genuinely curious. He was being kind. Supportive. I had no idea how to respond. But my body did. After I shut the car door, I started to cry.

"I-I don't know…" I began. "Between the murder scene and his erectile dysfunction, I don't even know where to begin."

Nate's smile faded, and he muted his enthusiasm. "Oh."

It felt like a dam had burst inside me. "He's not a good kisser. Like everything I thought would happen didn't and I just never expected him to…"

I stopped myself. I knew Nate didn't want to know the sexual details of my dates. That wasn't fair to him. I focused on the emotions.

I wiped the tears streaming down my face. "And to top it all off, I'm sad because I don't know if I'll see him again. I feel this strong connection with him but… gosh, this is not what I expected."

Nate lovingly held space for me. "I understand."

I threw up my left hand. "Like I have no idea if he's interested in seeing me again."

"Do you want to see him again?"

I nodded. "Yes. I want a relationship with him."

We continued to talk. Nate was so gracious to let me process my feelings as we drove the thirty minutes back to our house.

Later that night, Max texted me that he'd made it home.

ME

> If you want to text me later, after you eat and stuff... but if you just need to do your own thing I understand.

MAX

> How was your day?

ME

> Good. Just processing our time together. When my husband asked me how it went I got emotional. I cried a little. I can't explain it. I'm so drawn to your energy. I think you are kind and funny and sweet and I love touching your body.

MAX

> You cried because of me?

ME

> I feel safe with you. Like I was so moved by our time together and it felt scary when I told you I wanted a relationship with you and you didn't respond. Which is of course totally fair. You don't owe me anything. But I want to make this work. I want to make time for you. I just don't want to keep you from something better.

Something better.

Looking back, I see how completely unaware I was of what I had to offer someone. Subconsciously, I thought I should just be grateful to get the attention and approval of a man I desired.

I pushed for a relationship quickly with Max because I craved security. I didn't want to feel the ache of rejection I had with Andreas again. I didn't want to be basically used for a good time and then discarded like I didn't matter. Purity culture ingrained in me that sex was supposed to be special. Meaningful.

And if it's not, then you got used. Played. And that left me feeling foolish.

MAX

> I want to see you again. I just don't know when and if you say you want a relationship with me what that means. You want to see me often? Which won't be possible. Also the reason that I appeared so defeated is because of this problem. It has nothing to do with you. I had that with other women. And it is always more. And that makes me depressed. And I know that it will bore you if that happens again.

I acknowledged his feelings and offered a solution—meeting halfway.

That next week, Max called me his girlfriend. It was music to my ears.

Finally! This was the kind of arrangement that would make me happy.

Max and I talked every day and figured out what weekends we could spend together. Nate and I agreed to me seeing Max every two to three weeks.

We met one other time halfway, and two other times I went to Munich. Max always took excellent care of me. He booked the hotel—paid for everything. Even surprised me with a private spa experience one time in Munich.

I could feel myself falling in love with him.

You may be thinking, whoa, whoa, whoa. You've known this guy for like two months and you're in love already? Well, you'd be right to be concerned. I believe if I had fallen in love, it wasn't with Max, but rather his potential.

It's important to remember that I was dealing with feelings and experiences most people work out in their twenties as a single person. Not as a married mom of three approaching forty who grew up in purity culture and had very few sexual and relationship experiences.

It's easy to balk at my intense behavior (trust me, I know I have plenty of cringe moments). But I was so insecure, repressed, unhappy, confused, and full of shame. Max was a safe harbor as I was building this new ship with Nate and sorting through decades of living according to someone else's (ahem, patriarchy) plan for me.

I knew he adored me, and I was grateful for that. But it often felt like trying to connect with someone through a window. No matter how close we got, there was thick-paned glass between us. And I couldn't quite figure out why it was there or if it would ever go away.

Max's birthday was coming up in mid-November so I asked if I could come to Munich and spend it with him. Nate said I could spend three nights with him since Max's birthday was a Friday and I wanted to be there the morning he woke up. Before I left, I drove forty-five minutes one-way to France to get Max a birthday card in French, bought his favorite salted butter, and a few of his favorite bottles of French wine. I ordered a book he had been wanting to read off Amazon France and had a picture of the two of us framed. I was ready to celebrate my boyfriend.

When Thursday night arrived, we had sex within ten minutes of me walking in the door of his apartment. It felt so good, but once again, our passion was interrupted when he lost his erection. No matter what we tried, the sex with Max never got better. The erectile dysfunction issue never resolved. It was a source of frustration in our relationship because I wanted him to see a therapist and he, ironically, didn't believe in therapy.

I had only come with Max a handful of times. When we first started texting, he had shared that he had a "fetish for licking pussy." I thought that was great because I'm a big fan of oral sex. After a few weekends together, Max shared that he actually struggled with going down on a woman. "Sometimes I love it and sometimes I find it disgusting."

Awesome.

When I was in high school, the boys on the bus talked about how some girls smelled like fish tacos, and they would resist the idea of eating a girl out because they acted like it was beneath them. They didn't give a shit about a girl's pleasure and merely saw a woman as a sexual object. They were the products of patriarchy and purity culture, where a man's needs and desires are elevated above a woman's.

I had no idea what to do with Max's confession or my memories from hearing young men talk about women in such a derogatory way. Anger simmered in me. I felt misled by the types of things he had told me at the beginning of our relationship. The reality was that he oversold himself and instead of calling him on it, I ignored it. He was the safe escape I needed from my marriage and life; I wasn't willing to walk away from this because then I'd have to start this whole process over. At least Nate liked that I had Max. Who knew how long it would take me to find another Max?

Looking back, it saddens me to know that I thought this way. But that is easy to say when I'm no longer trying to escape my life and marriage. At the time, I didn't think I could find anyone better than Max.

I saw myself as one of those discounted, dented cans because I was a married woman trying to find a serious partner (that doesn't really compute with the whole mono-heteronormative narrative). What good and decent man would choose to "share" his partner when he could find one that he could have all to himself? One where he's not embarrassed about what his parents or colleagues think of his married girlfriend. Instead of seeing myself for the prize that I was, I saw myself as the pathetic, participation ribbon who should just be grateful she was let out of her cage to play.

Later that night, we went to dinner at a nearby restaurant. Max couldn't stop smiling. I loved seeing him smile. I loved being the reason a grin would spread across his face. He noticed me playing with one of the rings on my finger. I never wore my wedding ring when I went on dates, but wore other rings. Not because I was ashamed of being married. But I didn't want it to intimidate whoever I was out with when they saw the symbol of the other man in my life.

Max's smile grew bigger, and he leaned a little across the table. "If you weren't already married, I'd fix that."

I love hearing that. I love having him in my life.

A huge smile spread across my face. I knew what he meant, and I didn't need to use words to respond. I leaned across the table and kissed him.

Later that night, when Max and I were in bed together—his long arm wrapped around my bare back, our legs intertwined, and our bodies covered partially by a crumpled bed sheet—he opened up to me.

"A school."

My head lifted slightly off his muscled chest. Sensing my confusion, he continued.

"If I could do anything, if money didn't matter, I'd build a school."

I lowered my eyes and then my head back to his chest. I could sense the sadness in his statement. "School was hard for you?"

"Not academically." His fingers continued to stroke the strands of my hair that had fallen into my face.

I knew what he meant. Growing up as the lanky, highly intelligent, introverted kid hadn't been easy. Max had shared he didn't have many friends as a kid; he had even fewer as an adult.

"Kids shouldn't have to worry about being bullied in school. They should get to learn in an environment that feels safe, you know?"

I nodded and snuggled in closer to his body, inhaling his faintly musky scent.

"I hope you get to see your dream come true."

His hand moved from my hair to my back as he pulled me tight against him. "My dream has already come true. Being with you. I was lonely for so long and then I met you. You're an amazing woman, Courtney."

I lifted my head fully off his chest and met his brown eyes. They seemed to search mine. For what? I had no idea. But I hoped this, what was building between us, was the answer.

My lips met his. I leaned my forehead against Max's and said, "thank you."

He pulled back a bit. "No, thank you. I was so hurt by my last girlfriend. She used me but I didn't really care. It just felt nice to have someone, you know?"

I did. I knew what it was like to sacrifice parts of myself to feel needed. To feel loved.

I ended up doing that with Max. Even though I never ended up having the mind-blowing sex I desired with him, my intellectual connection with Max was fantastic. I had traded one need being met for another (I was definitely getting my sexual needs met by Nate at this point).

My conversations with Max were stimulating and engaging. We'd stay up for hours texting and talking each night. I loved when he challenged me on an opinion I had. It was like having a verbal sparring partner. And damn, that was hot.

Despite a few tender moments, my emotional connection with Max... was... underwhelming. He was not the most emotionally aware individual and had no interest in improving that. Overall, the stability of having another partner that Nate actually approved of was wonderful.

Nate didn't have an interest in meeting Max or having him be a part of our life together. I respected that. I was grateful that Nate was supportive of the time I spent with Max and how he added value to my life. Nate could see me falling in love with this younger, taller, European man and he never once acted like he felt threatened by that. He never told me I couldn't love someone else. I think Nate knew that preventing that was impossible. Because really, you can't help who you fall in love with.

The night of his thirty-fifth birthday, Max drew us a bath, lit some candles, and opened a bottle of the wine I had gotten him. Over bubbles and red wine, and as the flames danced in the darkened bathroom, I told him I loved him. I was so confident and unwavering when I said it. I knew he wouldn't say it back, and he didn't.

Looking back, I'm not sure if I can characterize what I felt for Max as love. I had such an intense desire for emotional closeness with him that was one hundred percent rooted in my anxious attachment. I overlooked his shortcomings and excused behavior that I would never tolerate now. But when I told him I loved him, I genuinely meant and was detached from him reciprocating that sentiment.

He simply said, "Thank you."

Surprisingly, I didn't feel rejected by him not reciprocating my words. I was proud of myself for sharing my truth with someone I cared deeply about. I was grateful to have someone like Max that I could love.

On our last night together, we went to an Irish pub in downtown Munich to watch a big rugby game. The bar was packed, and I managed to grab us a table next to a group of guys. At some point, the guy next to me, who looked to be in his late twenties, leaned over and said something in German. I didn't understand him so I looked at Max. Max responded for me in German, and they began talking a little.

I scrunched my nose slightly. "I'm sorry, I don't speak German very well."

The German man waved his hand, kindly dismissing my apology. "It's okay. So you guys like on a first date?"

I shook my head. "No."

"Second date?" he asked.

I kept shaking my head. "Nope."

The guy raised his eyebrows. "Third?!"

I laughed. "No."

He laughed a little, too. "Oh, okay. I see. So you think you'll get married? My buddy here does wedding videography so if you need someone for that…"

Who is this guy? What?

Max looked at me, and I saw him thinking what I was thinking. We stared at each other for what felt like a minute.

I nodded at him. "Go ahead. Tell him."

CHAPTER TWENTY-SIX

MAX DIDN'T BREAK eye contact with me. "She's already married."

The guy furrowed his eyebrows and shook his head. "What?"

I started laughing.

The guy said something to his two friends in German.

He turned back to me. "But you're like getting divorced, right?"

I shook my head and smiled. "Nope."

He spoke to Max in German for a few minutes and then finally said to me, "He's a lucky guy."

Yeah, Max is. But I don't know if he knows that.

I leaned in closer to him. "You should tell him that."

He nodded at me and made eye contact with Max. "Hey, man, you're a lucky guy. She's beautiful."

Max smiled, and a little smirk spread across my face. It was the first time Max had been associated with me by someone else, let alone in public. It felt great to know that people knew we were together. I wanted him to be proud that I was his girlfriend. That I chose him. And that he chose me.

We left the bar shortly after, slightly tipsy, and headed back to Max's place. We got ready for bed, turned off the lights, and lay next to each other in the dark. It was my last night in Munich, and I was craving my boyfriend.

I ran my hand across his defined abdomen.

"I'm not in the mood," he said flatly.

Slight embarrassment caused me to remove my hand. I rolled over, defeated.

Without moving, he said, "And I don't want any drama about it."

Seriously?

We had argued about me wanting sex more than he did in the past, but tonight, his comment felt harsh.

It's our last night together, and this is how it's going to end?

I was used to Nate being too tired for sex. Used to my sexual advances being rejected.

Maybe it's me. Maybe I'm the problem.

Discouraged, I gave up and went to sleep.

In the morning, I called Nate as he was driving himself to the Frankfurt Airport. We checked in, and I discussed my potential plans with him. I didn't enjoy this part of having another partner —managing another person's schedule. It often felt like I was trying to figure out where all my puzzle pieces went, and I frequently wondered if a few had accidentally fallen off the table.

I never knew who to ask first. Do I ask the person I'm interested in spending time with first and then check with Nate? Or ask Nate first to see how he feels about it then ask to see if the person is even able to go?

I sat down on Max's bed to chat on the phone with Nate while Max made breakfast in the kitchen. "So, my birthday is less than a month away. I'd really like Max to be part of it. Would that be okay?"

Nate's tone was short. "I haven't seen you in three days. I'm leaving for North Carolina in a few hours and won't see you for another ten days, and you're asking me about this now? Are you serious?"

Annoyed, I fired back, "It's never a good time to plan with

you, Nate. I'm here now so I'm trying to figure out when I'll see Max again."

"You want to spend your birthday with him?" Nate asked. "What about the kids and me?"

"No, I want to spend *some* of my birthday with him. Even if it's not the actual day. It's just that based on our current schedule of seeing each other every two to three weeks, my birthday falls in that timeframe."

Nate shut me down. "I can't think about this right now. Just do whatever."

And he hung up.

I refused to let that phone call ruin my morning with Max. When I walked into the kitchen, Max had set a plate of eggs and toast he'd made me on the table.

I put on a smile. "Thanks, babe."

Max plated his own food and joined me at the table.

I picked up some eggs with my fork. "So, I was thinking… What do you think about spending my birthday with me? My mom and sister are flying in and I'd love for you to meet them."

Max waited a few seconds before responding.

Quietly, he said, "I don't think I'm ready to meet your family."

My heart dropped. "Oh. Okay. Um, what about spending my birthday with me somehow?"

Max took a bite of his toast. "I'm not sure, that's a month away."

I set down my fork. "Okay… um…"

I don't get it. What am I missing? Does he not want to see me again?

I considered if I should end this discussion or continue.

My anxiety was building, and I couldn't wait. "Well, then can we look at the calendar and figure out when we can see each other again?"

Max put his fork down and looked down at his plate. "I don't know. I don't ever have time on the weekends for just me anymore. I work all week and I just need some time for myself."

I clenched my nails into my left palm.

No time for yourself?! You're single and live alone! And we see each other every two to three weeks. What?!

I refused to back down. I wanted to address this now.

I leaned my head down, looking him in his eyes. "It feels like you don't want to see me again."

I did not see his next words coming.

CHAPTER TWENTY-SEVEN

MAX STOOD up and started to pace the kitchen.

I stared at him, wondering what was happening. My heart-beats quickened with his every step. After what felt like forever, he walked behind my chair and put his arms around me.

"I don't think I'm ready for this."

I jerked against him, but his arms didn't move.

Is he saying what I think he's saying?

I stared forward, his arms still holding me, and asked the words I had never anticipated. "Are you breaking up with me?"

Max released his arms and began to walk away from me.

He stopped, turning toward me, his face flushed. "I thought I was ready for a relationship. But I'm not. I can't do this."

A sea of emotions churned within me. Waves of anger. Embarrassment. Confusion.

Am I in the fucking Twilight Zone?

I raised my voice at him. "Were you planning to end things this whole weekend? Were you just waiting for me to leave so you could end it?!"

"No! Of course not."

He turned and walked to his bedroom. I stood up from the

kitchen table and followed him, watching him sit on his bed. Tears streamed down his face.

This can't be happening.

I crossed my arms in front of my chest, hoping to hold my breaking heart together. "No. No, we are not breaking up. No."

Max and I talked and argued and yelled and cried for almost an hour.

"I'm sorry," he said. "I never meant to hurt you."

Desperation rose over me. "Please don't do this. Please."

As the words came out of my mouth, I instantly regretted them.

I will not beg to be with this man.

A switch flipped, and the waves made their final crash.

Anger overtook me. "I'm leaving."

I shoved my belongings into my bag, leaving behind the Lindt Advent Calendar he had bought me the day before.

As I walked out the door, I glared at him. "You're making a huge mistake."

I grabbed my crutches—that I should have been using and not carrying—and walked as quickly as I could down the three flights of stairs, out the door, and to my car.

Max never moved from his bed. I slammed the car door shut, sitting there, simmering. Wondering if I should go back in there and fight for our relationship. But something told me not to. I wanted to call Nate, but he was already on his nine-hour flight to North Carolina. So, I called my mom instead and told her what had happened.

I didn't go back inside. I turned on my car and made the four-hour drive home from Munich in tears. Replaying our weekend. Analyzing where it went wrong.

Why doesn't he want me? What's wrong with me?

When I arrived at my house, Nate was not there and wouldn't be for ten days. Seeing my car pulling up, my thirteen-year-old daughter came outside, and I tried to hide my red, swollen eyes through the windshield.

Addison waved, her smile wide. "Hey, Mom!"

Her excitement vanished when she saw my face. "Oh… are you okay?"

I rolled my window down slightly and told her timidly, "Yeah, I'm fine. Just give me a minute."

Addison slowly retreated back into the house.

I can't let them see me like this. Get it together, Courtney.

I sat in my car and wondered how they would react if they knew the truth. Would they feel sorry for me? Would they think that I deserved to be in pain? Would they be grateful that I would no longer be taking time away from them to spend with someone else? It never crossed my mind that they could genuinely accept and love me. Because the truth was, I didn't fully accept and love myself. How could I expect anyone else to?

How can I hide this heartbreak from them? How do I pretend like everything is fine when I'm not?

I tried to put myself together, sweeping my broken heart aside, and walked into the house where my three kids were waiting for me. My kids, who had no idea the man their mom just told she loved didn't want to be with her anymore.

A few hours later, Nate finally landed. I went into our bedroom, closed the door, got under the covers of our bed, and called him. I started sobbing the minute I heard his voice.

"Hello," Nate said distantly.

"He dumped me," I managed to say in between sobs.

"Wait, what?!"

I grabbed a tissue and blew my nose. "Max. He broke up with me. Right after I talked to you. And then I couldn't call you because you were on your flight…"

The tears continued.

Nate's tone changed. "I'm so sorry. I'm so sorry I can't be there to comfort you. Why? Why did he end it?"

I shook my head and pulled the blanket tighter around me. "He said he wasn't ready."

Nate did the best he could to try and support me despite

being on a different continent. He knew how much Max meant to me and was genuinely confused as to why Max would be "so dumb" to end something so special.

Later that night, Max texted me.

MAX

Please tell me that you made it home safely.

ME

I did. I didn't think you'd want to know.

MAX

Of course I'd want to know.

ME

Why? Do you want to know that I cried almost the entire way home? That I sat in my car hoping you would come stop me? That when my kids asked me how my weekend was, I had to lie and tell them it was great? I'm sorry that sounds angry. I'm not angry.

MAX

I feel depressed about my life and know that I'm not ready to receive love. I understand that you're mad at me. I'd be mad too. I hate myself that you feel so sad because of me, but I never wanted to hurt a kind and rare person like you. I feel incredibly lucky that I had the chance to meet you. You can be angry... I would be angry in your place. Life angers me. I feel so guilty for what I've done.

ME

Why do you feel guilty?

MAX

Because you are a wonderful person. I tried to appear more emotionally stable than I am to convince myself. I lied to myself, and it makes you sad.

ME

You think I didn't know? Do you think I couldn't see through it all? You may not believe in what I do professionally... but I saw you. And I loved you anyway. You insulted me when you said I didn't even know you. I know people. And I know pain.

MAX

I never meant to insult you. It's hard for me to speak about what I feel.

ME

I can't explain it but I have a connection with you. But of course I saw your pain. And I thought when he's ready he will tell me. I'll show him that I care by being open with him and creating space where he feels loved and valued. And that freaked you out. Because it triggered your nervous system. Just like we talked about with women who go back into chaos. Yours is just the opposite but that's another thing. I'm awesome at what I do. I have a gift and of all the people in this entire universe, you ended up with me. With me, Max. But you were too scared and too proud. And I won't force myself on you. But don't ever believe that I never saw you and your pain. Because I did and I fell in love with you anyways. You don't win anything for running the race alone. Or finishing miserable. There is no prize for that. You deserve so much love and happiness. I truly wish that for you. And I know a part of you still wants that.

He didn't respond, and I was left with a hole in my heart.

Over the next couple of days, my feelings oscillated between understanding and anger. And instead of feeling them, I went immediately back on the dating app. I needed to numb my heartbreak—to forget that I wasn't wanted. I felt like a fool.

Of course, this wouldn't work. What was I thinking?

Nate thought I should grieve differently. He thought I needed to take a break from dating and heal. I felt like he was trying to control me and had no intention of following his advice. This plan did not go well.

I texted with Nate that evening.

ME

I have a phone date tonight. He's looking for a secondary partner also.

NATE

I had a bad feeling most of the day so I figured something like that was happening.

ME

What do you mean?

NATE

You have been without a second partner for what? Two days and you are zero to sixty with texting multiple guys, dates, and trying to replace Max. You can't just slow down can you?

ME

I'm only getting to know him. The intention was that it's not something flippant and casual. You said you wanted me to tell you. I'm not trying to replace Max. I'm not meeting anyone. I'm just open to it. That's all.

NATE

You just can't stop. I am working my ass off, and you are continuing to date and text multiple dudes. You can't even take a break. You are unbelievable. I don't even want to talk to you.

You never want to talk about this!

NATE

You can't just slow down. I can't support you when you are of control like this. Night.

ME

How am I being out of control? I'm not doing anything! I thought if I did this while you were gone it would be better!

NATE

You can't even stop for a single day.

ME

I did!

NATE

You know that it makes it even worse for me.

ME

Why?! I'm not even meeting anyone.

NATE

Just stop talking to me. I am so pissed right now.

ME

What did you want me to do, Nate? Please tell me.

NATE

Just fucking slow down. You can't even do that, not ever.

ME

What does that mean? Slow down. I'm not setting up dates. I'm just talking. That's it. What am I doing wrong?

NATE

You are out of control to fill some need to have a second, or a third, or even more. You don't even see it because you are like obsessed. You are totally out of control.

ME

I told you what my desire was. To have one other partner. I lost that this weekend. So how is exploring out of control? How long did you want me to wait? Until you got back? I don't want a third or more. That's hurtful. Can we please talk?

ME

Hello? I don't want to fight with you.

He didn't text me back that night.

My patience with my husband was waning by the day. I wanted him to be supportive—to understand how hard all this was for me. I was walking a tightrope between keeping the peace with Nate and embracing who I was. At any minute, I could lose my balance and plummet. Not to my death, but to a darkness I had fought so hard to get out of.

Maybe Nate was right. Maybe I was moving too fast. But I had no interest in slowing down to find out.

CHAPTER TWENTY-EIGHT

December 2022

TURNING FORTY WAS UNDERWHELMING. My birthday always falls eight days before Christmas, so no one usually does much for it. Nate asked if I wanted a party. I said no. My mom and sister flew in on my birthday and we spent the night in Frankfurt, just the three of us. We explored the Christmas market, drank Glühwein, and stayed at a fancy hotel. Despite the fun I shared with them, depression crept in. Something was missing. A large part of me wanted to have a boyfriend by my side to ring in this new decade.

That night, I reflected on everything I had been through the past six months. As I did, I couldn't help but feel defeated. Empty. A bit adrift. Nate and I continued to have massive ups and downs. Dating wasn't going well. Men would just stop communicating with me or never set a date to actually meet up. I was discouraged and didn't see things improving. And on top of all of it, I missed Max.

On Christmas Day, I decided to message Max.

ME

I went back and forth on sending this to you but my instincts told me I should. So I am. After you broke up with me, my marriage kind of imploded. And I blamed you for it. I was so angry for what you did. And I've been angry for weeks. Not all the time, but enough that I can feel it bubbling beneath the surface. And I hate it.

I have to take responsibility for my choices and not blame them on you. And I have to let go of the anger because it's not who I am. It's slowly poisoning me.

I don't want to be angry at you and in order to do that, I have to forgive you.

So this Christmas, that's my gift to myself—forgiveness. I'd be lying if I said I didn't miss you. Maybe someday we'll be friends. Who knows. I still get emotional when I think about how things ended. But I'm not angry anymore. I want you to be happy. So, so happy. I hope you have a fantastic Christmas with your family. I tell my clients to use this Hawaiian forgiveness tradition whenever they want to forgive someone. So I'm using it here with you. 'I'm sorry. Please forgive me. Thank you. I love you.' Merry Christmas, Max.

He read it but didn't respond until two days later. As the months went on, we continued to stay in touch but only sporadically. Our conversations were casual with the occasional compliment or sexual innuendo from Max. He never asked to meet up or expressed any desire to see me again.

CHAPTER TWENTY-NINE

January 2023

NATE and I continued to struggle. My happiness was so dependent on how things were going with the men I interacted with online. When I got attention from men I was interested in, I was happy. Elated. Playful. When I wasn't getting any matches or guys would suddenly ghost me, I was frustrated. Nate was on the receiving end of all of this.

I truly believed that if I just had another partner, an occasional escape from my life, more so my marriage, then I'd be happy. Then the pressure would be off of Nate to be everything I needed him to be. Which was impossible for any one person. This belief fueled my behavior. It justified my actions. It propelled me back to the app time and time again.

When I wasn't doing well or when Nate and I had normal (non-dating) arguments, he would tell me that he felt far from me. He would share how sad he was watching me get my needs met talking to other men. I hated hearing that. It felt like he was trying to clip my wings. Keep me in the golden cage I had spent my entire life in. I wasn't interested in being trapped again.

I was desperate to find another partner. Not just because I craved another man in my life. Nate didn't enjoy the revolving door of men I seemed to go through when I was dating. During this stage, our marriage would feel even more strained.

I spent so much time establishing strong connections with men who were serious about getting into a relationship with me. But I kept attracting men who only wanted casual dating, or friends with benefits. I wanted to feel what I had with Max again. I was chasing that and felt that once I found it, all my problems would go away. Couldn't Nate see that I was looking for stability again?

CHAPTER THIRTY

February 2023
Germany

DATING PICKED BACK UP in February and I became more confident in what I was looking for. My marriage continued to feel like a never-ending roller coaster ride. It was getting harder to hide my dating from the kids, and Nate didn't like having to lie for me.

After another disappointing date, I came home, hopped into bed but struggled to fall asleep. I stared at the ceiling wondering if this is what dating was going to be like. Having mediocre conversations but good sexual chemistry. Or like with Max, having a great connection but underwhelming (and often dysfunctional) sex.

Why is it so hard to find both? Am I asking for too much?

Something else struck me while sleep eluded me. For the first time in my life, since opening the marriage, I felt free. I wasn't with Nate out of obligation. I didn't stay with my kids because I felt like I had to. I wanted to be here. I wanted to make this work. To create something beautiful and fulfilling, even if society had told me that it was wrong to want it.

I couldn't give up. On any of it. My marriage. My family. But most importantly, myself. I had to believe I would find love again. That I *deserved* to find it.

I continued to search for connection on the dating app. Nate was traveling more for work which was a nice break for me. It allowed me to stay up late and chat with guys I had matched with and not worry about annoying Nate.

I had connected with a single thirty-year-old German engineer who lived about an hour away from me. He worked long hours and the only time we could talk was at night. With Nate being out of town, I decided to take the call in our bedroom instead of downstairs like I usually did.

It was nearly ten p.m. when I heard the faint knock on my bedroom door.

I lowered my voice and quietly told Thomas, "I have to go. I'll text you later."

I hung up and responded to the knock. "Come in."

Addison carefully opened the door. She slowly stepped into my room, a concerned look on her face. "Are you okay?"

I scrunched my forehead, pouted my lips slightly, and tilted my head. "What do you mean?"

"It sounded like you were upset with someone."

My anxiety rose, and my heart started to beat faster.

Had she heard me? She can't know. Can she?

"Oh," I stated calmly. "I was just talking with a client."

Addison wasn't budging. Her curiosity wasn't satisfied. "I heard you say something like, 'I can't trust you.'"

My hand waved, dismissing her inquiry. "I was just role-playing with a client. That's all."

I walked past her, avoiding eye contact, and headed to the bathroom.

I hated lying to her. I wanted to tell her the truth. But I couldn't. I was terrified of what she would think of me.

Addison followed me into the bathroom. She pursed her lips. "Just wanted to make sure you were okay."

I walked over to her by the bathroom door and wrapped my arms around her. "Thanks for being concerned about me, but I promise I'm alright."

I stepped back to look at her. Such a mature young woman stared back at me through those pale blue eyes.

"Get back to bed. You have school tomorrow." I kissed her on the head. "Love you."

She said, "Love you," as she walked back to her room.

I shut the bathroom door and walked over to the sink. My hands gripped the lip of the smooth, white porcelain. I released a deep breath. One that I felt like I had been holding since Addison asked me who I was talking to. I looked up into the mirror and considered my reflection.

What kind of mother am I? Who does this to their kids? Lies about their behavior. Meets random men. Why couldn't I just be a normal mom?

But I had come too far to turn back.

Once Nate and I are in a good place or once I have another partner, then I can tell the kids.

I tried to reassure myself with these beliefs, but my head hung in defeat. It would never be a good time to shatter my kids' world. What was I thinking?

CHAPTER THIRTY-ONE

I HAD SPENT the past two and half weeks texting a graduate student from Poland, who was getting his master's degree about an hour away from where I lived. This guy checked all my boxes. He was intelligent, tall, gorgeous, athletic, and had this snark to him that made our conversations fun.

Nate wasn't a fan of his age though.

"What could you have in common with a twenty-six-year-old?" Nate had asked me.

Nothing, and everything. Something about us felt... fated, the chemistry electric.

Seeing Poland in person for the first time was the biggest roller coaster of emotions I had had in dating. I was curious and cautious. Excited but hesitant. But most of all I was happy.

Watching him walk to me across the parking lot was like watching one of those movie scenes in slow motion. Dark sunglasses sat on his sharp nose, accentuating his raised cheek-bones. His 6'2" athletic body was dressed in maroon corduroy pants and a collared, navy button-up, complementing his slightly olive-toned skin and chocolate-brown hair. He looked like he had fallen out of one of those Hugo Boss magazine ads. Seeing his charming smile when he saw me sent waves of pleasure and anticipation throughout my body.

We spent most of the date talking, kissing, and touching. The world seemed to disappear during our time together. After we had coffee, we went for a walk in the village, stopping every few minutes to make out.

After three hours together, I told him I had to go home. He walked me to my car and continued to kiss me there. Every fiber of my being wanted him and I wanted him to know that.

My hands gripped his shirt. "I want you."

He looked at me and smiled. "I know."

I stepped back, pulling our bodies apart. "I mean it. I want you. I want all of you."

With a serious tone, he said, "I know."

I knew that tone. My heart sank. "Have you thought more about what I'm wanting?"

By this point in my polyamory journey, I knew I wasn't interested in merely a friend with benefits. I wanted a boyfriend. A relationship. Someone to add value to my life. Someone for whom I could add value to theirs.

He nodded. "I just don't know if I'm ready for what you're wanting right now."

My excitement deflated like a week-old balloon.

Had he not been on our date? Had he not been present the past two weeks of us messaging all the time?

I put my hands to my side. "Okay. I should go."

Poland held my door for me as I got into my car. "Text me when you get home," he said before he quickly kissed me goodbye.

As he walked to his car, he tucked his hands in his front pockets. I watched him get into his car before I backed out of my parking spot.

I drove the thirty minutes home in silence. Numb.

The next day, I messaged him and asked him to choose me.

To choose us. He said he needed a few days to think about it. So I said I would give him the space to process it.

As promised, he messaged me a few days later and told me that I was important to him but that there were too many factors impacting his ability to be in a relationship with me.

I don't understand.

ME

Why did you pursue something with me if you knew you couldn't give me what I wanted?

POLAND

I told you I wasn't sure about everything. I was simply confused, wanted you, but wasn't sure about my feelings. Maybe I should have stopped it earlier. But I wanted to meet you.

ME

Meeting me clearly didn't change how you felt about me.

POLAND

That's just one meeting. I like to get to know the person in many different situations.

ME

I've dated a lot. I know we have a connection.

POLAND

Yesterday was my first date. Ever.

What?!

ME

I didn't know that.

POLAND

I know it's kinda funny. You were my first one.

ME

Most dates don't go like that. I know you feel
something for me. I saw it. I felt it. Someday you
will understand.

POLAND

Maybe...

I'm so tired of this.

ME

Then don't.

POLAND

What?

Anger took over the driver's seat with Hurt riding shotgun.

ME

Never mind. I don't see what more time will give
you. You've made your case. Your cons outweigh
your pros. And as you said you're not that
emotionally attached so ending this should be
easy for you.

POLAND

It's not. There will be moments when I regret it a
lot. I know that.

ME

Good. You should.

POLAND

But I think it's the right thing to do.

ME

Women like me don't come around often.

POLAND

I know it. But I like doing the right thing too
much.

ME

It's not the right thing.

POLAND

I am sure you will find somebody more suitable for you that will deserve way more the things you have to offer than I do.

ME

I'm so tired of men telling me that.

POLAND

Well your situation is a very specific one.

You knew that before we even met!

ME

I want you. And you don't want me. And that's fine. I respect that.

POLAND

I don't know what to say. I think you should date other people.

My heart sank. Disappointment and sadness spread through my body, causing my legs and arms to feel heavy. My head hung in defeat.

I don't understand. I don't want to date anyone else.

There was something about Poland that just made sense even though absolutely nothing about having a relationship with a twenty-six-year-old should. But he was definitely not a typical guy his age. And this was definitely not a typical situation. This felt special. Like a gift that I had to now put back in the box.

So I did.

I knew there was nothing more I could say to Poland. I wasn't interested in trying to convince him that we should be together. After that, our communication decreased, but we still kept in touch. I was disappointed he couldn't give me what I wanted. He was everything I thought I was looking for.

If he could just see that we're good together...

After scrolling for a while, I put my phone down. I laid down on the bed and stared out the window, watching the clouds drift by.

I don't get it. Why is it so hard to find someone who wants to be with me? What is wrong with me?

I had been on thirteen first dates since things ended with Max four months ago. And to some extent, I kept being told the same thing. "You're beautiful. You're amazing. But I can't give you what you're looking for." Maybe Poland was right. Maybe I was too demanding. Maybe I was asking for too much.

I let those thoughts percolate. After a few minutes, something shifted.

You know what? Screw it. Let's have some fun.

I matched with a cute thirty-year-old Dutch guy, Bram. We agreed to meet later for a drink, after he got off work.

While I waited for Bram to finish work, I took myself out to dinner. I had never been intimidated to do things alone. Nate was always busy working so my independent nature had served me well.

I savored the steak as it melted in my mouth. The flavors activating each of my taste buds. Despite my exhaustion from traveling and another romantic connection not working out, I found myself anticipating the date with Bram. A couple of hours talking with a cute Dutch guy over a few drinks? Throw in some flirting and some kissing? Sounds like a great time to me.

On my date with Bram, I wasn't prepared for his forwardness. I didn't expect him to propose going back to my hotel room after only an hour of talking. And instead of sticking with my well thought out plan, I gave in.

Isn't this what I wanted? The freedom to be sexually carefree and spontaneous?

Isn't that what polyamory was all about? In all honesty, I had no idea what it was about because I wasn't connected to a polyamory community. I mean I knew what polyamory *could* look like, but I had no idea how to actually get there.

I ignored my sister's suggestions of getting on Reddit or TikTok and finding other people like me. I had tried one afternoon and got overwhelmed by the hateful comments. I was already full of shame—I didn't need to be reminded of why I felt ashamed on a daily basis.

Additionally, I thought I could figure it out on my own. I believed I already had a quasi-poly community that consisted of Abby and Carlos, even though their polyamory looked vastly different than mine. At the time, they both identified as non-monogamous, not polyamorous. They weren't looking for long-term partners so they didn't face the same struggles I did.

Also, it didn't feel safe to put myself out there and look for community. Most people still didn't know I was polyamorous, which led to me feeling further isolated. Yes, I had freedom to have romantic relationships with other men, but I felt alone in understanding how to navigate that. I no longer felt the protection from the security blanket of monogamy, and I didn't fit into the free-for-all love that some polyamorists portray online. Since I didn't know how to navigate this, I didn't. Instead, I went for the easy win—the dopamine hits.

Bram's presence and performance in my hotel room were short-lived. I found myself more satisfied by my steak dinner than by this brief encounter. And while I didn't regret my decision, I was disappointed.

Disappointed that my pleasure didn't seem to matter.

Disappointed that my husband couldn't be happy for me.

Disappointed that despite me telling this guy I didn't want a one-night stand, that's exactly where I ended up.

How naïve I was. When I was in my twenties, I didn't have friends who had one-night stands (or if they did, they weren't talking to someone like me, who had been raised in purity culture, about it). None of my clients dealt with these kinds of dating issues. They were mostly in unhappy, long-term relationships.

For my previous sexual encounters, I had made excuses for their poor performance. With Andreas, we were in a sweltering car. With Amsterdam, we had both been drinking and it was hot. With Max, he had a sexual dysfunction. But deep down, I didn't believe that I was allowed to be disappointed. I had fought for freedom and escaped my golden cage.

Now, I wanted extramarital sexual and relational satisfaction on top of it? Asking for a lot there, Courtney.

It's important to remember that I wasn't raised with women who modeled how to advocate for their needs. I was surrounded by women who were praised for shrinking and sacrificing. Who accepted the emotional unintelligence and feeble attempts at being emotionally available from their spouses. Who complained to one another, ultimately shrugging off their unhappiness, "What are you gonna do?"

And I get it. That generation of women needed men to survive. Women were just getting some autonomy over their reproduction (access to birth control) and financial access (being able to open a credit card or take out a loan without a man). Our mothers faced sexual harassment, pay inequality, and outright discrimination far more than my generation has. So they chose to partner with the best man they could find. Some chose well; others didn't.

Despite growing up in the seventies during the women's movement, my mom longed for the *Leave It to Beaver* perfect family. When she met my dad at the age of nineteen, she was ready to create that. And in a lot of ways, she did. My younger sister and I always wore perfectly coordinated outfits with matching hairbands or ribbons. We excelled in school and sports —went to church. To outsiders, we looked like a successful, happy family.

A large part of that "success" was my mom's role as my dad's cheerleader. Her life revolved around supporting him and his dreams. I never saw her ask for much that wasn't related to her appearance (like getting her hair and nails done regularly). When he died, she not only lost her partner; she also lost her sense of self. She didn't have any hobbies or things she did that were fun. Being productive and serving others was how she operated for over half a century, oftentimes only receiving breadcrumbs from others in return. But she rarely complained. Instead, she'd plaster a smile across her face and robotically say, "Everything's fine."

No wonder I was so disconnected from my body. My eyes would observe the treatment my mom and other women endured, my intuition would tell me something's not right here, but the feedback I received from them was, "It's fine. Don't worry about it. Move on to the next thing." And being the obedient girl that the church raised me to be, I did. Again and again.

Bram kissed me goodbye, and I was left alone. I checked my phone and noticed a text from Poland. I replied.

ME

Just got back to my room.

POLAND

Where were you?

ME

On a date.

POLAND

With a new guy?

ME

Yes.

POLAND

Did you have sex with him?

I considered telling him the truth but I knew he was not a one-night stand kind of guy.

> **ME**
> I gave him a blowjob.

I wanted to evoke jealousy in Poland. I wanted him to regret letting me go. I hoped my words would hurt him like he hurt me by not choosing me.

> **POLAND**
> Ok. You'll see him again?

> **ME**
> I doubt it.

I continued to text with Poland until I went to sleep. The next morning, I flew home to Germany. Nate wasn't responding to my phone calls or texts. Finally, when I was on the train, he responded to my message.

> **ME**
> Can you please talk to me? Please.

> **NATE**
> I don't understand this cycle where you lie to me and not do what you say. I get upset and have feelings about it, and then you get mad for that and I end up being the one who is the bad guy. Why can't you just do what you say you will do? Why?

> **ME**
> I never lied to you! I never hid that I was on a date!

> **NATE**
> You never indicated to me that you planned on going on a date.

Nate was right. I hadn't. It's not that I was hiding it from him. I just wanted something for myself. I didn't want to have to explain myself or answer questions. I didn't want accountability.

I wanted freedom. I wanted a husband who said, "Have a great time. I trust you. Do whatever you need to do. I'm here to support you."

Because that was something I never got—no one in my life had ever trusted me to make decisions that felt good to me. There was always a level of fear or an element of shame that influenced my decision-making process.

Purity culture and the patriarchy are relentless at convincing women that we can't trust ourselves. Despite the years of trying to untangle and heal those core wounds that I wasn't enough, and I wasn't deserving of pleasure outside of what was prescribed to me by society, I was still operating from that unhealed place.

For the first time in my life, I bucked against that. For the first time, I prioritized my pleasure. I pursued things that brought me joy. That made me feel good. And not just good. Liberated.

I was so tired of men telling me what I could and couldn't do with my body. Pastors, school administrators, boyfriends, my dad. When did I get to decide? I was forty years old. At what point in my life did I get a say?

It seemed like my happiness always came at a cost to others. It didn't feel fair. Is this the price one pays for a life that looks good on paper? I had signed on the dotted line to be a wife at twenty-two. I didn't realize that the whole "forsaking all others" also included forsaking myself.

Why does this feel so hard? Why can't Nate get on board with this?

I truly believed that non-monogamy was the only way to keep our marriage together. But nine months into it, I wondered when it would get easier.

I can't keep doing this up, down, up cycle.

In the following days, I searched for couples that looked like Nate and me in social media. In books. On websites. It was next to impossible to find others in our situation. Mono-poly. Parents. Professionals. Married. I needed evidence that we could make this work. I needed reassurance that this was not a dumpster fire of a decision I made.

I found myself getting angry—jealous—when I saw polyamorous people posting openly online. Talking about their partners and how supportive of a community they had. I'd fight back tears when Abby and Carlos told me how they felt incredibly close since opening their marriage. How Carlos and Abby had gotten drinks with one of Abby's partners. I was happy for them. I wanted to be happy for me, too.

Would I ever have that?

I asked myself that often. Because I was too scared to ask the real question:

Do I believe I deserve it?

CHAPTER THIRTY-TWO

April 2023

MY ACTIONS in Amsterdam had hurt Nate. We continued to argue, and I felt suffocated by him again. I didn't realize it then, but he represented forty years of men who dictated my actions. So when I fought back against him, I was fighting every man who had ever tried to keep me small. My dad who sheltered me because "you can't trust other people." My pastors who preached that women were responsible for keeping men's lustful thoughts in check by not parading around and trying to tempt them. Any man who had shown interest in me but labeled me as "too much." Male friends who never saw me as their equals.

It was incredibly unfair of me to put that on Nate. And I still hurt for that version of me who wasn't able to make that connection and communicate her pain.

When we'd argue, and Nate really wanted to hurt me, he would tell me that when I left to go on dates, I was abandoning him and the family. It was like he knew the number one way to break me was to insult me as a mother.

We still hadn't told the kids. It felt harder and harder to even fathom what that conversation would look like. Nate would bring it up, and I would dismiss it. It was like a game of Duck Hunt. Nate would hurl the clay pigeons, and I'd shoot them down. I would tell him, "One more round, then I'll be ready." He'd grow tired of asking, and I'd have bought myself some more time.

Poland and I continued to text often. Nothing seemed to change despite the fact that we both wanted different things. But Poland said that when he went home for Easter, he would talk to his best friend about our situation. He wanted his opinion on what he should do.

ME

Did you make it?

POLAND

Yes. I'm out with friends now.

ME

Thanks for letting me know. Have fun.

POLAND

I'm sorry, babe. You didn't ask me to let you know.

Poland had never called me babe before. Isn't that what you call someone you're in a relationship with?

ME

We always have told each other when we travel. But you're right. I didn't.

POLAND

I'm so sorry.

The next day, we exchanged our Instagram information. Until that point, I didn't even know his last name.

Calling me babe last night and telling me your last name today. Feels like we unlocked a new level in this thing.

POLAND

Sounds like an enormous step indeed.

He had talked to his best friend, who encouraged him to give things a shot with me. Poland seemed to be ready for a relationship, so I paused my profile on the dating app and ended things with other guys I was talking to. It felt like things were finally going to work out.

When Poland came back to Germany, we agreed for me to meet him at his place. I asked Nate what time I had to be home, and after arguing for thirty minutes about it, he asked that I just be home before the kids got up the next day. He was tired of lying for me, and I still wasn't ready to tell them.

Great.

I had wanted to spend the night with Poland for the past two months. Not just have sex with him, but share a bed. Share an evening.

I texted him that I had made it, and he said he would meet me outside. I spotted the handsome Polish man wearing dark jeans and a lightweight orange sweater. When he saw me, that charming smile spread across his face, revealing perfect small squares of white. We hugged briefly and then walked up the two flights of stairs to his flat.

When I walked into his flat, I noticed that there was no warmth to his home. No color. No beauty. It contrasted the man I had grown to care for these past two months. I looked at the bare white walls and then back to him.

Gosh, he is gorgeous.

My eyes roamed over his smooth, olive skin. His perfectly trimmed beard. His dark hair that playfully fell into his golden-brown eyes. And those thick, luscious lips.

All of me wanted him. A tingling spread inside me like syrup being poured on a pancake. His body felt like a magnet. The pull to be near him. To touch him. I was grateful we were inside because it felt like I might float away on the slightest breeze.

"I brought you something back from Iceland!" I shared excitedly.

"You did?"

I pulled the chocolate out of the bag first. "Here. I haven't tried it, but it looked good."

He accepted the chocolate, turning it over in his hands. "Thanks."

"And then this guy!" I said as I handed him a small stuffed puffin.

He smiled. "Is this the one from the picture you sent me?"

I shook my head. "No, that one was much bigger."

He set the puffin on his desk, near his bed. I could tell he appreciated my gifts, and that made me happy.

I sat in his desk chair that wheeled and spun around in it a few times. When I was around Poland, I was more playful. Curious. Less inhibited.

He sat on his bed, and I wheeled myself closer to him. We were a foot apart as we talked about school, work, and life. My heart raced as I tried to gauge the sexual temperature between us.

To relieve some tension, I spun myself in the chair. When my rotation hit three hundred sixty degrees, he stopped me. He put his hands on each armrest, trapping me in between his arms. Our eyes locked.

I waited for what felt like hours to see if he would put his lips to mine. Poland moved toward me and did what I had been longing for since our first date ended. He kissed me. Hard. Passionately. As if my lips were his oxygen. I grabbed for his shirt and lifted the sweater over his head. He did the same to mine. I unhooked my bra, standing before him. His lips moved to my breasts, and I let out a small moan.

He unbuttoned my jeans, and I stepped out of them. He admired my black lace panties, running his fingers slowly along the trim. I ran my fingers through his thick dark hair and cupped his face to look up at mine.

My body ached for his. I straddled him on the bed and returned my lips to his. He flipped me over onto my back, towering over me. My hands moved to his jeans as I bit my inner lip. I rubbed the outside, feeling his hardness before unzipping. He briefly sat back to remove his pants and boxer briefs before he returned next to me, naked. He held me in his arms, and I laid my head on his bare chest.

"I feel safe with you," I told him. "I hope you feel safe with me."

Coolly, he replied, "I do, but you know, you can't trust people."

I took my head off his chest and looked him in the eyes, furrowing my brow. "You can't trust me?"

Poland didn't move. "I trust you more than most people. But not like as much as I do my parents."

What a weird thing to say in this moment.

I put my head back down on his chest. "Obviously."

"It's just, you never know with people."

I rolled my eyes. I had heard this before. A hundred times. With my dad, who raised me to believe that you can never trust anyone. Because they will always hurt you or disappoint you or leave you. The problem with this approach is that when we keep people at bay, we keep out the love, too. And at some point in my life, I chose love and trust over fear. Even though I knew it would mean heartache. But it also meant I was open to joy.

Poland continued, "I don't know the kind of people you hang out with."

Is he questioning my integrity? Seriously?

I was undeterred. "You know people tell me their secrets for a living. I'm one of the most trustworthy people you'll meet."

Why am I trying to convince him that I am trustworthy? Have I not spent the past two plus months showing him that I am honest, open, and authentic?

It didn't feel like enough. I didn't feel like I was enough.

I was so tired of having to prove my worth. Prove I was lovable. Self-doubt crept in, and I began to question myself. I wondered if I was doing something wrong. Scratch that. The question that I had been asking myself since this all started surfaced.

What's wrong with me?

Poland wasn't making any bold moves. He seemed a bit hesitant and was quieter than usual.

His hand slowly caressed my bare back, and my desire grew. There was something about Poland's touch that short-circuited my cognitive functioning. No matter what dumb thing he had said or how socially awkward he seemed, when our bodies made contact, all bets were off.

I tried to assuage his nerves. "We don't have to have sex if you don't want to."

"No, I do want to. I'm just not that experienced. I've only had sex with one other person a couple times."

I knew he wasn't experienced; I just didn't realize he had only had one other partner.

"Okay. I don't care about that."

He stuttered a little, "I just... I don't think I'll last very long."

"That's okay. Do you want me to suck you off before we have sex?"

Poland raised his eyebrows. "Sure. You can try."

His muscled body moved to his knees on the small twin bed. I sat up slightly so his hard cock was now eye level with me. I licked my lips and titled my head. My hand slowly caressed his thigh and inched towards where my mouth was about to be.

I had never seen Poland's dick before this meeting. He wasn't a fan of sending dick pics or doing anything live on video. Being inches from this part of him, stirred even more desire within me. Before I wrapped my mouth around Poland's dick, I looked up at him. His eyes met mine as I took his hardness all the way in. I expected him to moan with pleasure. Instead, his body pulled away a bit, as if the sensation was too much.

I didn't understand. After twenty seconds of sucking his throbbing cock, I stopped. "Is it too much?"

Poland glanced down at me briefly. "I think so."

"Do you want me to go slower?"

"Sure."

My mouth movements slowed, but I could still see him wince out of the corner of my eye. I didn't want to hurt him, and this didn't seem enjoyable for either of us.

"Okay, why don't we just skip this then."

Without saying a word, Poland got off the bed, went over to his dresser, and grabbed a condom from his bag.

Walking back, he handed me the condom. "I want you to put it on."

I took the condom from him and smiled. "With pleasure."

I slowly unwrapped the latex down his long, thick shaft. His brown eyes watched me intently as the condom fit into place. He moved me onto all fours, his hand feeling my wetness before he slid inside me.

Finally.

I had fantasized about this moment for the past two months. Feeling him enter me, filling me, was incredible.

But after thrusting a couple of times, he pulled out.

Concerned, I asked, "Are you okay?"

Dazed, Poland said, "Wow, that was a lot faster than I thought it would be."

I was shocked. "You came?"

"Yeah."

I didn't know what to say. It had been like three seconds.

He pulled the condom off and threw it away.

Did that just really happen?

Poland tried to break the awkwardness with a joke, and ten

minutes later, we tried again. This time, he lasted about thirty seconds.

"Well, that was better than before," I said.

Ten minutes later, we tried for the third time. This time, he lasted closer to five minutes. I didn't come a single time.

After our last round, Poland asked me, "What can I do for you?"

I appreciated his offer. It seemed like he sincerely wanted to learn how to please me, and that was something no other guy I had dated was really that interested in.

I showed Poland how I liked to be touched and guided his hand for a few minutes. He approached the lesson methodically, focusing on my reactions to his technique. It was hard for me to focus on it feeling good so after a few more minutes, I told him I was fine.

He seemed relieved.

We sat naked with our legs hanging over the edge of his bed. I could tell that he was tired and wanted me to leave. Poland was introverted and had a limited social battery. It seemed that our sexual encounter had drained it.

So much for staying the night with him.

I didn't want him to feel embarrassed about the sex. I mean it wasn't ideal, but I wasn't upset about it. I cared about him so much. I believed the sex was something that could be improved.

I put my hand on his leg. "That's the beauty of a relationship. We can work on these sexual things together. Is that something you want to do?"

Poland didn't look at me when he said, "I mean, I guess. Yeah. But I can't guarantee it. I mean I could wake up tomorrow and change my mind. I probably won't but you never know."

At that moment, it felt like he had slapped me across the face. Fear flooded me. But this time, I couldn't escape it.

Change your mind? Did he value me so little that he so flippantly and carelessly dismissed the possibility of seeing me again?

That was the definition of casual—something I had told him

from the beginning and throughout our relationship I didn't want. Hearing him say those words caused anger to surge through my entire body.

I didn't know what to say. I wanted to push back. I wanted to tell him that this was the exact opposite of what I'd been asking for—security. Some sort of reassurance.

But all I could say was, "That didn't feel good."

Embarrassed and exposed, I grabbed my clothes and put them on as quickly as I could.

CHAPTER THIRTY-THREE

I NEEDED to get away from him. I needed to not be so vulnerable.

I slipped on my shoes, avoiding eye contact with him. "I don't need you to walk me to my car."

Poland ignored my anger. "I will."

Can he seriously not tell how pissed I am? Or maybe he doesn't care.

I completely shut down all my emotions.

I grabbed my purse, walked out of his room, and raced down the stairs. Poland followed me.

Why is he walking me out? I just want to be alone.

We walked in silence to my car. Normally, I would engage and tell him how his words hurt me. But I couldn't. I was so angry. So hurt. He finally spoke to me when we got to my car. I was so upset, I don't even remember the brief conversation.

How do I want to leave?

I felt stuck. Frozen. But before I could decide, Poland pulled me in and hugged me. I didn't move. My hands were glued to my side. He kissed my lips, but I didn't kiss him back.

I drove home in silence. Seething with anger. I couldn't remember the last time I was that mad.

Why am I so angry?

I kept replaying his words. "Change my mind."

Should I have said something? Would it have mattered?

No. Because I didn't matter to him. That had to be why he let me go so upset. He didn't care enough to know why I reacted the way I did.

I pulled into my driveway and saw that he had texted.

POLAND

Let me know when you get home.

I wanted to ignore it. I wanted to throw the phone across the road. I wanted to break something. Because I was breaking inside. I had put so much hope into this encounter. I truly believed that our having sex would give Poland the push he needed into happily entering relationship territory with me. Now it felt like all that investment, all that connection, was for nothing. And not only that, we were worse off than we had been before tonight.

I just wanted things to work out with someone I really liked. I wanted this chase for another partner to end. Why did no man want a relationship with me? Why couldn't I be seen as the "valuable prize" my friends told me I was? It seemed like, once again, I chose wrong. I put my efforts into someone who couldn't or wouldn't choose me. And that pain pierced my heart.

I ignored my feelings and responded anyway.

ME

Home.

POLAND

Good.

Is he serious? He's happy right now? Maybe he's just happy I'm home and not with him.

I slipped into bed at 11:44 p.m. Hours before I expected to get home. I had argued with Nate about what time he wanted me to be home. I fought to stay for hours longer. A battle Poland had no idea I fought on his behalf. On our behalf. But it didn't matter.

I couldn't sleep. I was still fuming. I refused to text Poland "goodnight."

The next morning, I woke up and checked my phone.

POLAND

Good morning.

I was surprised to hear from him.

Do I respond? Do I tell him to go to Hell? Do I ignore it?

I didn't want to be rude, but I also didn't want to pretend like everything was fine.

ME

Morning.

POLAND

Plans for today?

ME

Work. Asher has football.

Come on. He's got to pick up on my frustration.

POLAND

So nothing new.

I wanted to tell him I was hurting.

You hurt me and you don't even care.

But I pushed back tears and responded.

ME

Nope.

For the rest of the day, I didn't hear from him. I decided I wasn't going to text him. He knew me well enough to know that I was upset, and if he wanted to fix things, he would reach out.

That night, I stared at my phone.

Maybe he'll text me tonight. Maybe he'll tell me goodnight.

He didn't.

I woke up at 3:00 a.m. I couldn't sleep. I checked my phone. Nothing.

See, he got what he wanted from you. You're such an idiot, Courtney.

Tears filled my eyes, and I tossed and turned for the next few hours.

Suddenly, I got an idea. Poland loved sports. I played a conversation over in my head, then texted him.

ME

> I've been on the court, in the game, this whole time. And I see you, on the bench, wondering when you're going to join me. I keep wondering, when will I be enough for you to want to play with me? When will you see that I want you as my teammate? I'm tired of playing alone. I'm tired of being vulnerable and open and getting rejected. So I'm putting the ball down. I'm not going to ask you anymore to play with me or be my teammate. I shouldn't have to. I deserve someone who sees my talent and wants to get off the bench and get into the game with me.

Tears poured down my face. There was no anger left in me. Just sadness.

A few hours later, he responded.

POLAND

I knew very well why you were angry but didn't understand it because that was just a remark to the fact that it was a bit of a crazy thing we did, at least for me, and I don't do crazy things too often so I knew there was a very small possibility that I could regret. That didn't eventually happen btw. And that's the whole story. I texted you because I wanted to show you that I still care but you went cold on me so I decided to give you time and I wasn't sure if you still wanted to talk to me. And I'm not sure if you will ever find this security with me and I don't know if my actions would be the reason for that or your insecurity that you are being used. I still don't know if I can give you what you want.

My frustration festered even more.

ME

Then I can't keep doing this. Because there are too many moving parts in my life.

POLAND

Okay, it would be sad for me but I think it's probably best for you.

ME

I don't know what else to do. You don't have to take any risks and you get all the rewards.

POLAND

How?

ME

You get your needs met. Without having to commit. I don't even care if I'm your gf. I just want some predictability. That you consider me in your plans.

POLAND

I do consider you in my plans, I just don't plan anything besides three days more or less.

ME

My life doesn't work like that. But that you could so easily think that you could wake up tomorrow and not want me anymore. Damn, that hurt.

POLAND

I don't like people doing so much for me. I never said that I didn't want you anymore. Never. Literally never.

ME

You said you could change your mind tomorrow. How else was I supposed to take that? Also, I'm not 'people!' I'm supposed to be different.

POLAND

I said it about the thing we did and that I may regret it but not because of you. Don't know how to explain it better. I just didn't mean at all that I don't want to meet you again. And you are different. But I wouldn't want even the closest person to do that for me, especially knowing that you have your busy life here.

ME

I make time for people that matter to me. That's what you do for your teammate.

POLAND

I am an individualist even though I love team sports.

ME

Why would you regret having sex with me?

POLAND

I don't know, maybe I would think "omg, I fucked a married woman" or would just regret that I lost control... But it didn't happen.

ME

There's no point to this then. You're not interested in changing. You don't want me. Well you do but you don't want to risk anything for me. You would rather lose me. Lose this. Than make concessions. And that sucks.

POLAND

I don't like risking anything at all.

ME

No risk, no reward. That's how sports are played. You know that.

POLAND

I just told you I don't like risks, and I don't understand, what do I risk here?

ME

Your heart! No one likes risks.

POLAND

I know but I always felt like I had a lot to lose.

ME

And I don't?! I don't know what else to say. This doesn't feel productive. You don't want to make any changes for me. You won't take a risk. For me.

POLAND

I have to seriously think about everything you told me. Cause it's a bit of a new perspective. I never considered that there is anything to risk here. But apparently there is.

ME

My concerns are still the same. I don't matter enough for you to risk. You would rather lose me than risk.

POLAND

You do matter to me. I just feel bad about
keeping you on standby.

ME

What's it going to take to move me out of
standby? Because I've been patient. I've given
you my mind, my heart, and now my body.

POLAND

I told you, it's about me, my emotions that don't
appear so easily. You never did anything wrong.

I wished I could believe that, but it felt like I wasn't enough.

Poland was my ultimate lesson in examining and healing my self-worth. At the time, I believed that if I could prove my worth to him then he'd finally see how great I was. How great we were together. But I couldn't (or didn't want to) override my dysregulated nervous system and the "chemistry" I chalked it up to. So I held on to hope when I should have walked away.

On my way home from soccer that night, I called Poland. We talked for fifteen minutes, and I made the decision that I wanted to be with someone who was ready to commit to me. And since he still wasn't ready, I knew that wasn't going to be him. I cried and told him that I thought he was making a mistake. He agreed but said he wasn't ready and didn't know if he ever would be.

We didn't talk for a week. I missed him. Deeply missed him. We had talked every day throughout the day for two months and now that was gone. I decided to send him a message about how I was feeling.

ME

Here's what one week without you has shown me. You played an important role in my life and I miss that. I miss our connection. And if there's one thing I know, it's relationships. Our connection is weird. It's uncommon, unique, unexpected. And a bit magical at times. We talked almost every day for over two months. That meant something to me. Even though you guarded yourself. And I didn't. I let myself love you. Don't freak out. I didn't fall in love with you. But I do love you. I do care about you. And I didn't realize that until this past week.

I will not ask for you to choose me. I promised you I wouldn't and I honor my promises. I am so grateful we met. I am so grateful for how you made me laugh. And how you saw me in a way most people don't get to. For challenging me and reminding me how important a person's integrity is to me. And countless other lessons I was meant to learn. This life is so short and when you meet people that are special you tell them that. You say I love you. You say I miss you. You say I care about you. And you are grateful as hell for the opportunity to do it because so many people never get it. I'm grateful I could love you, Poland. I look forward to when I can chat with you and my heart won't hurt.

POLAND

Wow this message really made me smile a lot. I am extremely happy that you started healing and it's so nice to read all these nice things.

Over the next month, we had minimal contact. My epiphany about the role Poland played in my life, that he was a teacher, someone who peeled back all my layers to expose the woman who existed underneath it all, eventually turned to anger. I was angry that I wasn't enough for him. That he wouldn't choose me.

What is wrong with me that he wouldn't want me?

I believed that if I had a steady partner like Poland, my

marriage would stabilize and things would be easier. I'd finally be happy. The past ten months had felt like one big chase. I kept trying to chase happiness, believing that it was something to be found. I couldn't accept that happiness was something within me that was longing to be uncovered. I didn't know how to receive it.

Even as I write this, I am reminded that happiness is not a state or an achievement. It's an opportunity to tune in to what is within us and what is around us. And experiencing this is something I still struggle with on occasion, though not nearly as much as I did when this all began. This journey is filled with a lot of unlearning. It's often a daily battle, being surrounded by individuals who only accept monogamy. I don't live in Berlin or Portland. Even online, showing up, there is resistance to be being a sexually empowered woman, especially by men.

So when I had found someone who was willing to wade into the waters of a non-traditional relationship and I was very interested in them, I held on tight. Oftentimes, too tight thanks to my anxious attachment. But I could feel Poland's resistance at reconnecting, so I decided I wouldn't text him anymore.

He had erected a wall between us. Our conversations had become short and cold. I had accepted that he would likely never be in my life again. But I wondered if I'd ever connect with someone the way I had with him.

I checked my calendar and saw that we had a soccer team trip coming up in a couple weeks.

Well, well, well. Looks like we're heading to Amsterdam once again.

CHAPTER THIRTY-FOUR

June 2023

IT'S OFTEN in the strangest places that things seem to magically unfold. For me, there must've been something with train rides to Amsterdam. Once again, I was on my way to meet my soccer team there, waiting at the Köln station to transfer trains, when he came into my life. Well, more specifically, my app.

I received a ping from Dr. W., a handsome forty-two-year-old American living in Köln. Turns out Bill, who has a PhD in molecular biology, and I were looking for the same thing—someone to add value to our lives and share the everyday with. We clicked instantly, and I spent the entire three-hour train ride messaging him. He shared with me how he and his ex-wife opened their marriage. They had both been polyamorous (by lifestyle, not by orientation) and enjoyed it. Unfortunately, they disagreed on the direction of their marriage which ultimately led to its demise.

Bill and I connected on a different level, the kind I had craved with Poland, but I knew that ship had sailed. Everything with Bill was deep. It felt so incredible to have someone truly understand me—all of me—my polyamory, being married, being a parent, being an intelligent, driven woman. It was as if the Universe was saying, "See, the kind of man you want does exist. Here he is."

I met Bill on my way back from Amsterdam in the same station we had matched in just forty-eight hours ago. I left that date feeling euphoric, a strong sense of peace permeating my entire being. As I sat on the train headed back towards home, I connected with a sensation that I hadn't in a very long time— what it felt like to be seen.

As much as I enjoyed the possibility of my connection with Bill becoming something more, I was concerned with how much his marriage ending would impact his ability to fully commit to me. And even though I shouldn't have, I still thought about Poland. Part of me longed for him, and I wondered when that would go away.

Even though we had both paused our dating profiles, Bill shared that he had a date later that week that he planned on keeping.

BILL

How does that make you feel?

ME

Mixed. I mean our date was hard to top. I want you to be happy and if that's not with me then it's not with me. My inner critic is saying, 'see.'

BILL

Yes. Nothing has ever approached what happened today.

ME

My inner critic says I should pull back.

BILL

Don't pull back. Date on Friday is a courtesy. I said I would come so I want to keep my word. Meet and greet. Usually about an hour or so and then I am on my way walking home.

ME

I appreciate you telling me. You didn't have to. I hope you have fun.

BILL

You are my focus. I'll will show you this week.

We did a video call for about fifteen minutes to discuss our concerns—his fear of ruining my marriage and my fear that he wouldn't be able to fully commit because of that fear. It felt like this was ending before it even began. I just couldn't shake that Bill hadn't fully come to peace with his past and it was going to prevent him from being able to commit to me.

I texted him after.

ME

I'm afraid that me being married and you wanting a long-term partner who's not married will prevent you from wanting to be with me. That you will be afraid to love me. To let yourself have something great.

BILL

This is the poly dynamic. I know what I am signing up for. We may not be forever partners but we maybe also. There is value in either alternative.

ME

Remember when I told you I didn't like the silent eye gazing? And you asked me why. I thought about why I don't like it. It's because I'm afraid you'll see something in me you don't like.

BILL

I'm afraid I will see something in you I can't resist.
And destroy your family.

ME

I would like to share something. Up until we met
yesterday, you were very excited and I could feel
your energy. Not like physically but just your
interest, I guess. After we met, it seemed to shift.
And today it feels like it shifted even more.

He chalked it up to being tired or back to work, but it felt
deeper than that. If there was something I had learned in the
past year, it was that my instincts were rarely wrong.

We continued to chat over the next few days. I kept waiting
for him to ask me when we could see each other again. But he
hadn't asked, and it was making me anxious. I called him on my
way home from an appointment.

During our conversation, I got a call from Nate. I stared at
the screen that made me decide whether I wanted to "ignore and
send to voicemail" or "accept." I ignored Nate's call. I wanted to
keep talking to Bill. I could talk to Nate when I got home.

Nate called again. This time, I figured I needed to answer it.

"Bill, one of my kids is calling," I lied. "I need to answer it."

"Yes, of course," he replied. "Call me back when you can."

"Hello," I said to Nate.

As if he knew I hadn't chosen him, Nate asked, "Did you
reject my call?"

"Yes."

"Who were you talking to?"

I knew if I told him it was Bill, I was starting a fight. But I
was so tired of hiding things from him and walking on eggshells
when it came to my dating.

"I was talking to Bill."

"And you chose to keep talking to him over me?! I'm your
husband. That's supposed to mean something."

"Why does it matter who I was talking to?! If it was my mom

and I didn't click over, would you be this upset? I was in the middle of a conversation, Nate."

"You know what, I don't care. Call him back. Enjoy your nice little chat with him," he snarked and hung up the phone.

I called Bill back and pretended like everything was fine. When I got home, Nate was still pissed. He wouldn't talk to me. The tension between us was so thick, it almost choked me. I tried to talk to Nate in the kitchen, but he refused. He walked outside to watch Asher jump on the trampoline.

Addison walked into the kitchen.

Standing in the doorframe, she asked frustratedly, "Are you and Dad fighting again?"

"We're not fighting. Just having a disagreement."

She crossed her arms and leaned against the doorframe. "What did you do this time?"

I shook my head. "I didn't *do* anything. Plus, I am not talking to you about this."

Addison shifted her weight. "Are you having an affair?"

CHAPTER THIRTY-FIVE

MY HEART DROPPED and my eyes widened. "What?"

It felt like time was moving at half-speed. I wanted to laugh. I wanted to run. I wanted it all to stop. All I could do was cry.

She took a step toward me, her face focused on my reaction. "Are you seeing somebody?"

Tears began streaming down my face. "I... I don't know how to answer that, Addison."

I put my arms on her shoulders. "Please. I need to talk to your dad. Go get your dad."

She obliged, and I began pacing the kitchen.

What should I do? What should I say? I can't lie to her. Is she ready to hear this? I'm not ready. I'm not ready. I can't breathe.

I bent over my knees and tried to focus my breathing. My heart was thumping in my head. I closed my eyes. Trying to think.

After what felt like forever, Nate came into the kitchen, and I returned to a standing position. I asked Addison to give us some privacy.

I pointed to the empty space where our daughter stood a few seconds ago. "She knows."

Nate furrowed his brow. "Knows what? Who?"

I stretched out my arm again, pointing to the other room. "Addison just asked if I was having an affair."

Nate didn't take his eyes off of me. "What did you say?"

I threw up my hands. "That I needed to talk to you. I just started crying!"

Nate kept his distance from me. This wasn't the united front I had hoped we'd have when we told the kids. I could still feel anger exuding from Nate, but we didn't have time to sort our shit out first. We needed to deal with this now.

Nate clenched his jaw. "We have to tell them."

I leaned against the wall, hoping I could fade inside it. Hoping this would all go away.

I closed my eyes and quietly replied, "I know."

The bottom of everything I had built threatened to give way. I knew we had to tell them. But what if they hated me? What if they thought I was some freak? What if they never wanted to talk to me again? I hadn't prepared to tell them like this.

Nate and I took our fourteen-year-old on a walk and explain things to her. And then we would consider telling the younger two.

We slipped on our shoes, and the three of us headed out our front door.

It was hard to form the words to explain to Addison who I was. How did I explain to her that my heart was capable of loving more than one man? We had raised our kids in a sex-positive home. We had had open discussions on people of all genders and sexualities, and we accepted and loved anyone regardless of how they identified.

In my career, I had spoken to thousands of people across all age groups about sexuality. And yet, I failed to know where to even begin with my own daughter. This felt like one of the most important conversations I would ever have with Addison.

What if I mess it up? What if this ruins my relationship with her?

But the idea of her thinking I would betray her father by

cheating on him... I had to remedy that belief as soon as possible.

Nate kept reassuring me it would be okay. I wanted to believe him, but I couldn't.

We began to walk down our hill.

"Your mom is really nervous."

Addison walked in between us. "Okay."

I drew in a deep breath. And began the conversation that would forever change my family. I could never go back once the words were spoken. And I couldn't undo what I had set into motion one year ago.

I swallowed hard. "You know how there's different sexual orientations: gay, bisexual... and different genders?"

She glanced at me. "Yeah."

"Well, there's also some people that have different relation-ship orientations."

I didn't want to get into how some people believed you're born polyamorous and other people think it's a lifestyle choice.

Stay focused, Courtney.

"Okay," Addison said, hoping I'd get to the point.

I put my hands in my pockets. "I'm one of those people. I'm non-monogamous. More specifically, I'm polyamorous."

Addison crinkled her nose slightly. "Wait, so like a threesome?"

I shook my head. "No. I mean, there are some polyamorous people who are in like a throuple, but it's different for everyone. But that's not how it is for me."

I'm not explaining this very well.

We walked by the park I used to take the kids to. Moments when life felt a lot simpler flashed through my mind. Times that seemed a lot more black and white. But this past year, my life had burst open with a kaleidoscope of color.

"I realized that I was not only capable of loving and receiving love from more than one partner, but that I actually need that to feel like my best self."

She looked at Nate. "What does Dad think about that?"

I nodded in Nate's direction. "You can ask him."

Nate looked at Addison as we continued to talk. "It's been an adjustment. But I love your mom and I'm here to support her."

Addison turned back to me. "So you're not cheating on him?"

"Oh, gosh, no. No, your dad has been aware of this since the beginning."

She looked back at Nate. "Are you guys going to get divorced?"

I hope not, kiddo. But I won't lie to you.

"That's not our goal. We want to keep the family together. I love you. I love your dad. We're still figuring everything out."

Addison tilted her head. "When did you realize all this?"

I looked at her. "About a year ago."

She pursed her lips together. "And you didn't tell us!?"

I sighed. "Your dad wanted to tell you but I was so scared that I asked him to wait."

Addison furrowed her eyebrows. "Why were you scared?"

I stared at the ground as I put one foot in front of the other. "I was afraid you guys would hate me. You'd think I was some monster or deviant or weirdo. I was so scared that you would be ashamed of me as your mother."

"Mom. We could NEVER not love you. I'm sorry you would think that. I don't care who you love. I will always love you."

Her words sent a sense of peace through my heart.

Tears streamed down my face. "I'm so sorry, kiddo. I didn't mean to keep it from you. I'm so sorry."

"It's okay," Addison reassured me. "I've suspected something has been off for a while. I even Googled signs of an affair. I wanted to ask you about it but I was too scared. I even started having panic attacks because I didn't know what to do."

Panic attacks?! Googling signs of an affair? What did I do?

My stomach churned, and my breathing became shallower.

"Oh, Addison, I am so sorry. I'm sorry I put you in that position. I wish I had done it differently but I was so scared."

She shrugged. "I understand. I told Avery about it a month ago, about my suspicions. She was scared you guys would get divorced, too."

What had I done to my kids? By hiding who I was, I placed the burden on them.

Addison stared at the ground. "So like how does it work? Do you date other married men or women?"

My breathing returned to semi-normal. "Oh. Well, I'm not into women so I only date men. But sometimes they're married or in a relationship. Most of them are single, though."

"And they know you're married?"

I nodded. "Yes, I'm totally up front about my situation."

"Do their partners know they're also dating?"

"I only date men whose partners know they're dating. I don't date cheaters."

She nodded. "Good."

She glanced at Nate. "Does Dad date, too?"

"I don't, kiddo," Nate answered.

Addison looked back at me. "Will we meet him?"

My heart began to race. This was an issue Nate and I had discussed previously but hadn't come to a solid conclusion on.

"Oh, um, maybe. Eventually. I'm not in a relationship right now but I would like him to be part of our life at some point," I said.

Nate interjected, "I'm not quite ready for that to happen yet. Maybe someday."

I pushed my cuticles back with my thumb. "I know you'll have a lot of questions and I want you to know that you can ask me about anything at any time, okay? Do you have anything else you want to ask now?"

She glanced between Nate and me. "Are you going to tell the other two?"

My eyes met Nate's. Without saying a word, we both knew the answer.

I looked at Addison. "What do you think I should do?"

"I think you should tell them."

I nodded. "Then I will."

We walked for a minute in silence. "I'm so sorry, kiddo. Gosh, I love you so much and I'm so sorry that I hurt you."

"I understand," she said with so much grace. "I just wish you would've told me. I feel a little betrayed that you didn't."

I bit my inner lower lip. "Thank you for your honesty. I can absolutely understand why you'd feel that way."

I put my arm around her shoulder.

She leaned in to me. "I could never hate you, Mom."

Tears filled my eyes again. "Thank you," I whispered, and then kissed her head.

We walked into the house and asked Asher and Avery to come into the living room. I was sitting on the couch, tears leaking from my eyes when they came in.

Avery, our twelve-year-old daughter, looked at me, then back to Nate. "Is everything okay?"

Asher, our ten-year-old son, followed behind as Nate ushered them to the couch.

Nate sat down in a chair across from me and the kids. "Yeah, your mom just has something to share with you guys."

Concern washed over Asher's face as he moved closer to me on the couch. Avery sat diagonally from me, her hands folded in her lap. A few feet away, at the kitchen table, sat Addison, ready to listen to what she had just learned about her mother.

"What about Addi?" Avery asked.

Proudly, Addison piped in, "They already talked to me about it."

Fearing I was worrying them, I began, "Everything's okay. I'm not sick. Your Dad and I are good. But there is something important I want to share with you."

I explained it to them the same way I explained it to Addison. I cried throughout the entire thing.

After I finished, Avery looked up at me softly. "It's okay, Mom. We still love you."

Asher grabbed my hand and didn't let go of it until we left the couch. "Yeah, Mom, we love you."

Relief flooded me. A sense of calm washed over me. I didn't know what to say. A part of me feared they would reject me. Be ashamed of me. But it felt like I could finally breathe again.

Avery looked at Nate. "Does the family know?"

I answered for Nate. "Everyone but Dad's parents do. But we will tell them soon. We don't want you to feel like you have to keep this a secret from anyone. We're not ashamed of who I am, but some people may not understand it."

Avery blinked a few times and nodded. "Yeah, that makes sense. How did everyone react?"

I smiled. "Thankfully, as supportive as you all. I'm lucky to have such an amazing family. And I'm sure Grandma and Grandpa will be, too. I just, I'm not quite ready to tell them yet. Do you have any questions for me? You can ask me anything."

Avery asked similar questions as Addison. She, too, was focused on the ethics of the situation.

"Well, if all the adults know what's going on, I don't see what the problem is then," she stated. She looked back at Nate. "Dad, are you okay with it?"

Nate sat up a little straighter. "Yeah, I mean it's an adjustment but I love your mom and we're committed to making this work."

I looked at Asher. "Bug, do you have any questions?"

He shook his head, not letting go of my hand.

Avery looked at the floor. "Addi told me about her concerns a month ago, but I didn't believe her. I understand why you hid it from us but I wish you wouldn't have."

I'm so sorry, kiddo. Ugh.

I nodded, tears welling in my eyes again. "I was just so scared you wouldn't love me anymore."

Asher squeezed my hand. "Mom, we could never not love you."

"Yeah," Avery said, as she got up and hugged me. "We love you. You're amazing."

The grace my kids showed me that day is something I will never forget. Their love and support felt like a total game-changer in my polyamory journey and in my relationship with them.

I shared what had happened with Bill later that night. It seemed to trigger something from his past. He told me he needed some time to figure out how he felt about all of this. I was discouraged and knew what that meant. The end was inevitable.

CHAPTER THIRTY-SIX

August 2023

I HAD AGREED to go on a girl's trip with two of my besties, Ashley and Sarah, to Paris. And boy, did we have a great time. Wine, *Moulin Rouge*, and an impromptu date with a sexy Frenchman made for some wonderful memories.

"Tell us about Paris!" our friend, Leah, exclaimed.

I had started hanging out with two of Ashley's friends, Liz and Leah, more regularly, and tonight was wine night.

I grabbed my glass of wine. "Oh, man, it was so fun! You guys need to come next time."

Ashley stepped onto her back patio, carrying a charcuterie board, and chimed in. "Yes! And I can't wait for you all to meet Christian. He's the best. I mean, Hugo was a close second, though." She winked at me.

Liz turned to me. "Who's Hugo?"

Sarah, who was sitting across the table from me, cleared her throat. She was prepared to deflect the question.

Do I tell them?

It had been over a year since I had begun my journey. I was tired of hiding and wanted to come out to more people. I wanted to normalize non-monogamy. Demystify it. Kind of hard to do when not many people knew I was polyamorous.

Here goes.

I looked at Sarah, then Ashley, then to Liz. "He was my date."

Liz pursed her lips and looked from side to side. "Date?"

I looked to Leah and then to Liz. "I'm non-monogamous. Well, I'm polyamorous. Nate and I have an open marriage."

Leah raised her eyebrows. "Oh. Okay."

Liz shrugged. "Okay."

They followed up with a few questions, but then we moved on to other topics.

It felt liberating to share this about myself and not have it be a big deal. I found that sharing my truth with others wasn't just liberating, it was also healing. Knowing that people knew I was polyamorous and still loved me. And I started to believe that maybe, just maybe, there was nothing ever wrong with me.

I saw a message notification on my phone.

Well, well, well.

I didn't know how to feel seeing this man's name on my screen. Historically, I would have gotten excited about receiving a message from him. But I had made peace with never hearing from him again. Now all those old feelings threatened to emerge.

I opened the message.

POLAND

I finally watched Ted Lasso and no wonder you
said we should watch this together, apart from
the unexpectedly accurate references to our
relationship, I really enjoyed the whole thing. I am
always amazed by how sometimes such cheesy,
simple, unrealistic stuff totally destroys the
cynical side of me.

I didn't even contemplate how to respond. I just dove right
back in. Heart first.

ME

I knew you would love it. What do you mean by
"unexpectedly accurate references?" Please
explain.

POLAND

Like the goldfish thing or the relationship
between the owner and the younger, intelligent,
however not so handsome, player. And I was also
surprised that there were two Polish people—the
waitress and Zava.

ME

Am I the intelligent and not handsome player?
And yes, I loved both those characters!

POLAND

No, you are the owner, Rebecca. I'm the
intelligent AND handsome player.

Of course you are.

Poland and I picked back up where we left off like no time
had passed. We started talking every day, and I could feel myself
falling for him again. Which also meant falling back into our old
patterns. But one night, something changed in me.

> I woke up this morning with an overwhelming sense of peace. Something shifted for me last night. And I'm still processing it. But here is what I know: you have been one of my teachers. And for a while, I've resisted whatever it is that you were meant to teach me. And last night, I just let go. And it felt amazing.

I was afraid that if I lost Poland, that version of me who was fun and confident would go away. Losing Poland didn't scare me, but losing who I became when I was with him, that did. And even though I had that clarity the next morning after our reconnection, I still wasn't ready to separate my revelation from his role in my life.

I let Poland see parts of me that I had fiercely protected from others because none of it ever seemed possible. So I thought, why not? Why not be bold? Why not open myself up? I didn't see it then but I opened myself up because I sought his validation and acceptance. He had an avoidant attachment, and our anxious-avoidant attachment tango was ready to take another spin around the dance floor.

Despite my feelings for Poland being rooted more in friendship, our sexual chemistry was undeniable. Sure, the sex we had had was, well, not great. But I thought we could likely improve that (sex is a skill, after all). We discussed the idea of meeting again, but he was headed to Romania for the next five months.

I had no idea what my future with Poland would look like. I made no pretenses that we would ever have the relationship I once craved with him or if I even wanted that anymore. But I wasn't ready to end our connection.

I continued to date in hopes of finding another partner and also talked with Poland daily over text.

This boat that I was building felt like it was coming along pretty damn good. It wasn't perfect, and Nate still acted like a disgruntled first mate most days. But I was hopeful.

Until one day, the ominous dark clouds rolled in unexpectedly. The wind picked up, and I could feel it in my soul that a storm was coming. For the first time in our marriage, I didn't know if the boat would be strong enough to withstand the weather that was headed our way.

CHAPTER THIRTY-SEVEN

August 2023

WE DECIDED to take the kids back-to-school shopping in Prague. It's a city our whole family loved, and things are somewhat cheaper there than in Germany. I asked Nate if he wanted me to turn off the app while we were in Prague, but he said he didn't care. I didn't know how realistic it was to have a potential boyfriend live five hours away from me, but I kept it on.

We arrived in Prague later than expected. Nate drove the whole way, even though I offered several times. After getting settled and getting ready for bed, I initiated sex with Nate by kissing his neck.

Without reacting, he continued to stare at his phone. "I'm tired."

"Come on..." I kissed his shoulder. "What if I..."

He turned to put his phone away and pulled the covers up. "No, I don't want to."

I fell back onto my side of the bed. "Fine."

Seriously? What is your problem?

I grabbed my phone and saw I had a bunch of likes from the app.

"Enjoy looking for your boyfriend," Nate said rudely before he rolled over and went to sleep.

I suppressed the anger that threatened to erupt.

Ignore it. Let it go...

The next morning, Nate came back from a run in a terrible mood. Normally, I'd try to soothe him or give him some space. But after last night, I wasn't backing down.

"What's your problem?" I asked him flatly.

"All you care about are your boyfriends. You don't care about me. You're just always on your phone. Looking for the next guy who will give you attention."

My anger simmered, and I wanted to hurt him as much as he had been hurting me. "Well, maybe if you paid attention to me and actually wanted to have sex with me, I wouldn't care about these guys."

Our arguing continued for several minutes before Nate's anger exploded.

He grabbed his jeans. Stomped into the bathroom to retrieve his toiletries. "I'm done! I'm leaving. I'm taking the train back to Germany."

I pointed to the door. "Great. Go ahead and tell the kids."

He tightened his jaw. "Fine. I will."

He flung the bedroom door of our Airbnb open. Asher, who was on the couch, sat up in surprise. The door to the other bedroom where the girls slept opened, too.

I walked out of the room with my arms crossed, waiting for Nate to explain his sudden departure to the kids.

He was packing his stuff when Asher asked him, "What are you doing, Dad?"

He didn't look at Asher but continued to pack. "I'm leaving. I'll find a train to take home."

Asher put down his iPad, and the girls walked into where we were.

Addison looked around the room and then at her dad. "What's going on?"

Nate continued to pack his bag. "Why don't you ask your mom."

Convenient.

I shook my head. "Your dad wants to go home."

Avery stepped forward. "We're leaving?"

Nate responded, "Nope, just me."

Addison looked at me, confused. "Why?"

Nate answered without looking at anyone. "Ask your mom."

Addison looked at me, and I just shrugged.

I stood there. Silent. Watching as my life felt like it was slowly falling apart.

Frustrated, Addison turned to me. "Do something!"

If you only knew what I've tried to do to keep this family together.

She looked at Nate. "Dad, why are you doing this?!"

In that moment, it was as if something broke in Nate. He lost it. Months and months of anger spewed from his lips. He blamed me for all of our problems. He hurtled accusations against me. All in front of our children.

"She only cares about her boyfriends!" he yelled.

The girls began to cry. Tears streamed down my face. Our family was fracturing. Time felt like it was slowing, and all I could do was witness the demise of the thing I valued most.

"This is all your fault!" Addison screamed at me. The tears dropped from her eyes to the floor.

"Addi, no," Avery tried to intervene. "It's not Mom's fault. Stop it!"

Asher remained silent, but I saw him wipe tears from his eyes.

For the next minute, amidst our children crying, Nate continued to say horrendous things about me.

My lips felt like they were glued together. My feet felt

anchored to the floor. I had no idea how to stop the nightmare I was in with the people I loved most in this world.

I saw the venom eventually dissipate from Nate's words. I saw his face the moment he realized he had gone too far. Finally, as if the floodwaters had subsided, he sat down in the chair next to the bags he had been angrily packing for the past ten minutes. His elbows fell to his thighs, and he stared vacantly at the floor.

For a moment, no one spoke. No one moved.

Avery broke the silence. "Are you going to get divorced?"

I didn't know if any sound would come out of my mouth. I shook my head and mustered a response. "I... I um, don't know."

Tears continued to fall down Addison's face. "Will we have to leave Germany? I'm not leaving Germany."

Speaking felt like walking through mud, but I knew I had to address their concerns. "We'd find a way to have you stay."

I could see Nate mentally assessing the damage he had caused. "I would never make you leave. I would get an apartment somewhere else but no, I wouldn't make us leave Germany."

He tried to reassure the kids—to offer some bit of safety. Overwhelmed, Avery ran to the bedroom. Asher followed after her.

Addison was left behind. She turned to me, looking me up and down in disgust. "I hope you're happy. I hope it was worth it."

Hearing her say those words, just two months after we'd told her I was polyamorous, was a punch to my gut—I struggled to breathe, to assess what had just happened. A tornado had touched down, and I was too overwhelmed to determine the damage.

Nate was still sitting in the chair, his head in his hands. I could hear him sob. I could see his shoulders heaving. I hadn't moved from where I was. I didn't know how.

Everything I had fought to protect... everything I had worked to preserve... I couldn't do it. I couldn't keep my family together.

My worst fear was coming true. I had failed.

My thoughts were interrupted by Nate's voice.

"What is wrong with me?" he asked, looking up at me with tears in his eyes.

I stared at him blankly before I uttered the words I had never spoken in our marriage. Words I never thought I would have to.

CHAPTER THIRTY-EIGHT

MY JAW TIGHTENED, and my eyes narrowed. I looked into Nate's bloodshot eyes like a hunter does before they pull the trigger.

"I will never forgive you for what you just did." I said the next words slowly and firmly. "I want a divorce."

Anger fueled my steps as I walked into the bedroom and closed the door.

I sat on the bed and replayed what had happened.

How did we get here? How did I ever believe that Nate and I could make an open marriage work?

He would never accept me. He would never be okay with this. There would always be something that he had a problem with. I could never be happy in this marriage.

I was exhausted. I had no fight left in me.

Despite wanting to crawl under the covers and disappear, I walked to the room the kids were in and knocked on the door.

"Come in," they all said.

"Hey," I said softly. "How are you guys doing?"

"I texted one of my friends," Avery said. "Her parents are divorced so she knows what I'm feeling right now."

Addison continued to look at me with disgust. "Are you guys getting divorced?"

I shook my head. "I don't know. But no matter what happens, we will put you guys first. You will always be our number one concern, okay?"

Asher got off the bed and wrapped his arms around my waist. I squeezed him tight, his long hair sticking to my damp face.

Addison sighed and rolled her eyes. "Whatever."

I looked at my watch and saw the time. Fuck. Nate and I had made an appointment at the beer bath place that was in an hour. We had already paid for it, and it was a twenty-minute walk. If we were still going to go, we needed to leave soon.

Spending time with him naked in a small tub filled with beer ingredients was one of the absolute last things I wanted to do right then, but we needed a plan. Sitting here sulking for the next thirty-six hours wasn't going to do any good.

I shut the door and left their room. Nate hadn't moved from the chair. His head was still in his hands, and his shoulders were shaking from crying.

I stopped near him. "The beer bath appointment is soon. Do you still want to go?"

He looked up at me, his eyes swollen from crying. "I don't care."

"We should go. There are things we need to discuss."

I told the kids we'd be back in a couple hours. They somberly agreed.

Nate and I walked in silence to the hotel the beer bath was in. The cheerful lady greeted us, showed us to our private room, prepared the bath, and said she would be back in an hour. As I undressed, I turned my back to Nate. I felt exposed, not just physically, but also emotionally. I had lost all trust in him and now I was to share a tub with him for the next hour.

I must be insane.

We got into the tub, and I became overwhelmed with the reality of where we were. I couldn't look in Nate's direction for the first ten minutes. My tears were a steady stream. My heart was broken. The wound was bleeding, and I had no idea what would stop it.

Finally, I broke the silence. "If you could please give me some time to find a job here, I would appreciate it. I have no desire to move back to the U.S. The kids want to stay here. Even if I have to work as a janitor, I will do anything I can to keep them here. Can you please give me time to find a job that ensures we stay in Germany?"

Nate didn't answer right away. Eventually, he said, "I would never kick you guys out of the house. I would leave. I'm the one who should leave after what I did."

I was in no mood to entertain his self-pity. "I would be fine if you moved to the first-floor bedroom. You don't need to move out. I have no problem being co-parents with you. Business partners. Whatever. But our marriage as we knew it is over. You are no longer my husband. If you want a legal divorce, that's fine."

"I don't want a divorce," he said.

"After what you did, I have no desire to stay married to you. You did the ONE thing I asked you never to do. The ONE thing that you knew would hurt me. I can't trust you, Nate. How could you do that?"

"My worst fear is happening," he began. "I've always been afraid that you and the kids would abandon me, and now that's what's happening… I deserve to be alone in a shitty apartment, away from you guys. I'm no good. Of course this was going to happen. I knew it would."

I had no empathy to give. "You… you broke my heart. I will never forget how our children's little faces fell. Their little hearts broke hearing those awful things you said about me to them. I don't know how to move past that, Nate. I can't."

He nodded. "I understand."

The rest of the time, we sat in silence. The knock on the door indicated our time was up. We got out of the tub, dressed, and checked out. We put on fake smiles and walked to check out.

"How was it?!" the receptionist asked.

I feigned happiness. "Great."

Nothing like talking about your marriage ending while sitting in a pool of beer ingredients.

We walked back to our hotel without saying a word. By the time we got back, it was dinner time. The kids were quiet but hungry. I could tell they were afraid to ask any questions. Make any requests. Just like me, they wanted to disappear.

Sensing their sadness, I suggested we walk to our favorite restaurant in Prague to see if they had a table. Thankfully, they did.

After we ordered, Nate spoke to the kids. "I need to apologize to all of you for how I behaved earlier. It was completely inappropriate. I should have never said those things about your mom. I was angry and hurting and it was unfair to say those things about her. It's not true."

They looked at Nate and then back at their drinks. Asher stirred his ice cubes with his paper straw, and I wished he was preparing a magic potion that would take all of this pain away.

Avery was the first to speak. "It's okay, Dad."

"No, Avery," he continued. "It's not. There's a lot of unresolved trauma I haven't dealt with. A lot from my childhood that has impacted me more than I realized. I'm not using that as an excuse, but it's definitely something I need to work on."

"What do you mean 'childhood trauma?'" Addison asked, annoyed. "Like you were abused?"

I interjected, "It doesn't matter what the trauma was. The point is that your dad is sharing that when we don't deal with hurtful things from the past, they can impact our ability to handle stress in the present."

"No," Nate said. "I wasn't abused. But I did have some things happen that I need to work through. And I am so sorry that I hurt you today. That will never happen again, okay?"

"Are you going to get divorced?" Avery asked.

Nate looked at me. I didn't want to scar the kids any more than we already had. But I didn't want to give them false hope. I felt resigned at this point. In my mind, our marriage was over. I was done.

"I don't want a divorce," Nate said.

He looked at me to offer some words. I had none to give.

Nate continued, "We need to meet with our therapist and figure out what the best next steps are."

The server brought our food, but before anyone ate, Nate offered, "I'm so sorry for what I did and said." Then, he looked at me. "And I'm sorry to you, Courtney."

I mumbled a half-hearted, "Thank you." I didn't want his apologies. I didn't want to be at this table with him. I wanted to run away from it all. Everything that I had worked to build and preserve for the past twenty years felt like it had been shattered in one moment.

The drive home the next day was tense. We barely spoke to one another, and when Nate spoke to me, he had an irritated tone. He had asked me the night before to reconsider what I had said about our marriage being over. I declined, and he was upset by that. I didn't care. His feelings were inconsequential at this point.

A few days later, we met with Dave, our therapist. I was actually happy to recount the events to Dave. I wanted Nate to feel as small as possible for what he did. I wanted Dave to lay into him and tell him what a piece of shit he was for doing that to his kids.

But Dave didn't. He listened, as he always did, without judgement. And after I had shared every last detail, I waited for Dave to tell me to leave Nate. It could finally be over.

"It sounds like that was really hard for both of you," Dave said.

No shit. Tell me something I don't know.

Dave sighed. "To be honest, it's not great, what happened,

but the fact that you repaired what you did with your kids, Nate, that was great."

What?

I was pissed. Was he actually commending Nate for his actions? I suppressed my anger and continued to listen to what Dave had to say.

"Obviously, we don't want to have those outbursts in front of our kids, right. But you didn't leave. You didn't abandon them. You addressed your actions in a short time frame from when they occurred. And we know that that's what actually matters for minimizing traumatic events like this. So I think they're going to be okay."

Even though I was a trained therapist, and knew the importance of immediate repair and reconciliation after a traumatic event, hearing it from Dave was reassuring. But that was only one element of our larger issue—the fact remained that I wanted a divorce.

We spent the rest of the session talking about Nate's abandonment issues and how me being polyamorous made those worse.

Fantastic. Of course, it's my fucking fault.

"Why are we doing this?" I finally asked Dave, irritated. "Like at what point is it no longer even viable? This marriage?"

Dave took a deep breath. "I know that you both love each other very much and that you're committed to making this work. You've come a long way in a year, and I understand that this can feel like a huge setback."

I wanted to say, "thanks for stating the obvious, Dave. But you can save your therapy bullshit for someone else." Instead, I just nodded once, sat back, and waited for the session to be over. I just wanted it all to be over.

CHAPTER THIRTY-NINE

September 2023

EVERY TIME we talked about what had happened in Prague and me wanting a divorce, it ended up in an argument. Nate didn't see why I couldn't just forgive him and move on. I refused to budge in my decision that we were nothing more than co-parents and business partners. I refused any sexual advances from him.

"You know that we are at our best when we have sex regularly," he argued.

"I have no desire to do anything with you sexually." I shook my head. "Stop asking me. It just turns me off even more."

Nate wouldn't let it go. He didn't think it was fair that I continued to date and be open to physical intimacy with other men when I wasn't giving him any.

"I told you. I have absolutely no desire to have sex with you," I told him flatly one night.

His jaw tightened. "Then you shouldn't get to have it with other men."

I raised my voice. "Well, I'm not currently. But you don't get a say in that anymore. You lost that privilege WHEN YOU BROKE OUR CHILDREN'S HEARTS. Do you know what it was like for me? To see their faces drop. Their hearts break when you said those terrible things. I will NEVER be able to forget that moment. For the rest of my life, I have to live with that, Nate!"

In that moment, something clicked for Nate. It was just like what happened a year ago when I told him I was polyamorous. His face softened. His shoulders relaxed. It was like I was seeing a new part of his heart unlocked.

He turned to me and said softly, "I get it. You're right."

I had no idea how to respond, but my body did. I began to cry. The energy in the room was different—Nate was different. It was as if all the darkness had lifted. The anger. The resentment. It just… vanished.

He walked over to me, a few inches from my face, and looked me deep in my eyes. "I'm so sorry for what I did. Take all the time you need. I don't want to give up on us. I know I let you down, and I will spend the rest of our lives making up for it. I'm so sorry."

He was fighting back tears as he took me in his arms. The anger I had felt toward him melted.

Both of us cried as he pressed our foreheads against each other. "I'm so sorry," he said several more times.

I could feel that he was. A sense of peace washed over me.

Over the next couple of weeks, Nate was my biggest cheerleader. He became the man I had dreamed he would be. He wanted to hear about all the guys I was talking to.

He encouraged me to go on dates. "It's been a while since you've done an overnight. What about that one German guy you went on a date with a few weeks ago?"

"Johannes?" I asked, caught off guard he even remembered.

"Sure," Nate said. "Why not see if he wants to do an overnight?"

Nate had never acted like this before.

I raised my right lip slightly. "I don't know. He's kind of boring. I mean he's attractive and a good kisser, but like he's a shitty communicator."

Nate frowned. "Hmm, okay. Well, it doesn't have to be him, but maybe consider it."

It wasn't a bad idea.

Nate continued to be incredibly supportive. And it felt great to not have to hide anything from the kids. I decided that I wanted to implement a new rule. Once a month, I would take each kid on a one-on-one date for lunch or dinner. They could pick the restaurant, and we would agree on a date. I told them that if I could give men who I barely knew my time, then I could give them dedicated time once a month.

At first, they said it wasn't necessary. They knew how busy I was and didn't want to add another thing to my plate. I insisted and told them that I knew how to make time for things that mattered to me. During our dates, I would check in to see if they had any questions about our new normal. The girls usually did; Asher didn't. And we always had interesting discussions about their friends, sexuality, relationships, gender, and religion.

Overall, our household didn't feel so heavy anymore. Nate and I rarely argued. Our sex life returned to its very active state. Things were on their way up.

The more supportive Nate was, the less I desired to get away. The more he encouraged me to go out, the less I wanted to. I knew this had been a dynamic before, but things were different since that night in early September. Before, I was willing to settle for fine. Now, I wanted someone who made me feel like I had been struck by lightning. Someone who was worth me spending time away from the family.

With Poland back in my life and things feeling much better with Nate, I became less interested in dating. I still wanted to find a partner, but I didn't feel the need like I had before. Nate thought I should still be actively looking. Why? Because he knew

I was at my best with two men in my life, and he believed I deserved the best.

I called Nate and told him what happened with the Dutch guy I had been talking to. We had met once, had a fantastic time, and planned to see each other again. But due to our four-hour distance, things didn't work out.

"I'm sorry," he said sincerely. "I know how much you liked him."

Another day, another failed attempt at finding a partner. I felt like a fool. This time it was a thirty-nine-year-old Dutch guy. This was the first time I had dated someone who was in a long-term relationship like me. He was non-monogamous, not polyamorous (meaning he didn't want to have another romantic or serious partner), and thought maybe he could "do the whole polyamory thing" for me. Spoiler alert: he couldn't.

Well, at least I still have Poland to talk to.

But I hadn't seen him in five months and our pseudo-relationship could only fulfill me so much. I was leaving for Spain for a women's retreat the next day and decided to take a break from the app till after I got back. Nate agreed it was a good idea and told me I should go and enjoy my time in Spain.

And I did. But I still texted with Poland every day. He continued to meet many of my needs and damn, was he pretty to look at.

After a few days in Spain, I found myself longing for Poland. So I suggested something crazy.

CHAPTER FORTY

October 2023

I TEXTED POLAND.

ME

What if I came to see you in Romania?

POLAND

I want to see you, but that's a lot of effort. I don't like people making a big effort for me like that.

ME

Well, I'm not most people.

At first, Poland was hesitant about it. But something inside me urged me to go see him. And no, it wasn't my nether regions. Okay, maybe a small part. But it felt like there was unfinished business with him. And after my dumpster fire ending with The Dutch Guy, it would be nice to spend some time with someone I felt safe with. Who I knew cared about me.

I brought the idea up to Nate when I got back from Spain. "I know this sounds crazy, but I'd like to go see Poland in Romania."

I braced for his response.

He nodded. "Okay. Can I ask why?"

Nate had never been a fan of Poland. He didn't like the roller coaster ride our relationship was. He didn't like that he was younger than me, and he definitely didn't like Poland's lack of effort.

"He meets a lot of my needs and it feels like there's something I need to figure out about our relationship. There's a small part of me that still thinks a romantic relationship with him is possible. Spending a weekend with him will help me figure it out."

Nate didn't hesitate. "If that's what you need to do then I support you."

I couldn't believe it. I fully expected him to push back and tell me how this was an insane idea. How I was wasting my time on someone who was incapable of giving me what I wanted.

"Are you serious?" I asked him in disbelief.

"Yes," he said and kissed my forehead. "You have great instincts, Courtney. I trust them if that's what you think you need."

Whenever Nate was supportive like this, it made me want other men less. It made me want to try and fit into the shiny, monogamous Instagram wife role I had been playing for almost eighteen years. It felt incredible to have his support and it made me less attached to the outcome of seeing Poland. I hadn't even looked at flights. Or hotels. I had no idea how much this would cost. I never thought I'd get this far.

Yet, here I was. Nate and Poland both on board with me going to Romania.

How is this my life?

After doing some research, I was surprised to see airfare was pricier than I expected. Discouraged, I went to Nate and told him, fully expecting him to be like, "Well, it wasn't meant to be then."

"Ugh, flights are like a hundred Euros more than I thought they'd be!" I told him.

"So?"

"What do you mean 'so?'"

"I mean if it's still reasonable, who cares? You want to go, so go."

Once again, I was flabbergasted by his response.

"Okay," I said quietly. "Yeah, sure."

I could have easily told Poland that flights were too much and he would have completely understood. But then I wondered what my eighty-year-old self would say to me right now: "You're telling me that you didn't go and spend a weekend with your lover in Romania? Over a hundred Euros? Bitch, please get out of my sight."

I couldn't have that happening so I marched back to my office and booked my flight and hotel for two weeks from Friday.

Before I headed to Romania, the kids and I were going to Milan for their fall break. I'd spend three nights there, come home for a night, then fly out freaking early the following day to Romania. I told the kids that I was going to be visiting someone in Romania after we got back.

Addison gave me the side-eye. "Who are you going to visit?"

I can barely explain my relationship with Poland to my friends, let alone to my daughter.

I bit my inner lower lip. "A friend. Sort of. We used to date. Now we're not. It's complicated."

When I shared with Avery and Asher that I was going, they just smiled and said, "Have fun."

This had become my new normal. And it felt incredible. My excitement for visiting Poland grew, even though I knew it would also be exhausting. Since I knew Poland wasn't an actual relationship option, I kept my app on while I traveled. It rarely resulted in successful matches, but I figured, what's the worst that could happen?

CHAPTER FORTY-ONE

ON THE TRIP to Milan with the kids, I was sorting through some of the matches I had made since landing. I waited a bit longer in the hotel lobby before going to the room where the kids were hopefully asleep.

You may be wondering why didn't I just stop? Take a break. Enjoy my family and friends. There are several reasons why I didn't but before I get into that, I want to say that I *was* enjoying my family and friends. Yes, a lot of my free time was consumed with searching for another partner. But I also enjoyed going to my son's soccer games, and getting ice cream with my daughters. Nate and I took on a massive real estate project and my business continued to grow. My life wasn't on hold, but I had fought so hard for us to get here, I was terrified of losing my freedom.

That's one reason I didn't take a break. Subconsciously, I was waiting for the rug to be pulled out from under me. Who gets to have their cake and eat it too? I felt like I had to keep going until Nate decided one day that my fun and freedom had cost him too much. Even though, we had numerous conversations about his happiness and our relationship, I had a hard time believing that he was the happiest he'd ever been in our marriage. I kept waiting for him to change his mind.

Second, that dopamine rush is no joke. When you're anxiously attached, there's an intense need to have this space filled. In securely attached people, they can detach from the outcome of dating someone. I wasn't able to do that. I saw my time as limited (because it was) and I was intent on what I wanted. Instead of trusting the process (or even enjoying it), it became a hunt. I just wanted to hurry up and "arrive" because I thought that would ease my anxiety.

But that's not how anxious attachment works. It doesn't ever turn off—there is no arriving—there is no point where it says, oh we can exhale now. There's always a fear of abandonment. A fear of pain. And I had already experienced so much pain in the past, so I was terrified of repeating it. So I pressed on because I wasn't ready to stop and heal my nervous system. I wasn't ready to do the work to be the healthy (mainly) secure woman I am now.

As I was scrolling, I came to a picture of a brown-skinned man with a shaved head and faint beard, looking off into the distance. He was sitting on some ancient-looking steps with a bright blue sky behind him. I could only see part of his face, and he was wearing sunglasses.

Normally, I'd ignore a match where I couldn't see his entire face, but his caption caught my eye. "ONS (one-night stands) are boring." I had no idea why I found that statement intriguing. Maybe it was because I had been propositioned numerous times by men for one-night stands, but I admired a man who boldly proclaimed he found those encounters boring. I decided to like him back.

MR. NO ONS

Hi.

ME

Hey.

MR. NO ONS

You are exactly what I've been looking for.

Bold first statement. I like it.

ME

Oh really?

I appreciated the confidence this twenty-seven-year-old had. I found confidence incredibly sexy.

ME

So you live in Milan?

MR. NO ONS

No. Lyon.

Holy shit that's far.

ME

France?! How did we match? I've been nowhere near Lyon.

Lyon was about a six-hour drive from my house. Sure, I had traveled a lot this month but not anywhere within a two-hundred-fifty-kilometer radius of Lyon.

MR. NO ONS

Don't know. Maybe it's destiny.

ME

Lol... maybe it is.

He asked if we could switch to WhatsApp. I agreed. I asked him what his name was, and he told me. I'd never met anyone with his name before, so I asked where he was from. He told me Morocco. So when I saved his contact in my phone, I saved it as Morocco.

For the record, I wasn't that sexually attracted to him. Physically, he was not the type of man I typically dated. Short. Shaved head. Glasses. Plus, he lived six hours away from me. I couldn't imagine Nate being supportive of that long-distance of a relationship. All these factors contributed to my hesitation when it came to this guy.

Morocco, on the other hand, was very interested. He texted me all the time. Complimented me. Told me how much he liked me. I could feel his enthusiasm, which at times was a bit overwhelming. His curiosity was attractive, and I liked how he paid attention to details. He asked thoughtful questions and was engaged in our conversations. He seemed genuine and not like he was just trying to get into my pants.

As I was getting to know Morocco and anticipating my trip to Romania, Poland and I hit a bump in the road. He told me that he had booked a flight to come to Germany the day before I booked mine to go to Romania.

ME

You're coming to Germany?

POLAND

Yeah, next month. In the middle of November.
But I will mostly stay in Mannheim.

ME

Clearly you're not coming for me.

POLAND

My university friends need some love too. But
maybe we can meet then. We will see.

ME

That doesn't feel very good.

POLAND

I know but since you are already coming here...

ME

But you booked your flight before we even
discussed me coming.

POLAND

It was very spontaneous.

ME

I don't really fit into your life, do I?

POLAND

What does that mean?

ME

It means I'm a weird extraneous variable that doesn't get considered. This is the epitome of me not mattering. Of knowing we have no plans to meet and you not even considering me.

POLAND

I know it sounded bad. But if I stay at somebody's place, I have to prioritize that person. And I won't stay at your place.

I was so tired of this conversation. I wanted Poland to make me a priority. I thought that if I modeled for him what that looked like, then he'd reciprocate.

ME

I don't know where to go from here. Part of me wants to just be done with you. I don't want to be in someone's life who doesn't want me. Who doesn't appreciate me. I feel foolish. I'm tired of feeling that way. Like I don't matter. So maybe it's best if I bow out of your life and wish you the best.

POLAND

I know I hurt you. I'm really sorry for that. I want you in my life but I won't force anything. You can't say I don't care about you. I talk to you a lot, ask about your life. I spend a lot of time with you, even virtually. I know I could do more but I could also do way less. We don't need to have sex, talk about it if you don't want it. But if you feel it's better to let me go, I will understand it.

Is no man capable of fighting for me?
Because that is how love was modeled for me. At home. In

the movies. A man would fight for a woman who was worthy of his love.

I kept hoping—praying—that some man would come along and fight for me. Save me. Even though I had distanced myself from purity culture and the patriarchy, I continued to chain myself to their ideals. I was only worthy if a man deemed me as such. I only mattered if a man said I did. I felt like a hypocrite. But actually, I was just mired in the mess of untangling my beliefs from what I was told I was supposed to believe.

Ironically, I was blind to the fact that Nate had been fighting for me for the past eighteen months. I considered his actions a form of self-preservation. If he lost me, he lost the person who had kept his life running smoothly so he could have a successful career. And maybe part of that was true, but I still discounted his love for me because I still struggled to fully love and accept myself.

I kept waiting for another man to do that. I thought if I was able to show someone like Poland (who I significantly overvalued) that I was worth loving, then I'd love and accept myself. It was the ultimate challenge for me to prove I was worthy.

ME

Where do I fit in your life?

POLAND

You know things about me and my personality nobody else knows, and you understand me quite well. I guess it's enough for being a friend. Doesn't matter if sex is involved or not.

ME

You guess?

POLAND

I'm sure.

ME

Why tell me you want to see me if you don't actually want to?

POLAND

How do you know I don't want to??

ME

Because your actions indicate otherwise.

My ticket was already booked to Romania, so I ignored the voice inside of me that said "this is never going to work."

CHAPTER FORTY-TWO

MOROCCO WAS PERSISTENT. He texted me "good morning" and kept me updated on his life. He asked about my adventures in Milan with the kids and told me he wanted to see me. I knew he'd had a relationship with an older, married woman before (whom he would see almost daily), but I was concerned that he wasn't prepared to handle the physical distance between us.

Morocco acknowledged the difficulty of physical distance and shared that he had dated long-distance before and could adapt.

MOROCCO

It can be frustrating sometimes because I like the physical touch. I'd want just a kiss or to cuddle in front of the TV, but I still find it a good dynamic because it definitely helps making the relationship healthy, alive, passionate and always « looking for » the meetings.

ME

I just try to manage expectations. Long-distance is a bit of work so I get if you're not wanting to make the effort. No judgments.

MOROCCO

> Ohh, I understand better now. Believe me, I so am willing to put the effort here... as I said, I have so much to offer and I'd give my 100% on the relationship... that's how I be and that's just who I am.

I had to get past his incorrect grammar.

He's not a native English speaker, Courtney. Let it go.

Morocco was attentive. And he knew exactly what he wanted —me. I enjoyed the attention he gave me, especially as it turned sexual. But then he did things that annoyed me.

ME

> I didn't forget. Here's the pic I promised.

MOROCCO

> I thought you'll forget. +1 to you.

He would say things like +10 or +50 whenever I did something he liked or enjoyed. And he kept calling me "hun." I found both those things incredibly annoying. After a day or two more of being called "hun," I told him I didn't enjoy it. Thankfully, he had no issue not calling me that anymore. Instead, he called me "babe," which I was fine with, but he used it a lot, which eventually also got annoying.

Even though he did small things that annoyed me, he would also do incredibly thoughtful things. Something I wasn't used to. When he asked me how I liked to drink my coffee, I told him that I ordered a special creamer online. He asked me to send him a pic of it because he was curious.

MOROCCO

> Babeeee... I found it. I'll order it now.

ME

> Haha you should video chat with me before you make that commitment lol.

The idea that he would order my coffee creamer to have at his place before we'd even video chatted, let alone met, seemed a little odd to me. He took that interaction as a prompt to ask me to video chat, which I agreed to.

That afternoon, I FaceTimed him for the first time. The man on the other end of the video wore thick-rimmed, dark, sleek glasses that framed his golden-brown face perfectly. His beard was finely groomed, and he was wearing a designer black sweater. I still wasn't sure how attracted I was to him. Usually, video chats sway me one way or the other. This one didn't help me.

I told him that I was repacking to leave for Romania. I had explained my situation with Poland to him, and he was undeterred by it. Morocco was incredibly confident in who he was and what he was offering. He told me that he was going to Morocco at the beginning of November and asked if I could meet him for a date in Paris before he left. I told him I needed to check with Nate, but the truth was that I needed more time to decide if this guy was someone I could see myself with.

Nate and I were doing incredibly well. I knew he wouldn't care if I hopped on the train to meet Morocco in Paris. But I didn't like talking to Nate about going on dates unless I was sure I liked someone. I had become incredibly protective of my time. When everything opened up sixteen months ago, I would do just about anything to escape my marriage. But Nate and I had worked ridiculously hard to get to the place we were at. I actually enjoyed spending time with him. I loved the life we were creating. I wanted a partner who would fit into our life, not one I felt was a distraction from it.

Morocco and I continued to discuss the possibilities of meeting in person. But it seemed like the Universe was conspiring against us.

Long-distance was complicated enough, but adding the travel to see each other was a whole other layer. Morocco was trying to be helpful. He told me that if I came to Lyon, I could stay with him and he would sleep on the couch, giving me the bed. I appreciated his offer, but I reminded him I didn't have sex on the first date.

This "rule" was something that emerged shortly before I started dating Morocco. I got tired of men expecting sex on a first date, and even though I did enjoy a sexual connection, I was often left dissatisfied, typically due to being misled by their over-confidence or impatience in this department.

Nate and I developed the three-rule system for our open marriage. This was completely driven by me because it gave me a sense of safety and security. Nate supported my decision to implement the following rules: video call before a first date, no sex on the first date, and use protection until we discuss otherwise.

My frustration with the situation grew as Morocco and I continued to discuss our first date.

ME

> I'm not looking to date endlessly. I want to find one guy I can have besides my husband. I haven't met anyone yet who is willing to commit and to plan and figure out how we can make it work. So when I hit these situations, being far from each other, it floods me with all those failed attempts. I don't want you to settle by being with someone you can only see one to two times a month.

MOROCCO

> I know I'm not settling... I just know that I like you, a lot. And I'm so willing to put effort to be that guy you have besides you husband...

> As we say in French, les débuts sont toujours difficiles... beginnings are always hard, but things only can get easy and better with time. I mean, if we both want it, we can make it work.

ME

> The reason I'm hesitant to wait to meet until after the 23rd is that that's a bit of time to invest in each other without meeting. And I've done that before, waited a month or so to meet and when I finally met him, it was not great... That's my hesitation also.

MOROCCO

> I completely understand that.

He sent me different train options from various cities near me. Frankfurt, Luxembourg, Metz. He was motivated, and it felt so good to see someone care about me so much. I decided to wait until after I got back from Romania to book anything. I wanted to enjoy my time with Poland and figure out my feelings for him.

Paris would have to wait.

CHAPTER FORTY-THREE

I WOKE up at 3:45 a.m. to drive to Frankfurt to catch an 8:00 a.m. flight to Cluj-Napoca, Romania. I texted Poland and Morocco when I landed at my layover in Warsaw, which was quick, and the flight from Warsaw to Romania was short. Even though I had fairly low expectations for my time with Poland, I was still nervous and excited to see him. The last time I saw him was six months ago, when he awkwardly kissed me goodbye after our disastrous first sexual experience together.

Will he still find me attractive? Still want me?

I shoved all my insecurities out of my head and walked out of the small airport with my carry-on in tow. Poland emerged from the parking lot. I could see his athletic frame walking toward me. His dark hair fell into his eyes, and he took his hand out of his pocket to brush it out of the way.

There was something about him that lit me up whenever I was around him. He stirred something inside of me that felt magnetic.

It was my unhealed childhood wounds that were being activated, which is incredibly unsexy (but insightful information as it helps you to avoid heartbreak).

I let go of my wheeled suitcase to hug him. The scruff of his beard gently scratched my face as he bent down to embrace me. Just a quick hug, no kiss. I inhaled his fresh, woodsy scent as I stepped back from him. He grabbed my suitcase, and I followed him back to his car.

I put my phone in my back pocket. "Wow, you parked. You could have just picked me up from the curb."

He shook his head. "No way. It was no trouble. How were your flights?"

"Easy."

"Good."

I was tired from being up for twelve hours, but the adrenaline from excitement kept me alert.

Poland looked at me from the corner of his eye. "You look good. You've lost weight. You look younger, too."

I shrugged. "Thanks. Yeah, I have. About fifteen pounds."

One of the things I appreciated about Poland was that we had always been incredibly honest in our relationship. You'd think that talking to someone so much younger about my body would be weird or uncomfortable, but it wasn't. It's one of the ways I felt empowered in my relationship with him. Because none of it (being in a relationship with him, having sex with him) ever seemed plausible, I never felt the need to be anything but authentic with him.

We got into his car, and he drove us to the hotel I had booked for us. We checked into our room, and I wondered if the desk clerk thought we were an odd couple. Or made any assumptions about us.

Can people tell I'm older than him?

The thought both unsettled and aroused me. We walked to the elevator and went up to our room on the third floor. I wondered how this, the next forty-eight hours together, was going to go.

I opened the door to our room. Purple, gray, and green striped curtains framed the large windows. The crisp white linens on the bed made it look so inviting. I slipped out of my shoes and literally plopped down on to the plush white comforter.

Part of me wanted to sleep, but the other part of me… the one who was in a hotel room alone with a gorgeous, younger man I had an uncommon connection with… That part of me was not tired.

I didn't have to wait long. Poland saw his opening and lay on top of me.

I laughed. "You're squishing me."

He ignored my pleas. "This bed is not that comfortable," he said as he pressed more of his weight into me.

I continued to laugh. "Oh my gosh."

His body was over mine, his breath against my neck. I knew that if I turned my head, we would be facing each other. I tried to buck my ass to push him off me. He didn't budge. I spread my arms out to gain some leverage. He put his hands over mine. I was trapped, and we both knew it.

My resistance crumbled. I closed my eyes and turned my head to face him. We were mere inches from each other. His breath warmed my lips, and the tension continued to build in my body. I opened my eyes to see him staring at me.

Gosh, he is beautiful.

I looked into his light brown eyes, contemplating the reality of where I was. I had flown a thousand miles just to see him. To touch him. To feel his hands on my body.

Just like before, he put his lips against mine. Our bodies moved as if they had been making up for the past six months. My hand grabbed the back of his neck while his hand cupped my breast.

Quickly, we took off each other's clothes, tossing them to the floor. I laid on the bed, wearing only my lacy maroon panties, as he moved over me. He hovered above me, his hands on either side of my shoulders, and we held each other's gaze.

My body ached for him. I needed him inside of me—to feel all of him.

He lowered his head slowly to my lips. Our tongues moved seamlessly in each other's mouth before he moved down to my breasts where he stopped momentarily. Cupping my breast, he took my erect nipple into his mouth, raising his gaze toward me as his tongue explored this tender area. My hips instantly jerked up toward him, grinding against his hard cock.

He continued to explore my body with his lips, moving to my stomach and then pausing at the top of my panties. My fingers ran through his dark hair, as he looked to me again. His fingers outlined the silky seam in my panties and my longing had turned to throbbing.

I want you.

As if he could hear my thoughts, he pulled my panties down, leaving me completely bare before him.

He rested his chest against the bed and spread my legs. Taking a leg in each of his arms, he moved his mouth to the place that would completely shatter me and began licking.

Geez, that feels good.

I could feel myself approaching. There was so much build-up in my lower body, but just as I was about to go over the edge, he released my legs, stood up, and went over to his bag to grab a condom.

What is happening? I should tell him to get back down there.

But I didn't. Despite being sexually empowered enough to ask for an open marriage, I wasn't strong enough to advocate for my own sexual needs. I was too afraid of his answer—too afraid of being too much. So once again, I shrank my needs for a man I cared about.

That's how powerful purity culture is. It convinces women that our job is to provide pleasure, not receive it. Our satisfaction should come from our ability to please the man in our life.

Just like before, he handed me the condom to open and put on. I complied, dismissing my frustration for him not letting me finish. I rolled the condom down his throbbing hard cock, and within seconds, he was inside of me.

I really hope this is longer than last time.

Apparently, the Universe heard my prayer. But I should have been more specific in duration, because after thirty seconds, his body shuddered, signaling release.

He pulled out of me and rolled onto his back, emitting a heavy sigh. My head turned to the right, and I watched his chest rhythmically rise and fall, his breathing slowly returning to normal. I considered if this was how sex with him would always be—short and focused on his pleasure.

What in the actual hell is wrong with me?

The shame of what I didn't do overwhelmed me. I talked to women about sexual pleasure FOR A LIVING, and here I was unable to advocate for my own? I felt like a hypocrite.

Looking back, I see that I still believed that I should be happy for what I got. How many women would love to be in my shoes? A kid-free weekend in another country with a gorgeous younger guy who makes me laugh? *Just be grateful, Courtney.* I continued to let the pressure of what other people thought dictate how I showed up.

Also, at a subconscious level, there was sympathy in the struggle. Most people don't want to hear that I'm married to a handsome doctor and dating a hot twenty-something year old who gives me mind-blowing orgasms. No. That version of me isn't relatable. I'm already "too much" in that my husband lets me sleep with other men. To have that bonus relationship also be incredible? Come on… It was more than I believed I deserved. More than any woman deserved.

Before I could fully spiral, Poland proudly stated, "Well, I lasted longer than before."

"I mean, that bar was pretty low. I wouldn't be bragging about your stamina just yet."

Poland smirked slightly, got up, and went to the bathroom to clean up. I laid there, feeling empty. I didn't know what I wanted from him. It's not like he was my boyfriend. We weren't in love with each other, but a part of me wanted him to treat me like he was. I wanted him to come back into bed, pull me into his arms, and tell me how much he missed me. Tell me how grateful he was that I had come all the way to Romania, just for him.

But he didn't. He came back to bed, spread out on his side, and asked if there was anything he could do for me. Physically, I was beyond aroused. Emotionally, I was drained.

I sat up and pulled my knees into my chest. "I'm fine."

"Are you sure?" he asked sincerely.

I paused before answering.

No, I'm not okay.

But his lack of skill wasn't going to suddenly improve, and he didn't seem motivated to figure out what pushed me over the edge.

I shared my feelings anyway, still holding my knees tightly. "Why didn't you stay down on me for longer? I would have come."

He shrugged. "I got impatient. I really wanted you. I couldn't wait any longer."

Seriously?

I decided at that point that I wouldn't ask anymore for him to pleasure me. I was tired of being disappointed. I resigned myself to connecting with him on his terms. Once again, I gave my power away. I didn't know who I was more frustrated with—him or me.

I had no expectation for how our time together would be. Other than "our relationship is complicated," I had no way of explaining our connection. We weren't together like a normal boyfriend/girlfriend but we were beyond friends. We existed in the in-between that had no tidy answer. Thus, determining expectations were, well, you guessed it, complicated.

Poland said he had found a place we could walk to for dinner. I appreciated his effort. I loved when men took the initiative to plan something. We walked to the restaurant.

After ten minutes, we arrived at our destination.

"It should be right here," he said, staring at his phone and then at the building where there was in fact, no restaurant.

My appreciation quickly turned to irritation. I was tired and hungry and now we discovered the restaurant no longer existed. He looked at me for a solution.

I sighed. "I don't know. I guess look something else up."

Even though I didn't have set expectations for today, this is not how I imagined our first day going. After searching his phone, he found a place. Forty minutes away.

Fantastic. Good thing I wore the wrong shoes. Whatever.

After dinner, we began the long walk back to the hotel. Poland was a chatterbox, with me mostly just listening. He talked about some of the women he had been talking to and even one he had had a date with. Even though he and I texted every day, we rarely discussed dating. We both knew we talked to other people but it wasn't something we actually conversed about.

Most of the women he talked to were around his age, but occasionally, he would match with someone closer to my age.

"There is this one woman I was talking to, who was like thirty-six," he began, "I liked her. I even offered to drive like four hours to go see her."

I physically stopped walking and looked at him.

"What?" he asked, confused as to why I had stopped.

I fisted my hands and tilted my head toward him. "Are you fucking serious?"

CHAPTER FORTY-FOUR

POLAND STILL HADN'T UNDERSTOOD my reaction. "What?"

I shook my head in disbelief. "I can't even get you to come and see me and I'm like an hour from you. And you offer to go see a woman you barely know who's four hours from you?!"

He paused before answering. "I wasn't going to actually go see her."

At this point, I was beyond frustrated. This was the third woman I had heard about on our walk, and it was the straw that broke me.

I shook my head, throwing my hands up. "You know what? I don't care. You want to drive to see her? Fine. Have a great fucking time."

And with that, I kept walking. Poland knew my moods, and he knew when I shut down it wasn't good.

After a few minutes, he said quietly, "I wasn't going to go see her."

My jaw tightened. "That's not the point. The point is that I will never matter to you the way I should. Just like when you booked your ticket to Germany without even talking to me about it!"

"I know. That was stupid of me, and I still feel bad about it. I'm sorry."

I was tired of the apologies. I was tired of not being a priority in his life. I was tired of my own bullshit.

Why do I keep putting myself in this position with him? Why do I value myself so little that I tolerate his minimal efforts? I just want to go home.

When we got back to our room, I slid into my side of the bed and cocooned myself under the covers. Poland pulled out a bottle of wine he had brought for us and asked if I wanted a glass.

Yes, I could use an entire bottle of wine right now.

I turned my head slightly to answer. "What kind is it?"

He shook his head, looking at the label. "I don't know. I think it's a semi-sweet red."

Not my favorite. And of course, he wouldn't know I only drank dry wine.

"I'm fine," I said and rolled over.

He put the bottle down and laid next to me on his side, spooning me. I wanted to tell him to fuck off. I wanted to scream at him. But more than anything, I wanted him to want me. To tell me how much I did matter to him.

He pulled me closer to him, his strong arm around my body.

This is going to be an awkward trip if I don't get past my frustrations.

I could feel his breath against my neck; it sent tingles down my spine and straight into my pelvis. His lips kissed the sensitive spot between my neck and shoulder, and within a few minutes, my body betrayed me. I flipped over to face him, running my hand against his trimmed beard, staring into his almond eyes. I ran my thumb against his pink lips, feeling their thickness, forgetting any frustration I had previously had with him. He kissed my thumb tenderly and then my lips. And just like that, once again, I gave myself to him.

The rest of the weekend was a mix of exploring Cluj-Napoca, having short sex, and talking. In a turn of events, I hadn't expected, Poland completely opened up to me. It was like watching a flower's petals unfold.

On our second night, we sat on the bed and decided to watch my current obsession, *Welcome to Wrexham.*

"I know how much you loved *Ted Lasso. Welcome to Wrexham* is kind of like that but the real-life version," I said.

"Isn't that the team that Deadpool owns?"

"Ryan Reynolds? Yeah, he co-owns it. Let's just watch an episode, then we can decide if we keep watching, okay?"

He shrugged, and I turned on the first episode. After thirty minutes, the second episode cued right up. We had binged three episodes when Poland said, "My mom wouldn't let me play football as a kid."

I paused the start of the fourth episode. "I thought you played growing up."

"I did, but she wouldn't let me play on an actual team. Said it was too dangerous. When I was fourteen, the coach even went to her and told her how good I was, but she wouldn't budge. She still said no."

"That must have been hard. Not being able to play the sport you love."

He sat up, straightening his back against the headboard. "Not as hard as losing my grandma."

"Oh."

I hadn't expected the conversation to shift to this.

"You know my mom blamed me, for her death."

Stunned, I sat up, crisscrossing my legs, and faced him. "Wait, what?"

"Her and my dad left for the weekend. My grandma wasn't feeling well and she went to bed early. When I woke up, she had died. My mom was so upset. She blamed me. Said I must have done something."

Tears filled my eyes, and I reached out to squeeze his hand.

"That's awful. I'm so sorry. It wasn't your fault. Sometimes people die when we don't expect them to. That was wrong of her to blame you."

His brown eyes met mine and he squeezed my hand back. "I know."

Poland continued to share things with me he had never told anyone. He was fully himself. I had seen it hundreds of times with clients. When they shift from being skeptical and aloof in our sessions to feeling completely safe enough to tell me their darkest secrets. Poland had made that shift, while I pulled back emotionally.

I didn't know how to interact with him in public. I didn't think he was embarrassed to be seen with me, and no one stared at us being together, despite our age difference. Sometimes, I wanted to hold his hand or kiss him, but that felt like something people who were dating did. And we weren't dating anymore. I had no idea what the hell we were actually doing, though, and I was too afraid to ask.

Never ask a question you don't want to know the answer to.

Morocco and I continued to text.

MOROCCO

Any plans for tomorrow?

ME

No idea. I'm a bit annoyed with him. I have to keep reminding myself that we're just friends.

In a way, I had unrealistic and unfair expectations of Poland. I hoped or expected him to be someone he wasn't. What I didn't realize at the time was that I thought that if I was pretty enough or charming enough or whatever enough, then I'd be able to get him to be the man I thought he could be. I wasn't able to accept Poland for who he was. I kept hoping he would be someone I needed him to be.

MOROCCO

Want to talk about it?

ME

He's just immature. He keeps talking about himself. It's just different than when we've texted. This is the most amount of time I've spent with him. You know how you have an idea of the relationship in your head and then you actually spend time with them. And it's completely different. That's my situation.

MOROCCO

Oh I've been there. I know how you're feeling now.

ME

I'm just disappointed in myself. Like wtf, Courtney?

MOROCCO

No. You should be proud of yourself! I prefer to be the one with the effort or extra effort and have the confirmation of disappointment in the person in front of me. You lost nothing from this experience but gained confirmation about the person and yourself.

Lost nothing? It sure doesn't feel that way.

ME

Thank you for your words.

MOROCCO

Please don't hesitate if there is anything I can do.

Morocco was incredibly supportive. He was available anytime I needed some encouragement. He wasn't insecure about me spending a few days with another man. He just poured into me and gave me space as I processed my time with Poland.

As my time in Romania came to a close, my feelings for Poland shifted.

I had given a lot of my time and attention to him, and I didn't regret it, but I realized that that relationship was no longer serving me. I was tired of giving so much to someone who couldn't meet my needs. I decided, going forward, to dial back the amount of communication I would have with him. I wasn't going to end things with him but I was tired of not being valued.

The next evening, Poland drove me to the airport. I told him he didn't need to walk me in and wait. He could just drop me at the curb.

He shook his head, not taking his eyes off the road. "No."

Once inside, we found a set of stairs to sit on. Our knees touched the entire thirty minutes we spent talking.

I pointed to the clock. "I should go."

"You have plenty of time."

"Fine. Ten more minutes."

After ten minutes, he walked me to the security line.

He hugged me, kissed me on the cheek, then kissed me quickly on the lips. Then he shoved his hands in his pockets and walked toward the exit.

I rested my head against the seat, looking out the window. A wide grin spread across my face. Sure, this trip had been emotional and not what I expected it would be, but damn, I was proud of myself.

I made this happen.

I had advocated for my needs with Nate to get here. I had advocated for my needs with Poland, and yeah, didn't love how that ended up. But there were also tender times Poland and I shared. Passionate moments. Inside jokes that were born. I didn't regret my time in Romania. Not one bit. I smiled, imagining my eighty-year-old self high-fiving me for this adventure.

Speaking of adventures…

I texted Morocco.

CHAPTER FORTY-FIVE

WHILE I APPRECIATED Morocco's support, I was a bit overwhelmed with his attention. Actually, I just didn't feel the chemistry I'd had with Max or Bill. And definitely not the chemistry I felt with Poland. Something was a little off with Morocco. I couldn't quite place it, but I didn't feel that connection—that spark, the desire to be with him—like I had with other guys.

Morocco and I still hadn't finalized our first meeting, and after my weekend in Romania, I wasn't exactly up for another disappointment. I decided I wanted to end things with Morocco.

MOROCCO

Babe, are you expected to work from home tomorrow?

ME

Yes.

MOROCCO

I ordered something and you might receive a phone call about it during the day tomorrow. I just checked again. They say they'll send you a message to let you know you have a delivery or the delivery guy will call you directly. This is the first time I use that website, I'm sorry if it's not so great or doesn't look nice as I would hope so.

ME

That was thoughtful to send me something.

MOROCCO

As long as it makes you have a smile on your face babe.

My heart sank. He must have ordered me flowers.

Ugh. I can't end it with him the day before or after I get the flowers. Who does that?

I reduced my communication with him. Maybe he'd get the vibe that I wasn't interested.

I landed in Frankfurt close to midnight and still had a seventy-five-minute drive home. Morocco offered to call me on my drive home so I wouldn't fall asleep or just to keep me company. I told him I was fine and that I'd text him when I got home.

ME

Please don't stay up for me. I value your sleep.

MOROCCO

Too late. I already decided that I am. I value my sleep too but nah. I'll stay awake till you reach home.

Morocco continued to message me, telling me how much he liked me. It was hard to ignore that he was everything Poland wasn't. But I still didn't find myself that attracted to him. Meanwhile, Poland had increased communication with me while I had decreased mine.

The next day, two dozen red roses were delivered to my house along with the message, *"Keep wearing your gorgeous smile."*

I couldn't stop saying, "Oh my gosh," as I put the beautiful flowers in a vase.

ME

They are GORGEOUS. Thank you!

MOROCCO

I'm soooo happy you liked it, babe. I really want to see your gorgeous smile. And I hope they included the message.

ME

They did!

I sent him a pic of me holding the flowers with a huge smile on my face.

MOROCCO

That's important, cuz damn, babe. I admit that I simply love your smile like, A LOT.

ME

Thank you. I love them.

Later that night, Morocco texted me, asking how I was feeling.

ME

I'm a bit introspective right now. I'm trying to figure out what my life looks like.

MOROCCO

More like an observation and an analysis of the present to figure out how you want it to be in the future?

ME

Yes. How all the pieces fit.

MOROCCO

And how's that looking so far? I know that can be a long process as well as a decision/idea you get in the instant.

ME

It's overwhelming and confusing. Honestly, my biggest hesitation with you is our distance.

MOROCCO

That is a completely understandable concern. However, I know myself and I know if I really like someone, I see the good in everything, not meeting much is an opportunity to have a different layer of intimacy with the person... plus I'm a big believer of wherever there is a problem, there is a solution. We can make it happen by meeting let's say one weekend in Paris, the following one in Lyon and in two to three weeks traveling somewhere to meet in a destination.

He always had a quick, logical solution to my concerns. I kept trying to find a point where he would be like, yeah, you're right, this probably won't work. But it never happened. I decided we needed to meet before he left for Morocco. And if we didn't, I would end it because I had no interest in this turning into a pen pal situation.

Nate was going to fly to the U.S. for a week. My mom was flying in on Friday to visit us. She asked me if Nate and I wanted to do an overnight while she was there. I had an idea but needed to talk to Nate about it.

"What if I drive up to Frankfurt with you Saturday, we stay in a hotel, I take you to the airport, then drive to Metz to catch the train to Paris to meet Morocco?"

Nate shrugged. "Works for me."

Well, that was easier than I thought it would be.

A part of me had hoped Nate would push back and say that he didn't want me to go, but he didn't. On the contrary, he encouraged me to meet Morocco for a few hours in Paris for a date.

He knew I'd been struggling with how I felt about him. "That way you'll know. You have great instincts, Courtney. But you should meet him. Obviously, it's up to you, but that's my thought."

I told Morocco my idea. He loved it and told me he would book his train ticket. I booked mine because I was afraid I'd change my mind. The next day, I texted him to confirm.

ME

Did you get your ticket?

MOROCCO

Yes. Yesssssss and if they cancel it, I am taking a flight, and if they cancel the flight, I'm renting a car and coming. I am so excited.

ME

They can't cancel it right?

MOROCCO

No, no they can't. Was just trying to express that nothing's going to stop me from coming.

ME

Does your family know when you have a partner? Or your friends?

MOROCCO

I definitely do share that with them when I've been dating someone for more than 2/3/4 months… but yes, they do know when I have a partner.

I was tired of dating men who kept me a secret from their friends or family. Hearing this lowered one of my walls. Slightly.

Maybe I was making mountains out of mole hills for no reason.
Maybe…

The day before we were to meet, Morocco texted me:

MOROCCO

WHAT THE FUCK. Yesterday I was messing that
they would cancel the train and now I received an
email and something saying they actually got
canceled.

ME

Wtf?

MOROCCO

Don't worry. I'm looking for another train now.
Don't cancel anything. I told you, I will be there.

He was a man of his word and found another train. Our date
in Paris was still on.

Nate and I headed to Frankfurt and had one of the best
overnights of our marriage. It wasn't anything special. We
grabbed dinner at a pub where another couple bought us a
round of shots, walked around the city, went to a store where we
bought beer and Ben & Jerry's, and had great sex. We laughed
and talked and touched and it was truly magical. It's how I had
hoped our marriage would have been all these years. We were
finally at the place I had desired for so long.

Maybe non-monogamy was our salvation. I couldn't argue
with the fact that we were both the happiest we had ever been in
our relationship. Our communication was top-notch. Our sex life
was incredible. Arguments were sparse. We were going on weekly
date nights. The kids also noticed. "Dad is a lot more open with
us. He's around more."

Nate had worked incredibly hard on himself. He was going to
therapy regularly. We were seeing our couple's therapist when
something flared up. He was sharing his feelings and validating
mine when I shared. My foundation felt solid for the first time in
my life.

I knew that I wanted another partner that would add value to this life Nate and I were building. I just didn't know if Morocco was that man.

After dropping off Nate at the airport in Frankfurt, I drove two and half hours to Metz, France to catch the ninety-minute train to Paris. I had no idea how I was feeling about it. Nate told me to have a good time and to keep him posted on how it went. My train arrived in Paris before Morocco's did. I texted him that I had just got off the train and asked where to meet him.

Nothing.

Five minutes went by and he still hadn't responded to my message. My anxiety spiked.

Would he not show? Wouldn't that be hilarious.

I found a seat and decided to wait until I heard from him. Ten more minutes went by and still nothing.

I texted again. He finally responded:

MOROCCO

Hey, sorry, my train was late. I'm walking to your station now.

I was annoyed. I'd been sitting there for twenty minutes wondering if he was going to stand me up.

Just cause your train is late doesn't mean you can't text me or acknowledge my message.

Of all the men I'd dated, he was the best communicator. Until now. Something felt off.

I walked outside to wait for him. He called me. "I see you. Look to your right."

I turned my head to see a short man with a shaved head in dark glasses and a large gray overcoat walking toward me.

CHAPTER FORTY-SIX

HMM... *He's shorter and less attractive in person. Not what I was hoping for.*

We hugged, and he kissed me on both my cheeks. He could tell my moods after just two weeks of texting.

"You okay?" he asked me.

I shook my head, trying to shake off my anxiety. "Why didn't you text me back? It kind of freaked me out."

He looked surprised with my answer. "Did you think I was going to stand you up?"

I shrugged. I didn't actually think he was that kind of person, but the thought did cross my mind.

"Not really."

He didn't seem pleased with my answer but shifted his focus to the line of taxis.

"I got us an Uber," he said.

"Why? We can just take the Metro."

"On a first date?! Absolutely not." He started walking. "This way."

We found our Uber and Morocco spoke to the driver in French, telling him where to go. After a few minutes of not moving, our driver got out of the car to see what was going on. He came back to the car and spoke to Morocco in French.

"What's going on?" I asked him.

"There's something wrong with the machine to get out of the taxi line so they're calling someone to fix it."

"Okay," I said, nodding like I had any idea what was going on. We waited for another ten minutes before finally leaving the train station.

It was a beautiful fall day in Paris. I had no idea where we were going and didn't even ask Morocco what he had planned. As we drove through Paris, I noticed that Morocco seemed tense.

"Are you okay?" I asked him quietly.

"Yeah," he said without looking at me. "Just not how I thought the start of our date would go."

I put my hand on his leg and squeezed it, trying to reassure him that it was going to be fine. I contemplated whether I should move my hand back or not.

If I'm going to give this a proper try, then I need to touch him.

I kept my hand on his leg.

The driver dropped us off in the *8th arrondissement*, and on the other side of the Seine stood the Eiffel Tower. We were far enough away that we weren't in the touristy area, but close enough to have a gorgeous view from the restaurant. Morocco walked up to the restaurant hostess, said something in French, and we were escorted back to our table. Linen napkins and tablecloths, candles, and luxurious decorations adorned the posh establishment.

After the waiter handed us our menus and walked away, Morocco said, "Order whatever you want. Do you want wine?"

Do I want wine? In this amazing place? Of course I do.

We ordered our wine and food. After the waiter left us again, I knew I needed to address something.

"First of all, thank you for arranging all of this. It's lovely. I mean…" I looked out the window to my left and saw the Eiffel Tower in the distance. "It's wonderful. Thank you."

"You don't need to thank me. This is what you deserve."

I leaned forward, putting my forearms across the table. "I know my communication has not been as open or consistent lately. I'm fully aware of that. I've had a lot to think about since coming back from Romania. I'm not used to someone communicating like you. I mean sure, I've dated some guys where we have some intense communication, but not like this. You seem sure of what you want, which is me, and to be frank, I don't know how I feel about you."

Morocco smiled. "That's really hot."

Did he not just hear what I said?

I scrunched my eyebrows. "What?"

"That's hot. That you brought that up. I wanted to discuss this with you. I planned on bringing it up on our date actually. But you beat me to it."

I sat back a little. "Oh… okay…"

I wasn't sure where to go next. I wanted to enjoy our date but I also felt like my walls were pretty high. I had been hurt so many times by guys who were incredibly excited in the beginning, and then…

"You have veins," Morocco said, pointing to my chest.

Suddenly self-conscious, I brought my hands to my chest.

He leaned back and waved his hands. "No! Don't cover them up. They're beautiful."

I laughed. "That's funny. My mom used to make fun of me because of them. Well, not make fun of me but tease me that you could see the veins in my chest."

"It's sexy," he said confidently. "You're sexy."

Our food came, and we continued talking. About past relationships, dating, our families. Morocco was so easy to talk to and he seemed to feast on every word I shared. After we finished lunch, we went for a walk, passing by luxury stores like Louis Vuitton, Gucci, Chanel… We didn't touch on the walk but I could feel the sexual tension between us building.

"Let's find a café," he said and we continued walking.

At the next intersection, my desire for Morocco increased. There was something about meeting him in person that shifted things for me.

Maybe there is something here…

We found a café and Morocco ordered me a cappuccino and himself an Americano. He set his backpack on the table and handed me a large water bottle. "I forgot to give this to you. I thought you might be thirsty from your travels."

I looked at him, a bit stunned. "You brought me water?"

"Yeah," he said, as he continued to look through his bag.

"Wow," I said, still a little shocked. "That was super thoughtful. Thank you."

Morocco shrugged. "You're welcome, babe."

Feeling happy, I took a sip of the water and saw Morocco pull a vape out of his bag.

My heart sank. "You vape?"

"Yes. Sometimes. I used to smoke a lot. I'm trying to quit." He could see my judgment. "Does it bother you?"

I bit my inner lower lip before answering. "Would you not do it if it did?"

"I would go somewhere else to vape if it bothered you," he said calmly.

I sighed. "No, it's fine."

No, it's not fine. Ugh.

Smoking bothered me. I didn't like how it smelled. I didn't like the taste of kissing a smoker. And it definitely didn't help my asthma. But I had never dated someone who vaped.

New territory, I guess.

Morocco vaped, resting his right arm on the table, and I sipped my cappuccino, holding the mug with both hands. Thankfully, his vape essentially had no scent so I ignored it after a while. Our date had been about three hours already, and I'd need to go back to the train station in an hour and a half.

Boldly, Morocco asked, "So what do you think?"

I put my cappuccino down and sat back in my chair. "About what?"

"About us," he said, motioning. "This. Me."

I need to call Nate. I need to ask him what I should do.

In all the dates I'd had, I'd never once had the urge to consult with Nate. But this felt different. More serious.

Morocco could see me pondering his questions. "Are you sure you're ready for a relationship? Like really ready to have someone be all in?" He paused and said, "Because I don't think you are."

CHAPTER FORTY-SEVEN

IMMEDIATELY, I smirked. My body was reacting to the truth of his words. Morocco wasn't wrong. I had been so used to dating men who said they were open to wanting what I wanted, but who actually weren't ready. I kept attracting the same type of man because I was insecure about who I was as a polyamorous woman married to a monogamous man.

I nodded. "I've been asking myself that question for the past five days."

Morocco picked up his coffee. "And what did you discover?"

I sighed. "I have this desire in me to have two men in my life who I love and who love me. Who I share my life with. Who I get to share their lives with. That feels like the truest thing to me. And I also know that I'm married to someone who doesn't experience love and the world the same way I do. It's a burden that I carry, knowing that my choice to have another partner sometimes hurts Nate. So I have to balance doing what I feel is right for me and what I feel is right for the man I've been with for over twenty years. And yes, he's given me his blessing on being who I am and creating a life that is definitely non-traditional. I just haven't met someone who was truly willing to wade into those waters with me. Until you. And that's a little jarring—to have desired something and been rejected and rejected and rejected, and then have someone show up who is choosing me."

I paused, waiting for Morocco to process my words. Waiting for myself to figure out what was holding me back.

"I'm scared," I continued. "Because I have loved in the past and been hurt. I've opened my heart and body to men to be told that 'actually, I can't give you what you want.' That sucks. So yeah, I'm letting my fear have some say here. And the fact that we live hours apart, our age gap, our cultural differences, our religious differences, are all screaming at me to seriously consider my choices."

Morocco put his vape away. "I'm not going to convince you that you should be with me. I will tell you that I have no interest in being just friends with you. So we're either together or we're nothing. It's up to you to decide what you want."

He stood up and went to use the restroom.

I sat there alone, mulling over his words. Over our conversation. Our date. Our chats for the past two weeks. When he sat back down, I knew what my answer was.

"I need to talk to Nate," I told him. "Then I can give you my answer."

He nodded. "Fair enough."

It's not that I needed Nate's permission; I didn't. But I did want his support. Nate and I had been in such a great place these past couple of months. Even though having a polyamorous wife was hard for him, he was committed to me living as my biggest and most authentic self. I was more in love with Nate now than I ever had been. And was so excited to see what was in store for us.

I had truly come to value Nate's opinion on the men I dated, something I could have cared less about in the past. So if Nate told me that he had concerns over this guy, then I would end it with Morocco. But if Nate gave his blessing… then I'd pursue a relationship with him. Unfortunately, Nate was on a flight to the U.S. so I couldn't just text him to see what he thought. This would have to wait.

"We should probably get back to the train station," Morocco said.

It had been over four hours and we still hadn't kissed. I was one of those girls who needed to kiss on the first date. I needed to gauge our sexual chemistry. Plus, kissing was fun.

Morocco looked down at his phone. "I ordered an Uber. It's going to pick us up a few blocks away."

We started walking, and I shared what I was thinking with Morocco.

"Why haven't you kissed me?" I asked him.

He looked a bit surprised by my question. "Well, I wanted to take things slow with you. I really like you and I didn't want to rush our sexual relationship."

I raised the right side of my upper lip, showing disapproval. "Yeah, so here's the thing. Even if there's a second date, I won't get to see you for what? A month? And I'm not interested in waiting that long to see what kissing you feels like."

He didn't make eye contact. "Okay. That makes sense."

We continued to walk, tension building between us, without talking.

We arrived at the meeting point and waited, and he took a step toward me. He looked at me, those brown eyes beautifully framed, staring back at me and asked, "Do you really want me to kiss you?"

I nodded my head. "Yes."

He put his hand behind my head and drew me in. My hands fell to my sides as our bodies pressed against each other. His thick lips pressed against mine and my entire body lit up. He kissed me, gently, before I put my tongue in his mouth, his scent luring me in even more.

How does he smell so good? Damn, he's a great kisser.

This moment, being here, in Paris, with him, a man who knew exactly what he wanted—me—felt magical. We pulled away from one another when the Uber arrived. Morocco said something to him in French and we headed to the train station.

After twenty minutes of sitting in traffic, I started to worry. He had the map to the train pulled up on his phone. Our arrival time kept getting later and later.

"We're not going to make it back in this traffic," I told him, trying to remain calm.

He spoke to the driver and told me to get ready to get out at the next stop.

He pointed out the window. "There's a Metro we can take but we have to hurry."

At the next light, we hopped out of the Uber and jogged to the station. Once inside, I interlaced my hands with his as we walked briskly to the Metro about to leave. We hopped on just as the doors slid closed.

"Made it," he said, letting out a sigh. "This will take us to Gare de l'Est and you'll have a few minutes before your train leaves."

I let out a big sigh. "Wait! Your train leaves from Gare de Lyon."

Morocco's face dropped. "Shit. You're right. I need to get off at the next stop. I'll try and find a different Metro to take me there."

He pulled out his phone and began looking at the metro maps. Twenty seconds later, the metro made its first stop. He kissed me quickly and got off.

I stood there, watching the sliding doors close with him on the other side.

Not how I thought the date would end.

A twinge of sadness came over me.

I didn't even get to hug him goodbye.

I dismissed any disappointment and focused on my mission—making it to the next station. I needed to make my train home. Thankfully, my metro got me to the train station with five minutes to spare. I grabbed a croissant for Asher, found my train car, and plopped down in my seat with a big sigh.

Later that night, after I got home, I called to talk to Nate about my date.

"How did it go?!" he asked

"Better than I expected, actually. He gave me some things to consider. He asked me if I thought I was actually ready for a relationship."

"Are you?"

"I don't know. In theory, I am. In reality, I don't know."

"What's stopping you?"

I paused. "I'm afraid of getting hurt again. I'm afraid of..."

"What?"

My top lip curled in. "Hurting you."

"I understand," Nate said sympathetically. "I haven't always been the most supportive in the past. But Morocco seems like a good guy and he's treated you well. You should go for it."

Excitement built in my stomach. "Seriously?"

"Yes. But it's your decision. I support you no matter what."

Later that night, I saw that I had a text from Morocco.

MOROCCO

Is it weird that I miss you so much?

ME

No. Why would it be weird?

MOROCCO

I don't know, just making sure. And I also feel another thing. Which is that I've known you from before and not just now or today.

ME

Have you felt that with other people? I know the feeling.

MOROCCO

I did but only very few people I felt that with, ended up so so so so so soooooooooo close. I don't feel it generally or with everyone but when I do, it's like a big « positive sign » for me.

I asked him if he believed in past lives. He had never thought about it, but offered that maybe we were partners in a past life.

MOROCCO

> We just got « lost » for a few years. Yet, here we are. Ahhh, I'm so happy that I met you today.

ME

> That's actually romantic.

The next day, I woke up to a text.

MOROCCO

> Just want to say that I loved meeting you, and I wish I could've had more time with you. Can't wait to hold you in my arms and kiss you again. Thank you for making it to Paris.

I asked for him to call me so I could discuss my decision with him. I told him that I was ready to be in a relationship. We agreed that it would be exclusive. Neither of us would date others (other than me being with Nate). We both deleted our dating apps. I finally had what I had been looking for.

CHAPTER FORTY-EIGHT

I WOULDN'T BE able to see Morocco again until he came back from visiting his family in Morocco, which was about five weeks. We continued to text and call every day. Even though he was staying at his parents' house, he still made time to video call with me. He didn't tell his parents or sisters that he had a girlfriend, but he would often get interrupted by them. They knew he was speaking English to someone. I didn't know how he explained our daily conversations. I never asked.

Morocco's communication was still super consistent and supportive. It was a weird adjustment.

ME

> I need to tell you how I'm feeling. I have never had a partner talk about being with me the way you do. Sometimes it overwhelms me. I'm not asking you to stop! It just feels overwhelming and it scares me sometimes. But then I love it at the same time. I don't think you understand how long I prayed for a partner like you. And now that you're mine, sometimes I get freaked out.

MOROCCO

> I have to admit that reading your words made my day and probably my weekend! I am yours and I am so happy to be it! You have no idea how much I'm into you, not just physically but mentally and emotionally and everything.

Daily, he would tell me how much he liked me. How happy he was that we were together. It felt incredible. But sometimes, it felt like I was being love bombed.

MOROCCO

> I feel like I am SO MISSING YOU!

> Daily Reminder: I LIKE YOU SO FUCKING MUCH!!!!!

It's not that I didn't appreciate these messages that I received almost daily. It was just the energy behind most of his messages. They felt a bit manic at times. He messaged me every couple of hours. Let me know he was thinking about me. Checked in on me. Asked about anything I had shared with him. He was attentive and thoughtful but it felt like a lot since we had only started dating. One night he even shared that he wanted me to fly to Marrakech to meet him. I told him I couldn't do it but the truth is that I didn't want to do it. I thought it was insane to ask me to fly to meet him on another continent after only a couple weeks of dating.

Even though we were together, I still struggled with our differences. Culturally, he came from a Muslim family. He was the eldest child and the only boy. And even though he didn't consider himself religious or have any interest in giving his parents grandchildren, I struggled with the idea that his parents would be fine with his decision to share his life with an older, non-Muslim, married woman.

ME

I really like you…

MOROCCO

But…

ME

But what?

MOROCCO

Come on, babe. I know you! I can tell when
something's off with you or be bothering you.
What's up?

Geez that grammar still kills me sometimes.

ME

It's just… you're only twenty-seven. You have a
whole life to live. Are you honestly wanting to
give all of that up, a traditional marriage, kids…
to be with me?

MOROCCO

Are you serious?

ME

Yes.

MOROCCO

Babe. Have I not sent you your daily reminder
today of HOW MUCH I FUCKING LIKE
YOU!!!!!???

ME

I know, but I don't want you to regret anything.

MOROCCO

I'd regret not being with you. I choose you. I want
you. End of story.

I wanted to believe him, but I didn't know how to fully accept
that he was willing to give all that up for me.

MOROCCO

> How I see us, or how I'm with you is this way:
> there is the rest of the world and then there is
> you, and with you, I came as I am sharing
> everything with you and feeling safe and
> confident to deliver myself in every situation.
> Distance or any cultural differences isn't going to
> make me frustrated AT ALL or make me tired. I
> know what I want and was looking for, and that
> is YOU.

I had to believe he meant every word.

Why didn't I deserve to be happy? To find someone who would choose me over the whole world? Isn't that what every woman wants? Why was I so skeptical?

I continued to text with Poland every day. We never discussed my relationship with Morocco. I didn't tell him I'd had a date in Paris or even that I had a boyfriend now. It didn't seem relevant since Poland and I rarely discussed my dating life. Morocco was aware that I had a friendship with Poland, but he never asked for details. He never asked how often I messaged him or what we talked about.

One day, I knew my relationship with Poland would have to change.

POLAND

> We're sex friends.

Something shifted in me. I was entering dangerous territory with this conversation.

ME

> Ugh. I don't like that phrase.

POLAND

Why?

ME

Cause it discounts what we have. I prefer lovers.

Be careful, Courtney. You can't make these conversations sexual with him anymore.

POLAND

Well you do love me. And I love you too.

I truly never thought I would hear those words from Poland. But seeing them there, I didn't have the reaction I thought I would. I'd expected to have a sense of excitement or maybe a feeling of accomplishment. But instead, it felt like a tiny ping in my stomach, a reassurance of a truth I had known for a while and he finally realized it himself.

ME

Wow.

POLAND

Or at least I try. I know my doubts about the word love and my ability to do it.

ME

Well that makes it less profound when you disclaim it.

POLAND

I know. Still don't tell you that many times.

ME

Didn't tell me many times what?

POLAND

That I love you. Or ever.

ME

You've never told me that. Until today.

POLAND

Yeah. Wow. Big thing.

ME

How's it feel?

POLAND

Good. I mean you said we are lovers. I don't disagree.

ME

I prefer that over sex friends.

POLAND

Sex friends is freaky but it's also nice. You are a friend that I make love with sometimes.

ME

And that you love.

POLAND

And that I also love to some extent. Yeah.

I knew he had never told a woman he loved them before, but even this exchange felt off. Maybe it was because I was in an exclusive relationship with Morocco and I could no longer give that part of myself to Poland. I should have told Poland that we couldn't have sex anymore, but I was afraid of losing his interest. And even though I was committed to Morocco, I wasn't ready to fully give up Poland.

I was aware that Poland's visit to Germany was coming up, but since I was with Morocco, I hadn't asked Poland about it. Morocco would be uncomfortable with me seeing Poland, and I didn't blame him. But Poland was acting weird. Weirder than usual and he felt distant. So I waited to ask him about it until I knew he was already in Germany.

ME

How's Germany?

POLAND

I don't know.

ME

What do you mean? Aren't you here?

POLAND

No.

ME

What happened?

POLAND

I realized I have tickets to Frankfurt Hahn Airport, not Frankfurt Main and I can't easily get to Mannheim from there within a reasonable price and time.

ME

Oh I figured your friend would've picked you up.

POLAND

My friends there don't have cars.

ME

Ah. You could've asked me.

POLAND

I know. I think it would be too much.

ME

Why didn't you?

POLAND

Because you obviously would have offered it.

ME

And you didn't want to see me?

POLAND

I didn't want you to sacrifice your time. You have enough things to do. So that's another reason why I was pissed. And still am.

ME

I wish you would've told me why you were upset.

POLAND

There were many reasons. But I just didn't want to talk about it. Or think about it. But I think you have enough duties.

ME

You don't get to decide that!

POLAND

Ok I should have told you. But I won't change it now.

ME

Do you not think you matter to me? Have I ever given you that impression?

POLAND

I know I do.

ME

I thought you didn't ask me because then you'd have to explain to your friends how you got to Mannheim. That you were embarrassed to be associated with me.

I didn't realize at first how much it would bother me to be someone's secret. I was able to rationalize it—sure, you probably don't want your family knowing you're dating a married woman. No biggie. But it was a big deal for me. I wanted my partner to be proud to be with me. Proud to be seen with me.

For Max's birthday, I had given him a framed picture of us. He told me he would put it on his nightstand but then when his mom came to visit, he would have to hide it. Instead of advocating for myself and sharing how those words stung, I swallowed them. Because I thought I should be grateful for a man who would even choose "someone like me" (a married mother of three) and shouldn't complain.

POLAND

I didn't even think about it. At all. But I understand why you thought this way. I'm really sorry. Honestly, I thought you would ask me about me coming there. But since you didn't, I thought you just don't remember the date or something.

ME

You made it clear you weren't coming to see me. Of course I remembered.

POLAND

I told you I wanted to meet you.

ME

You said it in passing.

POLAND

I couldn't stay at your house, right?

I can guarantee Nate would never let that happen.

ME

No. You mentioned once about us getting coffee and then nothing after that. And since the trip wasn't about seeing me, I figured if you wanted to see me you would actually make an effort. Otherwise, I felt like I was imposing on your plans.

POLAND

I didn't have too many. So you weren't. And I would do it.

ME

Great to know that you could squeeze me in.

POLAND

About the coffee. Omg. I knew it sounded bad but it wasn't the intention.

ME

> No, you say 'I want to fucking see you. When can we make that happen?' We make a plan. You didn't seem interested in that. I'm not going to beg for your attention.

POLAND

> You never say, 'I want to fucking see you.'

Mother fuc…

ME

> I never say that? What did I say most of September? I SHOWED YOU I WANTED TO SEE YOU.

POLAND

> You are right. But I also told you I wanted to see you.

I was angry and I shouldn't be. I had a boyfriend, and Poland wasn't him. Why did I care so much about mattering to Poland? Morocco was crazy about me, and I was pissed because my former lover didn't know how to show me that he actually loved me?

What is wrong with me?

I told Poland I didn't care. That I was done arguing with him about it. I was done with not feeling like I mattered.

And yet, a part of me whispered: *You're delusional for thinking you could ever truly believe that.*

CHAPTER FORTY-NINE

December 2023

MOROCCO RETURNED TO LYON, and we set a date for me to spend the weekend with him. The day before I was to leave, my train was canceled.

This cannot be happening.

ME

> Just got an email that my train tomorrow is
> cancelled. There's a strike or something. What
> should I do?

MOROCCO

> Check the website and try to reschedule on a
> different one.

Oh, like it's just that easy.

I sent him a voice note that I was frustrated and overwhelmed. I hadn't seen him in almost five weeks and now it felt like the Universe just didn't want us to see each other. I told him that if I couldn't reschedule, then I would drive to see him.

MOROCCO

> Just calm down!!! No need to be pissed. We'll find a solution. I don't want you to drive! It's so far and you've been driving A LOT lately!

No, he did not just tell me to calm down.

My anger jumped about thirty-three notches. If there was one thing I despised, it was being told to calm down.

Oh good, another man trying to tell me how I feel or what I'm allowed to feel.

ME

> If I said I want to drive to come see you, you would be okay with it? Or would you say no, you can't come if you're driving

MOROCCO

> It's not that you CAN'T come if you're driving, that's another thing. But I DON'T WANT you to drive this much! If you're going to stay at least five days then I guess it'd be okay with you driving but for this NO. You're already tired. I just checked. It's six hours of driving.

ME

> I'm aware.

MOROCCO

> Hell no you're not driving! You are tired! Let's just cross our fingers this train booking exchange works. Are you free for a call?

ME

> I don't want to talk to you right now. I'm upset.

MOROCCO

> Because I care about you, and I don't want you to be tired while you drive?

ME

No. I'm upset because I told you what I was capable of doing and you chose not to listen to that. And not seeing you for another two weeks is just insane.

MOROCCO

I'm not saying I don't want to see you! I'm saying I don't want you to be TIRED!

ME

I'm always tired! I'm fucking forty with a husband, three kids and a boyfriend! Welcome to my life.

MOROCCO

The boyfriend doesn't want to be a tiring thing for you :) He wants it to be a good relaxing thing (and he's aware there will be times when it's not relaxing nor good).

ME

That's not how it works. Do you know what it takes for me to make these weekends happen? Things I have to arrange and coordinate? It's a major effort. But you're worth it. We're worth it. So when you're like, oh just no big deal, if it doesn't work out, it feels like alllll that work I put in was for nothing. I'm not like your last partner. I don't live right down the road from you.

And there it was—my insecurities popping up. I was scared that if I didn't see him this weekend, he'd realize what a trouble it was to coordinate this long-distance relationship. I was scared he would compare me to his last partner who he could see whenever he wanted because they lived in the same city and her husband didn't care what she did. I knew he was trying to be thoughtful and caring, but the reality was we hadn't seen each other in five weeks and I couldn't wait two more.

I ended up changing my ticket but had to pay an extra

hundred euros. I felt defeated. Is this what my life was now? Praying my trains didn't get canceled and hoping I don't have to pay ridiculous amounts of money just to see my boyfriend for a couple days? Oh, and not to mention it was six and half hours door to door, one-way, if everything was on time.

This is never going to work.

Before I left for Lyon, Poland asked me what my plans were for the weekend.

ME

I'm heading to Lyon.

POLAND

What for?

ME

To see someone.

POLAND

Oh. It's a DATE.

ME

Yes.

POLAND

That's a long distance.

ME

Romania was farther.

POLAND

How long will you stay there?

ME

Friday to Sunday.

POLAND

Yeah I see. So I won't text you much.

ME

You don't text me much normally anymore. Sometimes I don't hear from you for a day or two.

POLAND

That's not true. I text you almost every day.

ME

Almost. You can still text me this weekend. I just won't be as fast to respond. But I have a five-hour train ride Sunday so plenty of time to catch up.

The next day, I took the earlier (and higher cost) train to Lyon. Morocco took the afternoon off from work. He met me at the train station, bought my Metro ticket, and we went back to his apartment. I was tired but I was more excited to see him. To touch him, since our first date five weeks earlier.

We climbed the three flights of stairs to his apartment. He opened the large wooden door and I stepped into his flat, admiring the beauty. His place was decorated with modern, stylish pieces. There was no clutter. Everything seemed to have a place, and for a moment, I wondered if I would have one here too.

The wooden floors creaked as I walked into the main room, noticing his kitchen table and pale-yellow couch. Huge windows let in the afternoon sun. I set my purse on one of his chairs and let out a deep exhale.

"I want you to feel at home when you're here," he said, putting down my bag. "This is your second home. You can leave your stuff here if you want."

He walked to the kitchen. "Do you want some coffee? I ordered your coffee creamer so you'd have it just the way you like it."

He actually did that?

"You ordered my creamer? Wow, thank you!"

Morocco tilted his head slightly and raised his left eyebrow. "Of course I did." He then walked into the bedroom and brought out a pillow. "I also ordered this for you," he said, handing me the pillow. "I know you prefer more firm pillows and mine are soft ones."

Morocco had also gone to the store to get me plain yogurt and berries for breakfast as well as sparkling water. He had gotten two blocks of French salted butter, our family's favorite, for me to take home. I was flabbergasted. No one had ever put this much effort in for me.

I stood there. Speechless. Seeing my surprise, Morocco walked over and wrapped his arms around me.

"You are so sexy," he said, kissing me.

I snapped out of my speechless trance and focused on the man in front of me. I was happy to show him my appreciation for all of his efforts.

Morocco had talked about his former lovers raving about his sexual prowess. He told me about the sex-filled weekends he had had with sex friends.

I was not prepared for him to only last a couple of minutes based on that information. I was even less prepared for him not making me come or asking me if I wanted to.

I let it go.

Maybe he's just excited and overwhelmed with having me here. I'm sure he'll go down on me next time.

When the next time came, a couple hours later, I did not. When the third time came, an hour after that, I did not again. I went to bed frustrated and defeated.

How was this happening?

I'd expected it with Poland. He was inexperienced and well, he wasn't my boyfriend. But with Morocco?! Come on.

The next morning, I woke up before he did. I went out to the kitchen, made coffee, and had some berries. My frustration had not eased from the night before.

Morocco came out and made himself a cup of coffee. "You okay, babe? Sleep okay?"

I shook my head. "No. I'm not. I'm frustrated, actually."

I could tell he was not expecting that answer.

"Why?"

I clasped my hands together and set them on the countertop. "Well… we had sex three times yesterday and I didn't come once."

He moved his head slowly, pursing his lips together. "Okay… I know."

"It bothers me that you don't seem concerned with my pleasure."

Morocco explained that he had never come that fast, and that he was embarrassed because he had. He was feeling weird with me sexually because of my job and felt like there was this pressure for him to perform.

I narrowed my eyes and squeezed my hands into fists. "So now my job is a problem. Since when?"

"I didn't say it was a problem. It's just intimidating knowing you're a sexpert and all."

"I can guarantee you've had sex with more people than I have! I'm not a sex coach. I can't believe this. I'm being punished because of my line of work?!"

I got off the stool and walked to the yellow couch, plopping down on it. "Since when is performance an issue? You've told me about these weekends where you just fuck for like two days. And yet sex with me is a problem?"

Morocco followed me to the living room, sitting across from me in the chair. "I didn't care about those women. I could separate my feelings for them. I can't with you. With them, it was just sex. With you, it's much deeper than that."

I pulled my knees into my chest. "But I'm being punished because you have feelings for me?"

"I want you to have orgasms. I just don't want the pressure to perform."

"I'm not asking you to perform! I'm asking you to get me off first sometimes. It doesn't even have to be every time. But it would be nice to be asked or considered."

He nodded. "You're right. I can do better at that."

For the rest of the weekend, something still felt off with us sexually. I wanted to have sex with him all the time, and I knew he was attracted to me. But... in a weird way, he resisted me. I could feel him holding back during sex. I didn't understand what wasn't working. I left that first weekend feeling slightly defeated and only somewhat sexually satisfied.

CHAPTER FIFTY

AFTER MY LAST conversation with Poland, something had changed. He was more argumentative and just kind of an asshole when we texted. A few days after I returned from Lyon, I brought up my concerns.

ME

> What's going on? You've been acting differently since I went to Lyon.

POLAND

I don't know. I don't enjoy our conversations recently.

ME

> It's like you're looking to pick a fight or something. It's like you're angry with me. And instead of talking to me about it you find ways to poke me. And yeah, I push back. I own that. But I have also tried to make jokes and you're just not that interested.

POLAND

When did I poke you?

Yesterday. The day before that.

Our conversation devolved. Poland acted like he didn't care about me, and I could feel our relationship ending. Even though I wasn't interested in anything romantic with him, I still loved him. He was still someone who mattered to me and I didn't like how things were between us. I knew he was jealous of my new relationship. He felt replaced but he lacked the ability to maturely communicate that to me. Instead, he pulled away and shut down.

My heart hurt. But I knew that I had to let Poland go. I told Morocco that I had gotten into an argument with Poland. He was surprised that I was so upset by it. I downplayed my feelings for Poland when explaining my reaction. I mean I would be concerned if Morocco reacted the way I had about a former lover.

Finally, Morocco asked me, "Is there something going on between you two?

My stomach turned.

No, no, no. I can't lose Morocco, too.

I was worried that he wasn't okay with my feelings for Poland. I needed to shut this conversation down now.

"What? No! Absolutely not. We are just friends. Or we were."

Poland and I were *never* just friends. Our relationship lived in the in-between. And while I set boundaries for myself in the kind of conversations and pictures I would share with Poland since Morocco and I became exclusive, I couldn't deny the magnetic pull we had toward each other. We would always love and desire one another, even though we both knew a romantic relationship would never work for us.

Poland was my safety net. No matter what men came and went in my life, I always knew I had him to fall back on. Not having him in my life felt scary.

Empty.

For me, Poland represented the athletic and attractive boys I couldn't date when I was in high school and college. The ones I wasn't confident enough to put myself out there for. The ones that purity culture said were dangerous because they'd cause me to compromise my values of saving myself for marriage. The ones who never chose me.

Patriarchy makes you believe that if you're not chosen by a man, there's something wrong with you. And the men I desired in my young adulthood didn't desire me back because I wasn't willing to sacrifice my principles. Now, I was being chosen by that archetype and that felt incredible. Sadly, I was too blind to see his shortcomings because I thought (thanks to my mom's messaging during my dating years) that I could fix him. Change him. He'd improve for me. He'd try harder for me. I just needed to keep showing him that I was worth showing up for.

When you're anxiously attached, you're drawn to emotionally unavailable people because they represent what you had during childhood. My parents were often physically present, but anytime I had big feelings, I was told to pray about it. Or to shake it off. Or I was told that God would provide. I never learned that my emotions made sense and it was safe to show them to others. I was told "big girls don't cry" and other adages that neither comforted nor consoled me.

Poland felt safe because he was a remembrance of my past at a physiological level. His behavior didn't signal the red flags it should have because my nervous system was wired as an anxious kid to expect and accept love from those who were not emotionally attuned to my needs.

I believe the Universe kept Poland in my life to help me heal that younger version of myself that was oppressed by purity culture. The young woman who didn't get to choose for herself what it was she wanted. And instead of learning how to advocate for myself, I flew back to the pretty cage time after time.

That is how powerful this conditioning is. Despite my years of education and working with thousands of women in this very area, I had to go through my own journey to truly understand what it meant to dance with the desires of my unhealed wounds. And come back to the truth that I am not in the business of convincing anyone that I am worth loving.

My tolerance for Poland's inconsistent behavior was all used up. And I had no reason to make things work with him when I had a boyfriend who was everything Poland couldn't be for me. I knew this logically, but at the time, I still felt like I had lost.

For my forty-first birthday, Nate suggested I spend it with Morocco. The goal was to see my partner every two to three weeks when we're long-distance, and my birthday fell two weeks after our first weekend together. The weekend after my birthday was Christmas. Then New Year's. Then Nate and my anniversary. It's a complicated time of year when you're polyamorous. Having Nate suggest this made my heart feel like it was going to burst out of my chest.

When I told Morocco about it, he was elated and surprised. "Tell Nate, thank you!"

I was hoping this would be a better weekend than our first one. Two days before I was to leave, I got very sick. I had no idea if I would feel well enough to travel. Morocco encouraged me to reschedule, but I was determined to see him. It would be another three weeks before we saw each other if I didn't make this weekend happen.

Morocco met me at the train station again, but he didn't buy my Metro ticket like the first time, nor did he take the afternoon off. We hustled back to his apartment so he could get back to work. I took a nap but still wasn't feeling great.

Sex was better this time, with him focusing more on my pleasure. It was something that still felt contentious between us. I was resentful that he had given his body to women he didn't really care about but was more guarded with me. I knew it was something I couldn't push with him. It needed to unfold in time, but damn, it was discouraging.

The first weekend we were together, Morocco made a reservation at a nice restaurant. For my birthday weekend, he hadn't planned anything. He did get me two bras, a pair of panties, and a Snuggie to keep at his place. But I was underwhelmed with his lack of effort. Birthdays are a big deal to me, and I was hoping he would have made more of an attempt to do something romantic. I was disappointed and still not feeling well.

On our way to dinner, I nudged his shoulder. "Oh! You wanted me to remind you about something."

Morocco didn't make eye contact with me. He shrugged. "Yeah, I'll tell you about it later."

Sometimes when we texted, he would allude to wanting to show me something or tell me something. When I reminded him in person, he would brush it off and say, "Yeah, later."

I knew what he wanted to tell me, but I wasn't going to push it. He was falling in love with me, but I didn't know how I felt about it.

Being in a relationship with Morocco was easy. Our biggest issues were navigating the long distance, the sex thing when we were together, and that most of his family and friends didn't know about me. But the day-to-day stuff, the emotional support, the communication, planning a future together, that was fun and easy. And boy, I did not miss dating. I was happy to have found what I was looking for even if it was a bit of an effort to make it work.

Our connection was deep, even if we had only been dating for six weeks. It was the same for Nate and me when we dated.

That night, Morocco and I went out for drinks at one of his favorite spots.

"You know how I've been saying I want to tell you something?"

I sat my beer down and straightened my posture. "This sounds serious."

He inhaled from his vape. "It is. I've only told a few people in my life about this but I want you to know so you can better understand me."

I nodded slowly. "Okay, I hope you know you can tell me anything."

"I do, which is why I want to tell you this."

I leaned over and squeezed his arm. A faint smile spread across his face.

"About six years ago this month, when I was living in Paris, my sister, the one that's just younger than me, was struggling with depression. She got into a fight with my parents and then tried to kill herself."

I sat, stunned by his vulnerability, and listened to him share the details of not knowing if his sister would live or die, how his parents dealt with the shame, and how he tried to navigate his relationship with her after she pulled out of her coma.

"I've worked through that part of it, but sometimes I struggle with having a real conversation with her. I'm afraid of telling her how I feel because I don't want to upset her. So everything just feels surface level. It's the same with my parents and her."

I knew that my job wasn't to fix this situation. It was just to hold space for him to share. And even though he said he had worked through some of the pain, I could still sense the guilt he felt for not being able to help his sister.

After he had finished sharing, I asked if I could hug him.

"Babe, of course. You don't have to ask to hug me. I'm your boyfriend."

"I know," I said, as I wrapped my arms around him. "I am just so sorry you and your family went through that."

"I'm so glad I could share this with you. Sometimes I get anxious around this time of year. It's like my body remembers what happens. So I didn't want you to think something was off with us. It's just this."

"Of course, your body remembers. And I'm so grateful you

felt safe enough to share this with me. Please, if there's anything I can do to support you during this month, or ever, let me know."

He leaned in to kiss me. "I will, babe. Thank you."

"You ready to go? I'd like to go for a walk before we head back home."

I gathered my purse and gloves. "Absolutely."

We walked arm-in-arm around Lyon, admiring the Christmas decorations in the windows, the lights adorning the cobblestone streets, and listening to the faint sound of *Silent Night* being played by a street guitarist.

Later that night, while lying in his bed together, Morocco told me he was ready to tell me something.

He looked at me with those beautiful brown eyes. "I love you." He bit his lower lip. "And I don't care if you're not ready to tell me that yet. Or if you ever say it, but I had to tell you how I felt."

I did love him. I just didn't know if I was *in* love with him. Maybe I was.

"I know," I said, calmly. "And I love you, too."

"You knew?" Morocco asked in surprise, lifting his head off the pillow. "What do you mean you knew?"

I kept my head on the pillow. "It's hard to explain. I just knew. When you kept saying you wanted to tell me something and you told me how much you liked me… I don't know. I just knew."

He seemed disappointed by my revelation.

"It's still a big deal!" I said, lifting my head off the pillow. "Hearing the words and knowing them are two different things."

He put his head back down on the pillow. "You're right."

He pulled me down to him and kissed me hard and long. And he explored my body with his lips and tongue, showing me just how much he loved me. Twice.

The afternoon I went back to Germany, Morocco asked if I had room in my suitcase to take back some stuff.

I raised my left eyebrow playfully. "Depends on what it is."

"I got the kids and Nate Christmas presents."

My chin dropped, and my lips curved. "You did? You didn't have to do that!"

He dismissed my comments by waving his hand. "I know, but I wanted to."

I smiled and made room in my suitcase. "That was incredibly thoughtful. Thanks, babe," I said, kissing him.

"You don't need to thank me..." he said, kissing me back.

I was hoping we'd have sex the morning I left, the morning of my birthday, but we didn't. Sex with him was still sporadic, and I didn't want to keep pushing that we discuss it. Once again, I was too insecure to advocate for my needs. I was afraid of rocking the boat and losing something that finally felt secure. I thought that hitting this stage of our relationship meant I could finally release the breath it felt like I had been holding since things ended with Max.

Hitting that love stage with Morocco triggered my anxious attachment even more. Now, I felt like I had even more to lose if he discovered I wasn't willing to let the whole wanting sex and orgasms thing go.

Those early stages of dating were not enjoyable for me. Reflecting now, I know it's because having fun, which often characterizes those initial dating phases, didn't feel safe. Growing up, there wasn't only a cost (whether it was money or calories) to having fun. No. There was often some type of penalty or punishment that accompanied fun.

For example, if I laughed too much or was too loud, I was scolded by a teacher or adult. Or if I had an orgasm from my boyfriend, I felt like God was going to smite me some day (oh the agony of a delayed consequence). Having fun never felt like the responsible thing to do (that's probably also from all the Capricorn in my chart).

I desired a partner I could invest in. I believed that loving someone meant you were committed to figuring things out, even when they felt hard. I believed that Morocco was worth it, and I didn't want to lose him because I was being "pushy."

On my train ride home, I saw a notification on my phone.

It was a text from Poland.

CHAPTER FIFTY-ONE

POLAND

Happy birthday.

ME

Thank you.

I HAD no plan to engage any more than this. He had deeply hurt me two weeks ago, and I wasn't going to pretend like everything was okay. But it did feel good that he remembered my birthday.

A few minutes later, he sent me a picture of himself shirtless, his muscled arm posed behind his head, and his wide smile revealing the white tiles of his teeth.

POLAND

Your birthday present.

Damn. Why does he have to look so good?

I could count the amount of pictures Poland had sent of himself on one hand. He'd never sent me one where he was shirtless. I hadn't heard from him in almost two weeks. It was the longest we had gone without talking since I ended things last summer with him.

He looked incredible in the picture, but I wasn't going to give that to him.

> **ME**
> Where are you?

POLAND
At a restaurant.

> **ME**
> You're half naked at a restaurant?

POLAND
Maybe.

> **ME**
> Who are you?!

POLAND
People change.

> **ME**
> You don't.

POLAND
Maybe I do.

A week later, on Christmas, I decided to text Poland. I still felt a shred of a connection to him and missed our conversations.

> **ME**
> Merry Christmas.

POLAND
Merry Christmas. And thank you.

> **ME**
> For what?

POLAND
For your wishes.

ME

Oh. You're welcome.

POLAND

:)

Poland rarely texted more than the minimum. So him thanking me was a bit out of character. It felt like he wanted to connect more, but didn't know how. I wasn't interested in finding out.

A few days later, he messaged me.

POLAND

I wanted to say sorry for my overreaction last time we talked. I had frustration accumulated that every second interaction we had was ending with you being hurt or sad or whatever and I thought what is the point of this if it doesn't bring anything positive. But you didn't deserve my reaction.

ME

Thank you. I appreciate your apology. But, why apologize now?

POLAND

It was growing in me. I had an argument with my parents which made me realize how you really appreciated me.

ME

What happened? What do you mean I appreciated you?

POLAND

Well you never told me that I have nothing interesting to say. Like my dad did once or twice. That's already something.

ME

I'm sorry he said that. He's wrong. When did that happen?

POLAND

Christmas.

ME

That's shitty.

POLAND

Not like it's the first time he implied that. Life. And
yes of course. Also, your Instagram post made
me think you rarely shared your downs with me.

ME

Well you weren't exactly the most sympathetic
person.

POLAND

How do you know if you shared it so rarely?

ME

You didn't seem so interested in my marriage or
my family. And we didn't talk for a few months.

POLAND

Ok.

ME

You missed me, these past few weeks.

POLAND

I did.

Hearing that felt good, but I was no longer interested in
opening my heart to a man who was incapable of giving me
what I wanted. What I deserved. I was committed to seeing
things through with Morocco.

Despite saying "I love you," the second weekend Morocco and I
spent together wasn't much better than our first one. And we
didn't know the next time we'd be seeing each other. Morocco's

uncle was visiting family in France and Italy and planned to stay with him during his trip. But according to Moroccan culture, he couldn't ask his uncle the exact dates of when he'd be there. That was considered disrespectful. So Morocco had to wait until his uncle told him when he'd be visiting.

ME

It's just hard for me not knowing when I'll see you again. And it also makes it difficult to plan other things. I keep trying not to think about it. But my mom asked me today, and I feel like a goddamn moron when I'm like I don't know when I'm seeing him again.

MOROCCO

Oh. You're pissed about it I guess.

Please don't tell me how I feel.

ME

I'm not pissed. I don't want you to put yourself in a bad or awkward position. That's not why I'm sharing it with you. It's just hard for me.

MOROCCO

Well, it's annoying you. And I understand that. It annoys me as well. But I'll see how I can handle that without being in a bad position.

ME

In my last relationship I was the one that always pushed seeing each other. And I feel that way sometimes with you. A lot of times actually.

MOROCCO

I love you.

ME

My insecurity is this: It takes a lot of work to see her. She's not worth it. This relationship isn't worth it. I could have a more "normal" relationship with someone else. That's my fear.

MOROCCO

IM IN FUCKING LOVE WITH
YOUUUUUUUUUUUUUUUUU COURTNEY.

ME

I know that. I love you too.

MOROCCO

And nothing will change that. As I keep saying, I
knew what I got in the first day I told you let's be
exclusive. And nothing's going to break or
change that in me or make me « frustrated » from
the relationship. I need you to know that.

ME

I believe you. But my thought was that you hadn't
dealt with it. Knowing something and
experiencing it are two different things. And now
you're dealing with the challenges that come with
the distance.

MOROCCO

Well, I'm experiencing it and nothing will change
what I told you day one. Moreover now that I'm in
love with you. Yes, I wish you were living in the
same city as me. Is there anything I can do to
calm the insecurity you be having about the
distance?

ME

Just remind me that we can do this. That we are
meant to be together and you love me. That I'm
worth the effort.

MOROCCO

I will. And you are worth the effort and I'm so
much in love with you and BIG YES that we're
meant to be together.

Nate could see I was struggling with not having a time to see
Morocco scheduled. So when he suggested something, it totally

caught me off guard.

"What if Morocco came here for New Year's?" Nate asked.

I laughed. "Wait. Are you being serious?"

He shrugged. "Yeah. Why not?"

My mouth hung open. "What do you mean 'why not?' You've never met anyone I've dated and now you're inviting him to join our family and friends? Where would he stay?"

Nate shrugged again. "I don't know. You guys could get a hotel in town or something."

I couldn't believe what he was suggesting. "You know how much it means to me that you even suggested this, right? Like, I never thought you'd be willing to do something like this so soon."

"Well, it just makes sense for him to come here."

"I don't know if he's ready to meet everyone. I mean all our friends, the kids, you. That's a lot of people all at once."

"Well, talk to him about it and see what he says."

I hugged Nate, thanking him. Nate had worked so hard to get to this point where he wasn't threatened by me loving another man. Where he didn't feel like he mattered any less if my boyfriend joined us for a holiday. Nate accepted that when I was living as my authentic self, I was like an overflowing cup. I had more energy and joy to share with others, especially with him. And seeing me in a confident and energetic state caused him to be more attracted to me.

My courage to break out of my cage had inspired Nate to break out of his too. It had never clicked for me until that moment that I wasn't the only one oppressed by the patriarchy; Nate had been also. Men may have created the system but they are not exempt from being impacted by it. They too are slaves to the system.

They're told that they should be enough for their wife. That real men don't let their partner date or have sex with other men. That male dominance is the only way; otherwise you're just a beta or a simp.

I hadn't cajoled or convinced Nate to step out of his cage. He had broken free all on his own. He had chosen the path of deprogramming from compulsory monogamy. And now, it felt like my dream was coming true. My husband AND boyfriend and my kids and friends, all celebrating a holiday together?! Could life get any better?!

I called Morocco to tell him the exciting news. He was just as shocked as I was regarding Nate's suggestion.

"Wow," he said. "I don't know what to say."

"I don't want to put any pressure on you, so would you think about coming here for New Year's?"

"Yes, of course. I just planned on staying home for New Year's. Every year I go out and party really hard and this is my first year in Lyon. I just wanted to be chill at home."

Seriously? Didn't he want to be with me and kiss me at midnight and finally meet all my friends he had heard so much about?

I knew that meeting everyone may be a little overwhelming, but it bothered me that he didn't agree to what Nate suggested. He loved me, why wouldn't he want to be with me? I wondered if it was the distance. He'd have to do what I had done, twice: travel six and a half hours one way to be with the person you love. I started to question if he was willing to do that. But I pushed it out of my mind.

Give him the benefit of the doubt.

Morocco's uncle told him that he would visit the first weekend in January, which meant that I wouldn't be able to see him until the middle of January, four weeks after our last weekend together.

I told Nate how frustrated I was.

"Isn't he off on New Year's Day?" Nate asked. "Take the train to see him for a couple days then. You can work from his house."

"You mean leave in like two days?"

"Why not?"

Excited, I texted Morocco.

ME

What if I came to see you Monday to
Wednesday?

MOROCCO

OF COURSE IT'S OKAY! But that's not too much
for you, right?

ME

I'd take the early train and get in around ten or
eleven.

MOROCCO

Babe, if that's not too much for you, then YES. It
works perfectly fine for me, and I can't wait till I
kiss youuuuu.

ME

You're worth it. We're worth it.

After ringing in the new year with our friends, I got up at 3:45 a.m. to catch a 5:30 a.m. train. I was so tired but was more excited to see Morocco. We needed a good couple of days together. I had zero expectations of our time together. I wasn't going to ask about sex or initiate. I would just go with the flow. I told him he didn't have to meet me at the train station so he could sleep in. He didn't meet me, which disappointed me a little, but I let it go because I told him he didn't have to.

Apparently, my easy-breezy approach worked well because our two days together were amazing. We laughed, we joked, we had great sex, we cuddled, we relaxed. Morocco made my pleasure a priority all on his own. Our relationship finally felt easy. It felt just like I had imagined it would. Leaving that Wednesday, I was confident that we had turned a corner in our relationship.

We talked about when to see each other again and agreed that I would come see him in two and a half weeks. Anytime I suggested he come to Germany, he would say, "Maybe I will. But

I want to surprise you. I'll plan something with Sarah and Ashley and just show up unexpectedly."

Part of me thought it was romantic. The other part thought he was being non-committal. It made sense for me to go to him. He had his own apartment. He paid for almost everything when I was there. We had our own space and it was convenient— for him.

His birthday was coming up in March, and I wanted to go on a trip with him to celebrate. When we were first talking, he had suggested that we could alternate meeting places, including going some place together. Now was that opportunity.

"Where should we go for your birthday?" I asked him excitedly.

"I don't know," he said nonchalantly. "Let me think about it."

He had traveled a lot, and had traveled with his last partner to London often. I wanted to go somewhere with him other than the usual cafés and bars we'd go to in Lyon.

"What if we went to Paris the next time I'm here?" I asked.

He shrugged. "Yeah, maybe. Let's see how we feel when it gets closer."

"Or what about visiting your uncle in Italy? You said that he would be cool with our relationship."

"Yeah, they just had a baby a few months ago. Now's not the best time."

I took the hint and stopped asking about going on a trip for his birthday. And I buried the nagging feeling that maybe he had misled me on what he was actually willing to give me.

CHAPTER FIFTY-TWO

January 2024

"I DON'T KNOW if I can do this," I told Nate as I paced the floor of our bedroom. "What if I disappoint them? What if they hate me?"

"Courtney, it's going to be fine," he responded calmly. "But if you don't think you're ready then we can wait."

I didn't think I was ever going to be ready to tell Nate's parents that I was polyamorous. But I couldn't keep putting it off. More and more people were finding out and I didn't want them to hear it from anyone else but Nate and me directly.

I inhaled and exhaled quickly and swung my arms in front of my body like I was warming up for a match. I rolled my neck and narrowed my eyes. "Nope. Let's do it."

I sat next to Nate on our bed, crisscrossed my legs, and waited as the phone rang on my computer. My stomach churned and I could hear my heartbeat thumping in my ears.

Maybe they won't answer.

"Hey… oh wait, hold on," I heard my father-in-law, Ed, say. "Let's switch to video."

"Hey, Dad. Is Mom there?" Nate asked.

"Oh, there you guys are. Yeah, sure let me get her."

Ed yelled for Nate's mom, Marian, and within a few seconds they were both on the video call with us. Nate's hand rested on my leg as he tried to calm my mounting nerves.

"Hey, so, Courtney wanted to talk to you guys about something. She's really nervous."

They both looked at me with concern.

I can never go back once they know. I can't undo this once I speak this.

Tears filled my eyes and my chin quivered slightly.

Marian spoke, "Is everything okay?"

I bit the inside of my lower lip and searched for the right words. *Where do I even begin?*

Nate answered for me. "Everything's fine. It's actually really great, but there's something Courtney wants to tell you."

This couldn't wait; I had to do this now. Before I lost my nerve. Before I became a puddle of tears. They deserved to know the truth. My truth.

"I um… I don't even know where to start."

I looked at Nate and he nodded in support.

"So Nate and I are fine. I mean, we're actually great. We're the best we've ever been. And we believe that's because I realized that I'm polyamorous."

Omg, omg, omg.

It was as if I had just rolled a grenade into the room, and I was bracing for when it would go off.

Ed and Marian both furrowed their brows in confusion.

Please don't make me explain it. Please don't make me explain it.

It felt like an hour had passed before anyone spoke.

Finally, Marian asked, "What does that mean?"

I let out a long exhale. "It means that I feel like my most authentic self when I have another partner besides Nate."

Marian slowly nodded, processing the information.

"Nate, are you alright with that?" his dad asked sincerely.

Nate smiled. "I am. We're still figuring it out but we've gotten to a great place and I'm really proud of the life we're building."

"Do you date women?" Marian asked.

"I don't. Just men. If you have questions, you can ask us anything."

"Do the kids know?" Ed asked.

"They do," Nate replied. "We told them a few months ago. Courtney wasn't ready to tell you guys. She was really scared."

Marian shook her head. "Why would you be scared?! Are we scary?"

I laughed. "No. Oh gosh, no. I just…" the lump in my throat returned. "I didn't want to disappoint you guys. I was so terrified that you'd be upset or disown me or I don't know. I mean, I didn't want to hurt anyone."

Nate squeezed my leg.

"Do your mom and sister know?" Marian asked.

Nate nodded. "Yes, and they are supportive."

Marian continued, "Of course we're supportive too. As long as you guys are happy that's all that matters."

Ed added, "We don't really get what polyamorous means but as long as everyone's good with it, then we don't care."

The waves of fear of losing these two people I had loved for over two decades began to recede.

"Nate, are you polyamorous too?" Ed asked.

Nate shook his head. "I'm not."

We continued to talk about what our new life looked like. I shared that I had a boyfriend who lived in France. His parents asked respectful and thoughtful questions. The conversation continued for a few more minutes before we said goodbye, and told each other how much we all loved each other.

I closed the computer screen. Nate turned toward me and shared how proud he was of me. He wrapped his arms around me and kissed my tear-stained cheek.

"I'll be down in a minute," I told him as he stood up to go downstairs.

"Take your time."

Nate shut the door on his way out, leaving me alone to process what had just happened. Everyone I loved in my life now knew I was polyamorous.

The whole world could now know and I wouldn't care.

I sat there, staring out the window, soaking in the reality that I had been accepted for who I was. Who I am. By the people that mattered most to me. I pulled my knees to my chest, hung my head, and let the tears of peace fall.

CHAPTER FIFTY-THREE

February 2023

NONE of my kids had ever talked with or met anyone I had dated. Even though I had come out to them months ago, I hadn't introduced anyone to them. One day after the kids came home from school, I was on a video call with Morocco.

"Hey, Bug!" I said to my son, Asher. "How was school?"

Asher stopped by my bedroom door and looked at me, slightly confused. "Are you on the phone?"

I nodded. "Yeah. With Morocco. Do you want to say 'hi?'"

He shrugged. "Sure."

Asher walked into my room, and I turned the phone to face him. Morocco's smile widened.

"Hey, Asher. *Ça va?*

Asher side-eyed me. "What?"

I laughed. "It means how are you. In French."

"Oh. I'm fine. How are you?"

Morocco nodded. "I'm good. Thanks."

Asher turned to talk to me. "I'm gonna go eat lunch."

He walked out of my room but stopped. "Love you."

Avery met Asher on the stairs. "Who's Mom talking to?"

Asher continued walking downstairs. "Morocco."

"Oh, I want to say hi, too," she said.

Avery walked into my room, and once again, I turned my phone so she could see Morocco.

Avery waved. "Hi."

Morocco's smile widened again. "Hey, Avery. How are you?"

"I'm good, thanks." She turned to me and said, "I'm going to go do homework."

I nodded. "Sounds good. Love you."

Avery kissed my head before leaving. "Love you."

I could see Addison walking up to her room. "Hey, do you want to say hi to Morocco, too?"

Addison didn't stop walking. "Nope."

I turned the phone back to me, raising my eyebrows and frowning slightly. "Maybe next time."

He saw my disappointment. "I'm not going anywhere, babe. She'll say hi to me when she's ready."

Gosh, that felt so good to hear. My kids were incredibly protective of me, with Addison being the most skeptical of anyone I was dating. I appreciated their love and care for me. And I had to believe that one day, it would be normal for them to have conversations with another man that I loved.

A few days before Valentine's Day, I went to Lyon for the fifth time to see Morocco. Since we wouldn't be able to spend it together, I still wanted to do something special for him. He had talked about getting a Polaroid camera and hanging pictures on his wall, especially ones of us. So I ordered a camera, wrapped it, and brought it to Lyon. Morocco told me he couldn't come to the train station to meet me and he couldn't work from home, so

I met him at a station near his office, got his house key, and went back to his apartment.

I knew he had to work late so I went to the store, got groceries, fresh flowers, and made him a romantic meal. When he walked in the door a couple of hours later, he was greeted by a vase of flowers, a gift, dinner, and me.

He couldn't stop smiling. "Babe! You did all this for me?!"

I wrapped my arms around his neck. "I did. Happy early Valentine's Day. I know we can't celebrate on the actual day so I wanted to celebrate early."

I let go of him and handed him the present. "Open it."

The look on his face when he unwrapped the camera and case was priceless.

He looked at me wide-eyed, his mouth open. "You got me a camera?! I've been wanting one of these!"

I smiled, pointing at the box. "I know. Is that the kind you wanted? I didn't know. There were so many brands—"

"Stop," he interrupted. "It's perfect." He looked at me, tears building in his eyes. "You're perfect," he said, hugging me. "I... I just have no words... Thank you. This means so much to me."

I hugged him back. "You're welcome. I love you. Happy Valentine's Day."

He pulled back from me. "But I didn't get you anything."

I shrugged, hoping to ignore the tinge of sadness those words triggered. "I hope you're hungry. Let's eat."

The weekend we spent together was one of our best. We laughed, made love, cuddled, went to our favorite café and bar, and dreamed about the future. Things with Morocco felt good. Secure. I was happy. It felt like I had finally curated the perfect life.

Then why do I feel so exhausted most of the time?

I felt like a juggler trying to keep all the balls in the air, afraid to neglect one for fear it would crash to the floor. Despite my relationship with Morocco feeling easy for the most part, I found myself drained from the anticipation of meeting, planning travel, ticket costs, and time away from my family.

When you're anxiously attached, you over-function. You're the planner—trying desperately to keep the connection alive. I was doing this with Nate *and* whomever I was dating. And I was starting to run on empty.

The morning of Valentine's Day, I woke up excited. I had hidden a card for Morocco in his apartment the day I left. I told him to call me before he left for work.

"Alright," I said enthusiastically. "Walk over to your bookshelf, by the front door. On the top shelf, next to that book... you should see something red."

He followed my directions and pulled out a large red envelope. His smile was priceless. "You hid this? When?!"

"A few days ago. When I was still there."

He opened the card and read it. I could tell he was moved by my thoughtfulness. It felt so good to share this with him and see his face. He put down the card.

"I don't know what to say," he said, a little emotional. "I feel bad that I didn't get you anything."

Once again, I shrugged, pretending like it didn't bother me. "Meh."

I refused to say, "it's okay," because it wasn't. Morocco had touted that he was a big romantic before we got together. And yes, he had sent me flowers twice in three and a half months and had done some thoughtful things. But I'd expected more from him on a day like Valentine's Day. Even though it was a stupid, made-up holiday. I still wanted to feel special. And I didn't.

Later that night, Morocco and I had our usual video call. He could tell something was bothering me.

"What's wrong, babe?" he asked.

I had learned that it was better to just be honest with him than pretend like nothing was wrong.

"It bothered me more than I realized that you didn't do anything for me for Valentine's Day. You talked a lot in the beginning of our relationship about being very romantic and at times, you have been. But it kind of feels like you're not that romantic actually, and that hurts."

I could tell that my words bothered him. I wasn't going to apologize for how I felt. He had talked about the extravagant things he would do for women he dated before we became exclusive. So yes, I had an expectation that he would also treat me similarly.

After our conversation, I texted him. I felt bad about how he took the words that I shared.

ME

> You deserve better than how I treated you earlier. I'm sorry for that. I think because we're not like public public with our relationship (like I can't tag you in stuff... yet) that I look for other external forms of validation so I can prove to others, and to myself, that what we have is real and amazing. It's like that will give me proof that our relationship is real and means something. Which is just ridiculous. Because I know it is.

I wanted this relationship to matter. I wanted all of my efforts to matter. Every damn train ride and fourteen hours of traveling to mean something. Because that's the programming of purity culture—relationships must have a purpose (usually that's marriage, or in my case, a long-term commitment).

Looking back, I see that I was unable to be present and enjoy each interaction, each journey, each opportunity for what it was. I was so focused on the future.

Where is this headed? What are his intentions?

It was all about managing. Controlling. Predicting. I needed to know if my heart was safe with someone who claimed they cared about me. I longed for closeness, but was terrified that it would disappear the moment I let my guard down.

I feared that feeling safe with him meant that he would stop trying. Because I had seen that. In my own marriage, and in the hundreds of couples I had worked with. Where safety was seen as a finish line, and the romance and fun just went away because they reached that point. I wanted to be worth the effort to make something special.

He didn't reply to my message.

I was discouraged. Despite having a husband and a boyfriend, I went to bed feeling empty on the day of love.

CHAPTER FIFTY-FOUR

DESPITE BEING GONE MORE, my relationship with my kids didn't suffer. If anything, they began to appreciate my presence more. I became more intentional when I was with them. I was more patient and even grateful for the mundane moments that I had previously resented.

This was also true for my relationship with Nate. When he was supportive of me in all aspects of my life (not only in dating), it made our relationship stronger. I desired to be intentional with him. I would set up weekly date nights. Our sex life continued to thrive. When I was able to operate and exist from an authentic place, life felt more abundant.

"If you go on a date, can you not do it in Landstuhl?" Addison asked me on our way home from IKEA one day.

"Why?"

"Because I have a lot of friends that could see you."

"And you don't want them to?"

"Well, they don't know you're polyamorous. They would think it's like cheating or something."

"How do they even know what I look like?"

"Because kids are weird and look up other kids' parents."

I blinked in confusion, laughing slightly. "Alright."

Addison laughed awkwardly. "It's not that I'm ashamed of you…"

I smiled. "But you kind of are."

I knew not to take this personally. Kids have it hard enough with figuring out their own identities. Having a polyamorous mom definitely didn't make fitting in any easier. But I would be damned if I made her respectful request about me.

"Do any of your friends know I'm poly?"

"Just one." She looked out the window and I considered dropping the subject.

"I know it's not easy, kiddo. We're the *Ausländer* in Germany already and I know this makes you even more different. I'm sorry about that."

She shrugged. "It's not your fault. I'm just not ready to share it with my friends."

"I absolutely respect that. I just don't want you to feel alone."

She looked at me. "I don't, Mom. Promise."

I reached over to squeeze her hand. My heart filled with so much love when she squeezed it back.

For Christmas, Morocco had gifted his parents a trip to Rome, just the three of them. He didn't get to spend a lot of time with just his parents and he wanted to do something special for them. The night before he left for Rome, we had a video call, like we normally did. He had been acting different (less lovey-dovey, less communicative) since Valentine's Day, and I thought it was just the nerves of being gone for a week and getting his house ready for his parents. They would fly back to Lyon with him and spend a few days before going back to Casablanca.

"Hey," Morocco began. "So, I'm not sure how much time I'll have to text you or call you and stuff."

Uneasiness turned in my stomach. Something felt unsettling about hearing him say that.

"What do you mean?"

"I want to focus on spending time with my parents."

"Okay… Does that mean like no phone calls or video calls?"

"Probably no video calls but definitely still texting and phone calls."

Sure. That seems reasonable.

Morocco had *always* made me a priority. I'm sure he would still find time to do so. I wasn't concerned, but the way he was acting felt off. Something didn't settle right. I ignored my concerns and tried to be the supportive girlfriend.

"I hope you have the best time with them! Text me when you land in Rome tomorrow morning."

"Of course. I'm going to finish cleaning so I'll tell you good-night. I love you, babe."

The next morning, he called me after he landed and shared how excited he was about the trip. I was genuinely happy for him and told him to have a great time.

For our entire relationship, the longest we had ever gone without texting each other (other than sleeping) was four hours. We were consistently in contact with each other. We shared everything. And that was mainly established by him in the beginning. Morocco would send me random pics of waiting for his train or a bowl of candy at the office. This type and frequency of communication was something I had gotten used to.

On his first day in Rome, he messaged me after I was cleaning up from dinner.

MOROCCO

So so so tired. Long day but I'm happy that the parents are happy as well. Thinking of you.

ME

Love you.

MOROCCO

Love you too.

ME

Will you rest now?

MOROCCO

No. More walking and then dinner later.

Later that night, he messaged me that he was finally in bed, exhausted from a day filled with walking around and told me he loved me.

He texted me the next morning. He talked about how stylish the Airbnb was and how they planned to do more exploring today.

ME

Send me pics of what you explore. I'd also love to see pics of your Airbnb. It sounds cool!

MOROCCO

Will do. I'm going to go wash my face and have a coffee.

ME

Ok. I hope you have a great day! I love you.

MOROCCO

Thanks, babe. I love you.

After not hearing from him all day, I decided to text him since I was going to sleep soon.

ME

I hope you guys had a lovely evening and dinner was delicious. I'm going to sleep. Goodnight, my love. Sweet dreams. I love you.

He didn't message back until after I was asleep. I woke up to the same kind of message: he's so tired, he loves me, goodnight.

I could feel something shifting, but I couldn't quite put my finger on it. Ever since, our Valentine's Day conversation, it felt like Morocco was slowing pulling away. I kept trying to reassure myself that he was just spending time with his parents and there was nothing to worry about. But that nagging feeling that something was off bubbled beneath the surface.

Later that night, when we video called, something was different. The way Morocco talked. The way he looked at me. His kind smile and warmth were replaced by a coldness I hadn't felt from him before. The stiffness in my body reflected the invisible fence that seemed to now be erected between us.

"How do you like Rome?" I asked him.

"It's great! I can't wait to come back here again and explore it more on my own."

My stomach dropped when I heard him say that.

Anytime Morocco went somewhere, whether that was in Marrakech or Lyon or somewhere he found online, he would say, "Babe! *We* have to go here." It was always "we." This was the first time he had ever talked about traveling alone. So I called him out on it.

"On your own?" I asked teasing him. "Where would I be?"

He shrugged. "I don't know. Maybe in Germany, I guess."

"Hmm. Okay."

Our call was brief. Only a couple of minutes. It was the first time I had felt like I was losing him.

I texted him after.

ME

I'm sorry I nagged you about that traveling comment. I just feel disconnected from you so I was trying to poke you. That was wrong. I hope you have a great night. I love you.

MOROCCO

Don't worry about it, babe. I love you too. Good night.

I went to bed that night feeling that something had changed in our relationship. After not hearing from him at all the next day, I sent him a "thinking about you" text around dinner time.

He messaged me before I went to bed, again with only one sentence.

My relationship seemed to be ending in slow motion and I didn't know how to stop it. I talked to my friends about it. They reassured me that he's just with his parents. It's normal for him to be texting less. Don't make such a big deal about it.

I texted with my friend, Sarah, to get an objective perspective.

SARAH

How are you?

ME

I'm better. I have to literally talk myself into "he loves you. Five more days. It's okay. Everything's fine." I hate feeling disconnected. I have this irrational fear that he won't go back to being my boyfriend after his parents leave. Because I miss my boyfriend. I miss our end of the day calls where he tells me about his annoying boss and all the office drama. I miss talking to him about my day and giving each other advice. I miss his smile and his support.

Nearly every night for the past four months, that's exactly what I did before I went to sleep. I'd video call Morocco, and we'd talk for an hour, sometimes longer. We shared about our childhoods and what it was like growing up with parents who had ridiculously high expectations of us. He'd gush about how much he loved being a big brother. I smiled when he talked about surprising his little sister in June by flying back for her high school graduation.

Each night, we'd laugh and debate and discuss. And we'd dream. About opening a coffee shop together one day. About traveling to Spain where he'd been born. He'd tell me how much he believed in me and the work I was doing. Morocco wasn't just my boyfriend. He had become one of my best friends.

And that was what I was afraid of losing.

CHAPTER FIFTY-FIVE

NATE HAD BEEN nothing but supportive the past two weeks as my relationship with Morocco unraveled. He encouraged me to do whatever I felt was right and told me he'd be by my side no matter what. I was incredibly grateful for him and our marriage. The support system I had created, those who knew about my polyamorous relationships, was beyond comforting. Knowing that so many people loved and supported me… it was a priceless gift.

Tuesday, the day Morocco's parents were supposed to leave, came and went. Morocco still hadn't messaged me more than goodnight that evening. I texted him the next day around noon.

ME

Hey, did your parents leave yesterday? I'd like to connect with you and figure things out for this weekend.

MOROCCO

Hi. They did not leave yet—they extended their stay. So I guess it's not possible for this weekend plus we need to talk.

When he called, I could tell things were over. He was cold

and detached. He was not the man I fell for. Not the man who oozed love for me.

He started, "So, I've been thinking about my trip to Rome with my parents. I realized after spending time with them that I don't really see a future with you. I want to get married and have kids. Give my parents grandkids. And I can't have that with you. My parents would never accept you. I think the only way to make this work is if we were to open the relationship."

His feeble attempt at wanting to keep a relationship with me stung hard. He knew that Nate and I agreed to me having only one other partner. I didn't have the interest or the time to date other men. And Morocco had always told me he was a one-woman kind of man.

"First of all, you have been adamant about us being exclusive from the beginning. YOU were the one pushing for exclusivity right from the start and now you want to open it? No."

"I re-downloaded Feeld when I was in Rome," he admitted.

You've got to be fucking kidding me.

My heart sank. My cool and collected demeanor immediately vanished. Now I was pissed. "You did what?"

"I know that what I did was wrong. I needed to talk to you about it first. I deleted it right away but I wanted to tell you I did."

"Do you want a gold star for telling me?"

"No. I just... everything happened with us so fast. We fell in love and everything got serious faster than I expected. I wasn't ready for it to happen so quickly."

"Are you kidding me?! YOU were the one who told me you loved me first. You told me I was the love of your life. We were planning a future together! I introduced you to my kids, my family..."

My mind went back to the numerous conversations we had had about my concerns with him giving up the opportunity to be a husband and father to someone else. He would act offended that I'd even consider that scenario and would reassure me that he didn't care what his family thought. "I only want to be with you," he told me countless times.

"The trip to Rome with my parents really changed things for me."

"No shit. You don't think I couldn't feel it? I KNEW something had changed. I kept telling my friends, my mom, and everyone was like, 'Oh no, you're just being paranoid. He's with his family.' I was supposed to be your family!" I started to cry.

"I don't know what else to say."

"Fight for us!" I pleaded, immediately regretting the words as they came out of my mouth.

"Don't do that," he said, with disdain. "Don't beg."

Hearing him say that felt like having cold water thrown in my face. His sentiments severed any desire I had to be with him. "I can no longer trust you. And I am not interested in being with someone I can't trust. We are done. Goodbye, Morocco."

I hung up before I could hear his final words.

CHAPTER FIFTY-SIX

AND JUST LIKE THAT, it was over. I sat on my bed, staring at my phone. As the tears streamed down my face, I noticed that something was different. Sure, there was pain. Heartbreak always hurts. Even as my shoulders heaved from sobbing, I noticed that the weight I had been carrying was gone. I knew I had done what was necessary. I had advocated for myself and spoken my truth. And yes, I lost something I loved because I wasn't willing to settle. That was the price I paid for self-respect.

As I sat on my bed, I reflected on the past few weeks. Discouragement surfaced above the heartbreak. I didn't like the woman I had become recently. Insecure. Anxious. Unsettled. I had yearned for a long-term, stable relationship so badly that I didn't trust those tiny voices whispering that something was off. I thought that if I just kept striving, kept trying, it would work out. And I'd be happy.

Once again, I kept chasing happiness. I had forgotten that happiness wasn't something to be found. And today, in this moment, after that weight had been lifted, I understood that happiness was something within me. I had continued to bury it because I was so unsure of how to hold on to it. But the truth is, you can't hold on to happiness any more than you can hold on to water.

And that felt so incredibly overwhelming.

How do you love someone without holding on to them?

Immediately, I thought of Nate. I thought of the roller coaster he had been on with me these past two years. The image of him begging me not to meet Andreas came to mind. I closed my eyes and recalled the fear he must have felt. Watching me walk out the door and wondering if the woman he loved would return.

He couldn't control me any longer. And that must have felt like trying to hold on to water. I guess the adage rings true: if you love something, set it free. And that's what Nate did so many times. Sometimes by force and sometimes by choice.

The woman he loved and set free in August of 2022 didn't return the same. Because what was stirred in me after my date with Andreas solidified my desire for another man in my life. And that version of me, Nate didn't know. Hell, I didn't know her. But we've both spent the past two years befriending and understanding her.

Ending things with Morocco pushed me into finally loving this version of myself. I now know that I am not interested in settling for someone who isn't able to make me a priority. For the first time in my life, I truly believe that that's what I deserve. I'm not too much. I have nothing to prove.

And there is nothing, absolutely nothing wrong with me.

I heard a knock on my bedroom door.

"Mom?" Avery asked hesitantly. "Are you okay?"

I had nothing left in me. I was raw and bare. Not just from my relationship ending, but from the transformation that was unfolding. "No, kiddo. I'm sad."

She walked into my room and sat on my bed. "It's okay, Mom," she said as she put her arm around me. "Can I sit here with you?"

I smiled, grateful for her care and love. "That would be really nice."

For the next hour, my thirteen-year-old daughter sat with me. Mostly in silence. She wasn't on her phone. She didn't try to start an awkward conversation. She literally just sat with me in my sadness. Sometimes, she'd reassure me, "it's going to be okay, Mom" or "it's okay to cry."

After an hour had passed, I grabbed her hand and told her, "I want you to know that what you did for me, sitting with me in my sadness, not being afraid to witness my pain, is a gift. Thank you, Avery. You're a great kiddo."

Without hesitating, she said, "You're a great mom." And hugged me.

All I could think at that moment was that I would go through a hundred heartbreaks to experience this with her again.

How did I get so lucky?

I thought back to just nine months ago, when I came out to my kids as polyamorous. Just like today, Avery's words flooded my heart with a sense of peace.

"Mom. We could NEVER not love you. I'm sorry you would think that. I don't care who you love. I will always love you."

Even in this pain, I was met with unconditional love. To encounter love in this way is indescribable.

Love, in any form, will turn us upside down and break us wide open. It is wild and unpredictable and scary as hell. I believe that it is the most powerful force in the Universe. So why would anyone ever open themselves up to such chaos?

Because love runs through our veins. It moves our heart to beat. It stirs desire and action and propels people to cross oceans to be with the ones they love. The difference between love and lust is that love will always lead us back to who we are.

Avery's gift of compassion and presence was profound. What I had feared the most—my kids hating me for being polyamorous, for changing how our family operated—was what connected me back to them because it connected me back to who I was. Who I had always been. When I accepted myself, the shiny parts society deemed as acceptable, and the jagged parts that some sneered at or shied away from, when I opened my heart to love in all its forms, I began the journey back home to myself.

No man was going to rescue me from my life. I didn't need saving. I needed to surrender to the truth that it was never about choosing. Or losing. Or pleasing others. All of this had been about coming home to myself and realizing that I was the one with the keys to my cage all along.

This may have been the end of one relationship. But it felt like the beginning of a whole new chapter.

I was free to be me and still loved by the people I valued most.

CHAPTER FIFTY-SEVEN

October 2024

"WHAT IF WE STARTED A YOUTUBE CHANNEL?" Nate asked me over dinner.

I laughed, rolling my eyes. "Yeah, okay."

"No, I'm serious." He put his beer down and leaned in toward me.

My eyebrows furrowed slightly. "I'm confused. You barely post on social media as it is. What would we even start a YouTube channel on?"

"On our life. How we got here. We could help others who are struggling like we were."

I softly smiled as I stared at this man. My husband. I wanted to ask, "Who are you?!" But I knew exactly who he was. His evolution had unfolded right before my eyes. I had witnessed him wade into the unknown of rewriting the rules of our marriage, not knowing how it all would end.

My smile spread. This was what we had been working towards. A life, full of love and possibility, and the opportunity to offer hope to those who don't fit into the mold of traditional monogamy.

"Neither of us know what we're doing when it comes to this," I told him.

He tilted his head slightly and leaned back in his chair. "When has that stopped us before?"

I laughed. "You are not wrong about that."

I swirled the pinot noir in my glass, staring at the red liquid, considering his proposition.

This is gonna be a lot of work. I don't even watch YouTube. Where do we even begin?

I set down my glass and reached my hand across the table. "Ok. I'm in. Let's do it."

He put his hand in mine and we both squeezed. "Together."

I nodded. "Together."

As dinner went on, we discussed episode ideas, equipment we needed to purchase, and other logistics.

"We need to come up with a name," Nate said.

I bit the inside of my lower lip, considering a name that could reflect our mission. I rested my chin on my palm as I drummed my fingers against my upper lip.

I dropped my hand and sat up as if lightning had struck nearby. "Oh! I know!"

Nate nodded expectantly.

"I want to design the logo first. Then you'll see."

"Nothing like a little suspense."

"Would you expect anything less from me?" I asked, winking at him.

He shook his head and took a sip of his beer.

I leaned back in my chair and marveled at the life I had fought so hard to create. It had been six months since things ended with Morocco. I had dated a little but nothing serious. No one that was worth me spending time away from Nate and the kids. That was how I now measured my interest in someone. Were they worth giving up my time with the ones I loved to explore something that could be?

Once you've had your heartbroken several times, you tend to

be a bit more cautious (jaded?) when it comes to who you let into your world. Ironically, Nate is the one who encourages me to date more. He's still not interested in knowing the details, but he knows that my polyamory is a large part of who I am. In fact, the more confident and connected I am to my whole self, including my polyamory, the sexier I am to him.

It's incredible, truly, that the man who reflected the shame I had for this part of me is now my biggest cheerleader. The man who asked me repeatedly, "What's wrong with you?" now wants to share our story—my story—with the world.

We finished dinner, and I headed upstairs to work on the logo for our YouTube channel. I scoured Canva for inspiration until I finally landed on the vision that had dropped into my head just thirty minutes prior.

Fifteen minutes later, I was ready to show it to Nate.

"Nate! Come here!" I yelled down the stairs.

"I'm coming. I'm coming," he said calmly as he made his way into our bedroom.

I turned the laptop towards him, watching his face for a reaction.

He nodded slowly, a warm smile spreading across his face. "I love it."

"What do you think of the name?" I asked expectantly.

"It's perfect," he said as he kissed me on the head and turned to go back downstairs.

"Wait! Where are you going? We still have to talk about the design. Is this the right color of blue? Do you like the yellow?"

Nate stopped briefly halfway down the stairs. "Courtney, I trust you. Whatever you decide, it's gonna be great. Try not to overthink it."

Does he even know me?!

"Ugh, fine. But I'm gonna ask you about it later so don't think this discussion is over," I said with a laugh.

He smiled. "I never do."

EPILOGUE
JANUARY 2025

WHEN I DECIDED to burn it all down three years ago, I had no idea what would be left once the embers cooled. As I reflect on all that has happened in the short span of this book, I see that so much of it is marked by heartbreak. But there is also an incredible amount of beauty and joy amidst these ashes.

After I realized I was polyamorous, I thought that path would save my marriage. Save me. And for a while I did believe that. What I realized throughout writing this book, and upon further reflection, is that nothing saved me because I wasn't in danger. There was no damsel in distress, despite how often I thought I was.

No. I was controlled. I was indoctrinated. Caged. Polyamory was the catalyst that propelled me to leave my cage and show me that the world is far more complex and beautiful than we are made to believe it is.

I thought that if another man just loved me the way Nate couldn't, then I'd be whole. I saw love as the answer. And it was. I was just applying it to the wrong question.

I kept asking, what is wrong with me? Why won't anyone choose me? All the while ignoring that little girl inside me who was the one asking those questions. When I came home to her, to me, that's when it all began to change. And I wish that process was easy, but through it all, it taught me that transformation happens one of two ways—love or suffering. They are two sides of the same coin.

I can't think of anything more terrifying than true love. To care for someone or something so much that you fear the absolute loss of it. And that's really the journey of love. Finding a way to fight the urge to control, regulate, manipulate, and ultimately hold on to that love for as long as possible.

But that's not love. Love requires freedom. Love needs trust. Love is born from vulnerability. All of which make us susceptible to suffering.

And boy, did I suffer these past few years. But I also loved. Greatly. Boldly. And it burst open a whole new chapter in my marriage and motherhood. It's odd to look back and recall where Nate and I used to be because those two people at the beginning of this book are so different from the ones we are today.

It was Nate's idea for me to write this book. To open our marriage, and my most personal moments, to the scrutiny of others. After our struggle to find familiarity, to find hope, in the faces and stories of others in our darkest moments, Nate knew that something needed to change. The face of non-monogamy needed another voice. One that was steeped in motherhood and marriage. One that looked like your average soccer mom who was just trying to keep all the pieces from falling off the table. Who loved a good Pinterest recipe and was also polyamorous. He encouraged me to share our journey. To share my story. With the hope that we would help others. It's what led us to create the MonoPoly Couple YouTube Channel. And it will lead to more collaboration as our community of the non-monogamy curious grows.

I can't begin to describe the transformation my husband has had and the immense pride I have for him because of it. He was willing to finally face his own trauma in order to heal from his fears. Watching him put in the work, tearing down the emotional walls he had spent decades building, was inspiring. The changes in Nate have been undeniable. My mom and sister, his brother and his wife, they've all noticed he's more patient with the kids, more present when he's home, and more thoughtful in his actions.

Nate discovered a whole new layer because he was willing to go within himself and face his fears. Through this process, he's become more empathetic to those who are suffering. He's less judgmental and more open-minded when it comes to relationships, love, and marriage. I truly believe this is because we restructured our relationship and reclaimed what true partnership is all about.

As for me, well, that's a constant evolution. I've fully embraced my polyamorous identity and have a vision for what my future love life looks like. My desire for another partner hasn't changed. It's weaved into my DNA as much as my blue eyes are. When and how that comes about... well, I guess we'll see. But I no longer bristle at the thought of being "too much." I know that I'm just enough and whoever I choose to partner with will see that, too.

So did non-monogamy save our marriage? Maybe, but I believe it was more of a catalyst that broke us out of our cages. It was the medium that allowed me to redefine what it meant to be a wife and mother. Polyamory was the source and the path that reshaped how I looked at pleasure, perfection, and purpose.

From the outside, my life doesn't look that different than it did when this all began. Same kids, same job, same husband. But from the inside, well, that's where you can feel the transformation the most. And if that isn't testimony to the power of love, I don't know what is.

ACKNOWLEDGMENTS

I am beyond grateful to have so many amazing people around me who have supported me through this process. And let me tell you, writing a memoir is a PROCESS. Thank you will never be enough to convey how much you have made a difference in my life. My eyes are filled with tears as I write each of these words.

To my husband, Nate. I'm so proud of us. Our life and love are bigger and better than I ever imagined. Thank you for seeing the biggest version of me before I could. Can't stop, won't stop.

To my kiddos, Addison, Avery, and Asher. Your patience, encouragement, and unconditional love has transformed me in ways you will never understand. Thank you for loving me for who I am.

To my mom. Who kept telling me, "You should write that down," when I'd share a disastrous date with her. I'm so proud of how much you've grown and for your unwavering support.

To my sister. Knowing that you'd love me no matter what is one of the best feelings in the world. *Liebe duck.* ;)

To my incredible book team, Ashleigh Renard and Jamie McGillen, this book exists because of your brilliance and support. Beyond grateful for the both of you.

To my family and friends who cheered me on along the way. You will never understand how much that mattered to me. Every word of encouragement, every time you asked for an update, it spurred me to keep going.

To the Johnsons. I would not be the same woman I am today if it weren't for your love, wisdom, honesty, and encouragement. Love you both.

To the women in this book. You poured into me and loved me in a way that has profoundly changed me. I am so honored to have you in my life.

To the men in this book. I have learned so much from each of you, and I am grateful for the lessons and adventures.

To my beta and early readers. Thank you! Your feedback and insights were invaluable.

To the woman who asked for a threesome at her anniversary dinner. Your courage and belief that you are deserving of more love changed your family for the better. Congratulations on creating a life bolder and bigger than you ever imagined. I love you. Thank you for not settling, Courtney.

ABOUT THE AUTHOR

Courtney Boyer, M.Ed., M.S., is a therapist-turned-relationship coach, writer, and speaker whose work centers on love, desire, and authenticity. Drawing on her background in mental health and sex therapy, she brings a unique blend of professional expertise and lived experience to conversations around relationships and identity. When she isn't writing or coaching, Courtney can be found chasing joy—traveling, reading, or savoring delicious coffee and deep conversation. She is passionate about helping women break free from shame, reclaim their bodies and voices, and create relationships rooted in honesty and autonomy.

Courtney lives in Germany with her husband and three children, where she is still learning, unlearning, and writing the next chapter of her story.

instagram.com/courtneyboyercoaching

facebook.com/courtneyboyercoaching

tiktok.com/@courtneyboyercoaching17

youtube.com/@TheMonoPolyCouple

linkedin.com/in/courtneyboyercoaching